A COE
IN

This is the one guide that anyone who works in an office—from clerk to manager—should put on the desk beside pencil, pen, typewriter, or word processor. Filled with expert advice and a wealth of informative examples, this valuable, easy-to-use handbook, designed for both instant reference and cover-to-cover reading, can help you solve any and all office problems you may face.

MARY A. DE VRIES has written ten books dealing with office procedure practices, including *The Prentice-Hall Complete Secretarial Letter Book* and *The Secretary's Almanac and Fact Book*. She has also revised the last two editions of *The Complete Secretary's Guide* and she is the author of *The Practical Writer's Guide* (available from Signet).

THE COMPLETE OFFICE HANDBOOK

by

Mary A. De Vries

A SIGNET BOOK

NEW AMERICAN LIBRARY

Copyright © 1987 by Mary A. De Vries

First Printing, July, 1987

1 2 3 4 5 6 7 8 9

To John G. De Vries

Contents

MESSAGE TRANSMISSION

BUSINESS WRITING

FACTS AND FIGURES

Preface

It's not easy being an office worker today. I know that sounds illogical, since new products and advanced technology have eliminated many routine, repetitive tasks. But with every step forward in the working world, it seems that some one has to learn a different task or how to do a familiar task differently. In addition to further formal training from time to time, self-education is an ongoing process; in fact, survival in the modern working world depends on it. This book aims to provide you with the basic information you need to function intelligently in the workplace today and to have enough insight into common office practices and procedures to work effectively at any level of activity—clerical, secretarial, administrative, or managerial.

An office handbook today has to be a blend of the new and the old. Although we are moving toward an electronic world and the truly integrated office is no longer just a futuristic concept, people still perform many tasks conventionally. They type correspondence conventionally and file the carbon copies or photocopies in regular file folders; however, in many large organizations, these folders are then positioned, located, and physically retrieved by electronic means. People also still place traditional letters in traditional envelopes and mail them in the conventional way via the U.S. Postal Service, which in turn delivers them to a traditional mailbox; but some people send their letters electronically over the telephone lines directly to a receiving electronic "mailbox," or computer file.

Therefore, when you read a book such as this one, you may get the impression that we live and work in parallel worlds, and to a certain extent, that's the way it is. At least we're in a period of transition, and office workers need to deal with both the traditional and the contemporary while keeping their eyes clearly focused on the horizon where even more advanced systems are being developed, and—one hopes—greater or even full standardization will one day emerge.

Perhaps the contents of this book best reflect the old adage that some things never change and some things never stop changing. For example:

You still have to conduct yourself properly and meet and work with other employees. Chapters 1 (etiquette), 2 (human relations), and 3 (meetings) give you some practical guidelines in that area.

All organizations must keep files and records, using either traditional procedures or advanced technology. Chapters 4 (filing) and 5 (bookkeeping and record keeping) provide basic information about the multifaceted area of filing, record keeping, and financial reporting.

In many businesses as much as 80 percent of the office activity involves word processing. Chapters 6 (typewriters) and 7 (computers and word processors) explain equipment options and provide step-by-step instructions for preparing text both traditionally and electronically.

Modern messaging and integration of functions is the topic of interest to managers and operators who are looking for ever faster ways to transmit text and graphics. Chapters 8 (conventional and electronic mail), 9 (facsimile and telex), and 10 (telecommunications) describe systems and procedures for rapid message transmission in the modern office.

Tips on how to prepare a variety of written material properly—a daily concern in most offices—predominate in chapters 11 (style), 12 (letters and memos), 13 (business reports), and 14 (press releases, articles, brochures, and advertisements).

For those who need to check miscellaneous facts and figures while performing other duties, a collection of reference material at the end of the book includes arabic and roman numerals; diacritical marks; the Greek alphabet; standard paper weights and sizes; standard sizes of common printed material; metric conversion guidelines; a table of common and metric weights, measures, and values; common technical abbreviations; common computer abbreviations; state abbreviations; and abbreviations of foreign countries and regions.

Since a handbook is largely meant to tell you how to do something, this book helps you to solve daily problems and to answer troublesome questions such as:

Whose name do I mention first when I introduce an important customer to my boss?

What should I say—or not say—if I have to fire someone?

Is it proper to type the meeting notice for a stockholders' meeting on regular business stationery?

Should I include seniority titles such as *Jr.* and *Sr.* when indexing and alphabetizing the names of persons on file-folder labels?

How do I compile a work sheet that can be used in preparing financial statements?

Is there an easy way to chain-feed envelopes into a typewriter?

How do you format a document with a computer or word processor?

How do you get mail out of an electronic "mailbox"?

If my office subscribes to a Telex I network service, can I still send a telex message to someone who uses Telex II?

How do I set up a teleconference?

Why is it incorrect to write *Rio Grande River*?

How do I type the subject line using a simplified letter format?

In report writing, how do you convert a topic outline into a sentence outline?

What is the correct way to type a press release?

Is there a simple formula to use to convert inches and feet to centimeters?

The fourteen chapters in this handbook are organized in five parts: Office Relations, Record Keeping, Word Processing, Message Transmission, and Business Writing. The tables and lists of reference material are collected in a concluding part, Facts and Figures. Generally, the practices and procedures described in these parts are those approved and recommended by respected authorities. Yet even these experts concede that people in different offices and professions use different procedures to accomplish essentially the same thing, just as letter writers often punctuate their correspondence differently. Since many offices have a preferred style or policy in some matters, you should follow the requirements of your own office. In all other situations, use the guidelines in this handbook to improve your performance and enhance your job status. To succeed, we all need to take advantage of any insights and suggestions that will make it easier to be an office worker today.

I appreciate all of the advice and useful information that I received from many persons and organizations, and my special thanks go to several people for their particularly important contributions to this book: Becky Arterbury, accountant, Sigafoos and Arterbury; Clare Gorman, advertising and promotion, MCI International; Brenda Hobbs, owner, Centralized Secretarial Services; Marsha Hollingsworth, research consultant; and Frederick Schultz, district representative, United Parcel Service. In addition, I sincerely appreciate the interest, efforts, and ongoing assistance of Richard Balkin, The Balkin Agency, and Hugh Rawson, New American Library.

OFFICE
RELATIONS

———◆———

CHAPTER ONE

Observing Proper Office Etiquette

There are rules for proper behavior in an office just as there are rules of etiquette at home and at social events. Those who violate these rules, unintentionally or deliberately, demonstrate their ignorance or lack of consideration for others. Either way, it is at best embarrassing and at worst difficult or impossible to gain the confidence, respect, and cooperation of others when widely accepted practices are cast aside.

To work successfully with others in a productive and congenial atmosphere, it is necessary to conduct yourself according to certain long-established conventions. Since the foundation of proper etiquette is respect for others, essential courtesies usually flow naturally and easily with a positive and thoughtful attitude toward coworkers.

IMAGE

Many attributes combine to make up your professional image—the way that others see you. Job skills such as capability in math are certainly important, but personal characteristics in particular create the portrait that others view.

Attitude

Very few things can be hidden from coworkers. It is especially easy to spot a cynical, unreasonable, uncooperative, thoughtless, or otherwise negative attitude. Experts believe that you must have a genuinely cheerful, positive, and confident outlook to handle your work and working relationships with an acceptable level of success.

People are uncomfortable around someone who views the world darkly. Perhaps more important, they distrust and want to avoid someone who often appears to be angry or unhappy, fearing that such a person might treat both work assignments and clients or coworkers unfairly and irresponsibly. Since your attitude can't be turned on or off with the press of a button, it is sometimes necessary to conduct a serious self-examination and even seek professional help if corrective measures cannot be implemented alone.

Ethics

Without a code of ethics, life at work would turn into a free-for-all. Matters of etiquette take a serious turn where ethics are concerned. For instance, it is more than discourteous to discuss with outsiders a coworker's secret romance. It is dangerous. Some competitors are not above blackmailing persons who have something to hide, forcing them to reveal company secrets.

Organizations must maintain a degree of privacy and secrecy. Therefore, it is considered taboo to discuss company affairs—even apparently routine, innocent matters— in public or with outsiders. It is even unwise to discuss business in one office with coworkers in another office. Gossip is undesirable in any case, but employee politics and competition might cause someone in one office to seek ways to take advantage of someone in another office. The only safe rule is never to gossip about coworkers and never to discuss company business outside the immediate office.

Security. Proper office safeguards go hand in hand with matters of ethics. Keep important documents and file folders locked in cabinets or other containers and hide the keys. Do not leave sensitive or revealing correspondence and other material face up on your desk where anyone might see it. Carefully safeguard drafts, notes, and shorthand notebooks, and do not allow outsiders to wait in someone's private office while he or she is away. Beware how you dispose of material too. Anything thrown into a wastebasket, for example, can easily be retrieved by someone else. Take time to destroy carbon copies and photocopies that are not used by shredding them.

Personal Habits

Both idiosyncracies and normal personal habits reveal much about a person to others. Annoying habits in particular, such as pencil tapping or mumbling, make an unfavorable impression on others. Some habits such as tardiness have an especially adverse impact on one's job. Employers put this at the top of the list of undesirable traits in an employee. But often people are unaware that they have bad habits that irritate others.

You may have to develop your sense of self-awareness before you can pinpoint and correct unpleasant personal habits. Try concentrating more on what you say and do. When you talk with someone, do you look directly at the person or stare at your feet? Are you still talking (or mumbling) after turning and walking away from a person? Do you rudely drum your knuckles on the desk when you become impatient or bored with someone? Do you smoke in the presence of nonsmokers who may detest your contributions to office air pollution? Do you interrupt people before they are finished speaking or impatiently complete the thoughts of slow speakers? If you seriously pay attention to your behavior, you may be surprised to discover some annoying and discourteous personal habits that you never realized you had.

Elevator courtesy. Since many people are in a hurry to get to or leave the office, elevators are often crowded. Common courtesy requires that you hold the doors and wait for others who are approaching (always thank those who do this for you). Men need not remove their hats in a crowded elevator, although it is considered good manners to do so in the presence of women when an elevator is not crowded. People with packages should take care not to stab and jostle others carelessly, and everyone should allow necessary space for others to maneuver and step aside for those who are leaving.

Never smoke in an elevator (it is often illegal and it is always inconsiderate), and never eat or drink in an elevator. This is not the proper place for meals, and a sudden stop could accidentally splash your beverage all over the people standing next to you.

Office housekeeping. Some people do not worry about housekeeping habits away from home. But neatness or sloppiness is highly visible in the office and has an immediate impact on visitors. It is easy for someone to associate an office in disarray with carelessness in work as well. A client might think twice about giving business to someone who appears to scatter files and other material around the office without regard for efficiency or security. Such a person might be as careless with the client's material. Similarly, coffee spills and bread crumbs all over a desk will not add to a visitor's confidence in your work habits. People like to deal with others who appear to be orderly, careful, and particular in managing themselves, their duties, and their work environment. Sloppy housekeeping habits present a poor image in this regard.

Appearance

The way you look—cleanliness, neatness, style of dress, and so on—makes an immediate impression on others.

Clothes. Experts recommend that you dress for the job you want, not the one you have. Thus if you are a staff assistant and you want to become an executive, dress like an executive. Although offices vary in the degree of formality observed, the properly dressed businessperson usually wears well-tailored, conservative, businesslike suits or dresses with jackets and a minimum of jewelry. Although generally, you should follow the example of others in your office, it is usually in good taste to be neatly and conservatively attired.

Grooming. Clothes are only part of the picture you

present. Good posture and cleanliness (clean hair, finger-
nails, and so on) are essential. Hairstyles should be relatively conservative too. In terms of hairstyle as well as
clothes, you should look as if you're on the way to a
business meeting, not a picnic or the opening of the
Metropolitan Opera season.

Neatness is imperative. Keep hair combed and nails
clean and filed. But never attend to such grooming at
your desk or anywhere in public—use the restrooms—
and wear clothes that do not easily wrinkle or sag out of
shape.

Avoid heavy colognes or perfumes, which are offen-
sive to many persons, and use a breath freshener frequently, especially if you eat spicy foods during lunch.
Chewing gum to control bad breath is ill advised (use a
tablet or spray). Many people view any form of chewing
in public, other than at mealtime, as a disgusting habit.

Health. Matters of health have a great deal to do with
appearance and performance. A healthful diet high in
fruits, vegetables, and whole grains will help you look
and feel better and more energetic than a junk-food diet
of coffee or soft drinks and refined sugars and white
flour. Exercise, too, will add to your vitality, and many
companies provide facilities and programs for employee
exercise periods. Alcohol is best avoided entirely during
the day. Also, late-night binges that leave you with a
hangover will not only cause you to look and feel worse
but will lessen your productivity and efficiency the following day. It is a widely accepted rule that optimum
health and performance are directly linked to personal
habits in diet and exercise.

MEALTIME ETIQUETTE

Your behavior during business lunches and dinners is
just as important as your behavior in the office. To avoid
embarrassing yourself and others, pay special attention
to the basic rules of mealtime etiquette.

The Company Cafeteria

Procedures at a company cafeteria are similar to those at a commercial cafeteria. You usually pick up plates and utensils, place them on a tray, and serve yourself or tell the attendants behind the food counter what you want. If meals are not provided in your work, you usually pay for your selections at the end of the food line before finding a table.

If no tables are available, stand aside and wait, but do not hover about other diners and appear to rush them. If you are at a table and others are waiting, do not linger unnecessarily. Also when many others are waiting for tables, it is inconsiderate to hold places for friends. If no busboy service is available, place dishes and utensils on the tray when you are finished and deposit them at the designated area.

Restaurants

You may have lunch or dinner with a friend, associate, or client in a restaurant outside the company. When you are hosting a large party, arrangements must be made in advance with the facility, and invitations should be mailed in sufficient time.

Invitations. Invitations to an important function with out-of-town guests should be sent at least four months in advance. Invitations to an informal lunch or dinner with local guests should be sent three to five weeks in advance.

Casual luncheon dates with a friend or associate are often made a few days in advance by telephone or even on the spur of the moment during a conversation. "Let me *take you* to lunch" means you will pick up the bill. "Let's have lunch *together*" means you each pay your own bill.

Be specific about details: date, time, and place, and reserve space at the restaurant. A spouse is usually not included in business luncheon invitations but is included in dinner invitations. For sample invitations see the models in this chapter.

Table manners. Offer your guest a drink, but do not take one if your guest declines. If your guest accepts, you may have either an alcoholic or a nonalcoholic beverage. Offer a second drink and suggest ordering so that the meal will be served when the drinks are finished.

Men and women in business both place their own orders directly, although a businesswoman, if she wishes, may allow a male host to relay her order to the waiter or waitress. In social settings, both male and female hosts ask guests for their choices and relay them, although, again, a woman host may ask a male guest to give the orders if she wishes, or she may prefer to make advance arrangements with the restaurant for everything except cocktails.

Although the host does not start until everyone is served, he or she should tell others to begin so that their food does not get cold. Let the guest, particularly a client or customer, make the first move to end the meal.

Payment. The host pays in the case of invited guests. Otherwise, each person asks for a separate check or pays an appropriate share of the total. An employer always pays for a guest employee.

Company policy must be followed in expense-account meals. Fill out the proper company form and get a receipt from the restaurant. Payment by credit card insures a proper receipt and statement.

Tip the wine steward and the waiter or waitress. You may also tip the head waiter in a small restaurant if he provides a special service. Give at least 15 percent in an ordinary restaurant and 20 percent in an expensive restaurant. A hat-check attendant is tipped by each guest individually.

OFFICE VISITORS

If you are an office visitor, act as courteously as if you were a guest in someone's home. If you are receiving a visitor in your office, act as thoughtfully as if you were greeting a guest at home. In short, dress appropriately, be punctual, and behave politely.

Greetings

The visitor. Be very punctual (telephone if an emergency will delay you) in making an office call. People at work usually have other appointments and need to stay on schedule. Always identify yourself; for example, "I'm Helen Braithwaite from First Industries." Give the receptionist a business card if you have one. The rule for women is to use *Miss* or *Mrs.* if you want to be addressed by that title. Otherwise, the receptionist or secretary greeting you will identify you as *Ms.* Then explain that you have an appointment or ask if you can see the person in question.

Dress neatly and conservatively for the office call. Wait until you are asked to be seated and then place your briefcase and packages on the floor or in your lap. Fold your coat over the arm or back of the chair if the receptionist does not hang it up for you. You may read or take notes while waiting (come prepared), but do not interfere with the receptionist's work or appear to read private papers on someone's desk.

When your host is ready, wait for him or her to shake hands and offer you a chair. Again identify yourself if the receptionist does not introduce you. If the receptionist hands you a note during the meeting indicating that you have a telephone call, suggest that you will return the call later. Otherwise, excuse yourself and be brief. If your host receives a call, offer to wait outside.

Do not overstay your scheduled appointment period, and thank the receptionist on the way out.

The office host. Do not keep callers waiting unnecessarily, and introduce yourself if they do not know your name. If you are not ready, offer them a place to wait with ashtrays and magazines. Offer to take their coats or show them the clothes tree or cloakroom.

In a large reception room visitors are not offered refreshments unless there is a coffe machine and they are urged to serve themselves. In a small office, however, if a secretary or the executive is having refreshments, he or she should offer the guest something too. Otherwise, refreshment breaks should be postponed until the visitor is gone.

If callers do not identify themselves, ask their names and the nature of their business. If it is your job to screen visitors, and you know that your employer is busy, suggest that the person make an appointment. If you know that your employer would not want to see the person under any circumstances or never sees people who refuse to state their business, suggest that the person write a letter: "I'm really sorry, but Mr. Clarke's schedule is so full for the foreseeable future that he's no longer making appointments. But you could write to him, and I know he'll be happy to receive your letter." Since office policy regarding visitors may vary from one office to another, follow the practices in your office; if you don't know what they are, ask.

If a caller overstays his or her appointment time, the secretary or receptionist could buzz the office or knock on the door and indicate that it's time for another meeting. This should signal the visitor that it's time to leave. For details on telephone courtesy, refer to chapter 10.

Remind visitors to collect their coats and packages and offer to show them the way out if the location of the stairs or elevator is unfamiliar.

Problem visitors. On rare occasions visitors who do not get their way become emotional and even threatening. If your company has a security system, ring for help. Otherwise, look for immediate assistance if your efforts to calm a visitor fail.

A female employee may need to step into another person's office or buzz someone on the intercom system. Even a male employee who can handle a physically violent visitor should have a third person present to avoid having the visitor misrepresent the situation later. In any case, seek help and remove the emotional person from the office as quietly as possible (in some situations a female employee may be able to calm a female visitor without further assistance). In instances of actual violence or direct threat of it, telephone the police immediately or, if you are unable to do so, make every possible effort to signal a coworker to do so.

Introductions

A few simple rules will help you handle introductions correctly and with ease. Names alone suffice in most cases, but include the person's rank, title, or other information when it is significant or will help to identify the person. Note that a person who formerly held an official position is introduced by that title ("This is former governor George Lewis"), and a retired military person is still introduced by rank ("May I present Major Tim Demerest").

1. Don't hesitate to introduce yourself or offer your name if someone seems to have forgotten it: "Hello, I'm James Upland—Jim."

2. "How do you do?" is always a proper response: "How do you do. I'm Martha Tennyson, and please call me Martha."

3. When you are uncertain about using first names, don't do it: "It was nice meeting you, Ms. Knox." Wait for the person to suggest it: "Oh, please call me Sherry, and it was very nice meeting you too."

4. When you introduce someone *to* another person, mention the name of the person being honored first: "Reverend Hill, this is my neighbor Phillip Klein."

5. Introduce an executive in your company *to* an executive of equal status in another company: "Mr. Brent, this is Jim Benson, our marketing manager. Jim, this is Paul Brent, advertising manager at Shipman Manufacturing."

6. Introduce a junior employee *to* a senior employee: "Mrs. Blackwell, this is June Pruett from accounting. June, this is Mrs. Lydia Blackwell, vice-president of production."

7. Introduce an employee *to* a customer or client: "Ms. Hammer, this is Don Jones, our sales manager. Don, this is Ms. Maxine Hammer, Newstate Services' representative."

8. Introduce someone in an unofficial capacity *to* someone in an official capacity: "Senator Black, this is Henry Fry, general manager at Four-State Productions. Mr. Fry, this is Senator John Black."

9. Introduce a younger person *to* an older person: "Mrs. McKenzie, this is Ms. Courtney Brewer, assistant dean of education. Courtney, this is Mrs. Mabel McKenzie."

10. Introduce a man *to* a woman when they are peers and none of the previous rules apply: "Jane, this is Ted Finley. Ted, Jane Osmon."

INVITATIONS

The Invitation

Many casual invitations (for lunch or cocktails or to address a meeting) are made by telephone, in person, or by business letter (see the model in chapter 12). A formal business invitation is typically engraved in black ink on white or cream card stock. Consult printers and stationery stores for samples. When a lot of events are held, fill-in cards may be used; otherwise, the invitation may be engraved in its entirety (see the examples below).

Some innovative businesses deviate from the traditional design and the classic engraved card. However, before any radical departures are made, one should consider the audience and whether the recipients might view anything but the classic form in poor taste and undignified (this is unlikely except in very conservative businesses).

Printers and stationery suppliers usually have samples of traditional styles for invitations, fill-in invitation cards, reminder cards, and reply cards (include an RSVP line on the invitation if you do not enclose a reply card).

In planning an event, schedule printing, checking of proofs, and so on in time to mail the invitations when required: at least four to six months for dinner with out-of-town guests, two to four weeks for cocktail parties and receptions, and three to five weeks for lunch and local dinners.

Model Invitation

BM

Brice Management, Inc.

In honor of

the Governor of the State of Vermont

Frank Beckett

requests the pleasure of the company of

Mr. and Mrs. Stanford Hart

at dinner

on Friday, the fifth of August

Nineteen hundred and eighty-seven

at half after eight o'clock

902 Lyle Avenue

Burlington

RSVP   Black Tie
17 East Drive   Dancing
Burlington, Vermont 05402

Model Fill-In Invitation

Daniel Jordan, President

requests the pleasure of your company

at *Lunch*

on *Friday, February 2, at 12:30 o'clock*

at *The Wilson Room*

RSVP *Oak Lane Lodge
2016 West Highway
Phoenix*

(602) 511-7000

The Reply

When a reply card is not enclosed, and the invitation has RSVP printed on it, reply in handwriting (typing is widely permissible, however, for a business reply) in the same third-person style of the invitation (see the sample replies on the following page). If a phone number is given, reply by telephone.

INJURY, ILLNESS, AND DEATH

Three unfortunate occurrences that office workers must deal with are injuries, illnesses, and death. In the case of injury and illness, observing proper procedure is essential for the welfare of the person involved. In the case of

Model Reply: Accept

Miss Ann Williamson
accepts with pleasure
Mr. and Mrs. Pasnelli's
kind invitation for
Friday, the sixth of May

Model Reply: Decline

Mr. and Mrs. Herman Asnette
sincerely regret
that owing to a previous engagement
they are unable to accept
Mr. Roger's
kind invitation for
Saturday, the third of October

death of a coworker or member of a coworker's family, observing proper etiquette is essential to help friends, relatives, and associates cope with a difficult situation.

Injury and Illness

When a fellow employee is injured at work or becomes ill, call a doctor immediately or telephone a hospital emergency room if the situation is urgent. Call the family of the coworker when someone is seriously ill or injured. If possible, someone from the office should go with the coworker to the hospital and wait until a family member arrives. Keep hospital visits short. Gifts of flowers are thoughtful. Food or candy must be approved by the doctor.

When a coworker has a minor illness (flu) or injury (paper cut) not requiring hospital care, offer local assistance. It may be necessary to drive someone home if the person cannot and should not be working. A first-aid kit is useful in treating minor cuts and scratches.

Offer to help take over some of the coworker's duties. You may be in the same position one day and need to have the favor returned.

Death

When an employee of a firm dies at work, someone from the company should immediately call upon the family in person. When an executive dies, members of the staff customarily offer to help the family in notifying others, in making arrangements, in providing newspaper notices, in writing the obituary, and so on. (Members of the company commonly prepare a newspaper obituary but send a copy to the family for approval before submitting it.) In large companies, internal announcements are commonly made by inneroffice memo. In small organizations the information may be transmitted by word of mouth. Someone also must notify outside business associates and advise receptionists how to handle incoming queries.

Observe the basic rules of the person's religion in

sending cards and flowers when an employee or member of the employee's family dies.

1. Observe the family's wishes in regard to sending donations, flowers, or fruit baskets.

2. If flowers are given send them to the funeral home, church, or cemetery according to the family's wishes. Include a white card with a handwritten message such as "With sincerest (or deepest) sympathy from friends and colleagues at XYZ Company." For a Catholic funeral, flowers go to the house or the funeral home, not the church. (The family should keep a list of what they receive to use in sending acknowledgments and thank yous.)

3. Send a fruit basket instead of flowers to a Jewish family if a memorial donation is not made. Bring kosher food when calling upon the family during the mourning period.

4. Mass cards to be sent to the family are available at Catholic churches. Make a donation to the church when you pick up a card.

5. Send letters of condolence regardless of the person's religion (see the model sympathy message in chapter 12). Strict social custom requires a handwritten (very brief) message to the family of a close friend or associate, and the reply from the family is also in handwriting. Business messages, such as a message to a company upon the death of a prominent executive, may be typed on business letterhead.

PRESENTS AND CARDS

Presents

Gifts may be sent to clients, customers, dinner hosts, secretaries, and assistants. Some presents are sent simply as a goodwill gesture and may be given at any time, not only on holidays such as Christmas.

When gifts are sent often to the same people, keep a record of the occasion, the date, the gift sent, its price, and any other pertinent information. This information will help you later in avoiding duplicates, deciding what to spend, and so forth.

When possible, always give a gift in person and enclose a thoughtful message such as "Hope this will help you celebrate your well-earned promotion in style!"

Although secretaries generally do not give their employers a gift, the boss always gives the secretary something on special occasions such as Christmas or a birthday. The amount varies upon the length of service and the relationship from about twenty-five dollars to one hundred dollars or more (some secretaries receive a generous bonus in addition).

Cards

Use general-message holiday cards ("Seasons Greetings") instead of messages associated with a particular religion ("Merry Christmas") to avoid offending members of a faith who do not observe a certain religious day.

Holiday cards, birthday cards, and other special-occasion cards are appropriate and desirable (remembering someone on special days is always a thoughtful goodwill gesture). However, adding a personal handwritten note of even a few words makes them doubly important to the recipient.

Some people prefer to send individually prepared letters to clients or customers—and important associates—on special occasions. A card is not necessary then since the letter takes its place. Keep a card address list and update it from year to year.

DONATIONS

Executives and their companies receive numerous requests for charitable contributions. How much is given and to whom or what depends on company policy or the executive's preferences.

Records should be kept indicating the amount given, the date, and the recipient. This information is useful in determining tax deductions and will be useful in future years in budgeting. Secretaries can help their employers by transferring amounts and probable dates of the donations to the executive's working calendar as a reminder for future contributions.

Since the demands for donations are numerous, the secretary or the executive will likely refuse many requests. Reasons given (if any) vary, but often the explanation offered is that the year's budget is fixed, and no additions are possible during the current fiscal year.

CHAPTER TWO

Dealing with
Human Relations Problems

It's an unfortunate fact of life that people do not always like each other. Hence a myriad of human relations problems arise at work; they range from petty, trivial disputes to devastating, irreconcilable differences. Sometimes problems develop for no apparent reason, although most difficulties at work occur simply because two or more people fail to make the necessary effort to communicate effectively and to cooperate with one another. There is considerable merit to the old adage that you don't have to like all of your coworkers, but you do have to get along with them. Usually, one has a lot to gain by fostering good human relations at work. Much more is accomplished when people work *with* rather than *against* others.

WORKING RELATIONSHIPS

Several types of relationships affect your performance and job satisfaction. Among the important ones are the relationships with your boss; with assistants, trainees, and other subordinates; with people in other offices and departments; and with your coworker peers. All of these relationships affect your performance at work, and all of them merit thoughtful attention and serious efforts from both parties.

A common but dangerous assumption is the belief that you only have to contribute to relationships with people of equal or higher job status, that in cases of people of lower job status, it's up to them to make the effort. But experience proves that *you* must contribute as much or even more time and effort toward developing good working relationships with subordinates if you want them to do their best on your behalf.

Employer-Employee Relationships

When you have one boss. Teamwork is the key to successful operations in a work environment. Your boss may not be perfect, but you should consider yourself part of his or her team. Your job is to assist and support your boss even when you have a different opinion about something. Certainly, you should feel free to contribute useful ideas, but if they are rejected, accept the decision gracefully and be prepared to support and carry out your employer's wishes with a positive attitude.

Loyalty in an office must be undivided. Your boss has a right to expect you to perform your duties without any betrayal of confidence or sabotage of activity. However, you should not do anything unethical or illegal, and if you are asked to do so, you should refuse. This may jeopardize your job, but committing a crime will place a lot more than your job in jeopardy.

To foster good working relations with your boss, keep the lines of communication open. Ask for clarification when you are uncertain about something. Don't hesitate to restate ideas and instructions to avoid misunderstandings. Above all, keep your boss completely informed about your work. This will insure that you receive credit for your efforts and also will help to keep activity moving on the path your boss prefers. As part of the information exchange, build your image by offering to take on special projects and demonstrate your willingness to be an active part of the team.

Very few employees escape at least occasional criticism from their boss. Learn how to accept such criticism as a favor to you. If you take it as a personal attack, you will be inclined to harbor resentment and may even be tempted to retaliate. Even if your boss is not very tactful, remind yourself often that your goals are the same—to be more accurate, more effective, and more productive.

If your boss points out an error you've made, be happy that you have a chance to correct it and improve your abilities in that area. If you respond in that vein, it will serve to make you a better employee, which is to your benefit.

Employers as well as employees make mistakes, and you should not hesitate to point out—*very* diplomatically—an error your boss has made. Choose your words carefully, for example: "I wonder if *we* have the right sales figures here, Mr. Blackwell. It looks like they might be the third-quarter figures instead of the fourth." Don't say: "It's a good thing I double-checked your report, Mr. Blackwell, because *you* used the wrong sales figures." In the case of minor errors, such as a typographical error or minor error in addition, simply correct it without saying anything.

When you have more than one boss. The teamwork principle applies whether you work for one, two, or more people. But the cooperative effort may require more skill in communication and scheduling.

When more than one boss competes for your time, you need to make all of them aware of your scheduling difficulties. If you simply devote more time to one person's needs or always handle that person's assignments first, the others will eventually conclude that you're "playing favorites." To avoid that, ask each boss for assistance in working out scheduling conflicts with the others. Whenever possible, anticipate incoming work and plan your day accordingly to accommodate the needs of each person.

Sometimes one boss holds a higher position than the others, and it is assumed that his or her work takes priority. In that case, use tact in any necessary delays of work for the others. Do not make them feel unimportant. You might say, "I should finish this assignment later today and will start your project first thing after that." Don't say, "Your project will have to wait until I finish my assignment for Ms. Lewis this afternoon."

When you work for a woman. Pronouncements about

the equality of the sexes sometimes are accepted more easily in theory than in practice. Responses differ among men who work for women. The most favorable situation is one in which a male subordinate does not feel threatened by a female boss but rather views the association the same way as any other business relationship. The least favorable situation is one in which the male subordinate cannot adjust to having a female boss. This person may become inefficient, unproductive, resentful, or even totally incapacitated. Even if he doesn't have negative feelings initially, the adverse remarks of family and friends may cause him to develop them. An astute boss will sense such a problem and take steps to foster a cooperative team spirit, but the employee must also contribute to the relationship.

To prevent or at least minimize the problems that could develop from working for a female boss, a male employee should recognize the potential difficulties and deal with the situation immediately, rather than deny it or pretend the feelings of hostility or inferiority do not exist. A male employee may have uneasy feelings about his manhood, about the security of his job, or both. Since the situation requires adjustment (for both parties), it is important to understand and accept any feelings of discomfort before trying to make the necessary adjustment.

The male employee can begin the adjustment process by setting a practical goal such as "developing a productive working relationship," which in turn will help him to perform more effectively, which in turn will enhance his career potential. In other words, shift the emphasis from simply trying to get along to working together effectively. Use a tactful approach in discussions; for example, offer to be of help but avoid sexist connotations ("since you're a woman, you'll be needing help from a man—feel free to call on me"). Let her indicate whether your relationship will be formal or informal, and do not misinterpret her friendliness as a romantic overture. Also let her set the time and pace for work-related duties. In short, do not be offended when a female manager does what she is supposed to do—manage. Finally, if you treat her with the same respect that you would grant a male executive and demonstrate the same willingness to cooperate, some of the most critical obstacles will be eliminated, and the chances for a successful working relationship will be greatly increased.

Women as well as men may have trouble adjusting to a female boss. Although some women form close relationships, others believe that personal relationships interfere with performance and avoid them. Some women will not work for another woman; others believe that women are more considerate. Attitudes vary widely, but basic requirements for the relationship do not. Women, like men, must cast aside personal feelings in the work environment and treat the relationship the same as any superior-subordinate situation; that is, a female boss is entitled to the same loyalty, cooperation, and respect that a male boss would receive. Unsupportive behavior will likely weaken everyone's performance, and this can only hinder an employee's prospects for advancement.

When you work for a younger person. Most employees who have a long career will eventually work with several or many persons who are younger. If you are an older employee, you may work not only with but for younger persons. Perhaps a younger person has more appropriate education or training, or perhaps management wants a younger person who will be with the company longer to be in charge. The reasons for selecting a younger person to be in charge vary, but it is a fact of business life that one may work for someone with fewer years on the job.

The younger boss should be sensitive to the older employee's feelings and openly show appreciation for his or her wisdom and years of experience. However, the boss, regardless of age, has a job to do, and the older employee must understand and respect this, assuming that the younger employee's appointment is legitimate and age discrimination is not involved. (The Age Discrimination in Employment Act prohibits employers from discriminating against anyone between the ages of fifty and sixty-five in matters such as hiring, firing, and compensation.)

An older employee can contribute to a relationship

with a young boss by treating the relationship as a matter of teamwork, whereby the two persons, age aside, have a common goal—to work together effectively in order to complete their mutual and respective tasks successfully. Although the older person may have learned a certain way of handling procedures or skills, the young boss may want to establish new practices. In such cases it will serve no useful purpose to cling to the past. Change is sometimes necessary, perhaps for reasons that are unclear at the moment, and it is important to support your young boss just as you would support someone closer to your own age. He or she may need your help and cooperation even more than someone older, just as you once did. On the other hand, do not hesitate to share (tactfully) your experience with someone younger. A capable manager will always welcome ideas and suggestions, even though it may not be possible to use all of them. Generally, a positive, helpful attitude will make your job more rewarding and your relationship with a younger person more enjoyable.

When you are the boss. Effective leadership is essential whether you have one or many employees in your charge. Although the nature of your business—and your office composition—will greatly influence the type of leadership you must provide, certain characteristics are essential.

You must motivate your employees to perform effectively. This may require a certain division of labor; it may mean the establishment of some type of reward system (bonuses, promotions, time off, and so on); it may involve more staff meetings; it may necessitate improved communications in general. You may even need to test different tactics and incentives to determine which practices best motivate your office personnel.

Sometimes you can stimulate creativity and enhance worker productivity with verbal rewards. Praise where praise is due is a proven way to recognize good work and encourage more of the same. Positive (constructive) criticism is part of this approach. Thus instead of saying, "This brochure layout is unacceptable. You didn't leave any room for a reply card on the back," you might say,

"Your design looks so nice that I hate to ask you to change anything, but I'm afraid there won't be enough room on the back panel for our reply card. If you can make space for that, I think it will be perfect." Above all, don't criticize an employee in front of other coworkers. Needlessly embarrassing someone will quickly breed resentment and discontent.

Many executives have an open-door policy to encourage active communication. People who talk—frequently—are less likely to let annoyances fester until they develop all out of proportion. In fact, misunderstandings of all sorts are less likely. Encourage employees to question instructions that are confusing and not to hesitate to discuss assignments that pose special problems.

Employees are likely to follow your example in many respects. If you are open, honest, and responsible, they are more likely to act the same with you. If you admit your mistakes, it is more likely that they will do the same. If you are consistent in your work habits and responses to their performance, they will be less hesitant about performing consistently. If you are punctual and respect your company's policies and practices, they will be more inclined to follow that example.

In general, treat employees fairly and equally. Displaying favoritism and discrimination is counterproductive and will discourage and antagonize most employees. Also, both mild flirtations and serious romantic involvements with someone in the office are distracting to everyone and can prompt a variety of responses (disrespect, gossip, embarrassment, and so on)—most of them undesirable. The best policy is to be equally respectful, courteous, and fair with all workers and to perform your own duties consistently and decisively.

Departmental Relationships

It can be difficult to apply the teamwork principle outside one's own office. Other departments and their personnel are even perceived as adversaries at times, competitors for a larger share of the company's budget, for certain promotions, and for other desirable benefits.

Although a healthy spirit of competition is usually considered an asset, it should not be allowed to develop to the point where departments become antagonists that try to block one another's efforts. Since the overall goal is the same—to promote the activity and welfare of the company—it is essential that one work *with*, not against, other departments.

Working relationships with employees in other departments should follow the same pattern as inneroffice relationships. Be courteous, respectful, and helpful at all times. When you need information or assistance from another department, respect its scheduling, priorities, and other influences. Thank the employees for their help and offer to reciprocate in the future. If you will be calling on others outside your office from time to time, you may find that it helps to establish a friendly contact in each department—someone you can call on freely as the need arises.

Coworker Relationships

Working with your peers. Coworkers in an office may seem like one's family away from home, and some executives encourage this type of atmosphere. A "family" approach at work can be beneficial, but it also can be harmful if it means that members of the "family" begin to take one another for granted, no longer feel the need to be courteous and thoughtful, and tend to fall into the habit of visiting (or bickering) during office hours. In short, it is usually unwise and counterproductive to treat office relationships completely with the same casual demeanor of relationships at home.

Teamwork, again, is the key to successful coworker relationships. Although you may be competing with your peers for recognition from your boss, for a promotion, for a special assignment, or for some other goal, you must balance this position with an open, friendly, cooperative attitude. No matter what your personal career aspirations may be, you must join your coworkers in advancing the cause of your organization. Clearly, any attempt to thwart their efforts is a handicap to the entire operation. Unity is a paramount need, and just as you help others do their job better, they will help you to perform better.

To help promote good relations among coworkers, be sensitive to the needs of others. Offer to help another coworker who is away from the office with an injury or illness. Take time to provide special friendship, guidance, and assistance to new employees. Be generous in compliments of others on their work, appearance, and so on. Always carry your share of the work load, and don't ask others to cover for you. Help to ease tension and stress with a cheerful disposition. Avoid potential conflicts by being a good listener and trying to understand the position of others. In general, be honest, fair, hardworking, and respectful of your coworkers. Aim for a spirit of trust and cooperation and refuse to participate in any practices that undermine good human relations at work.

PROMOTIONS AND RESIGNATIONS

Job changes in the workplace are common, and most people experience one or perhaps many such changes.

Promotions

Promotion strategy. Not many employees count on tenure or seniority alone as a basis for a promotion. If you are serious about advancement, you need to prove your worth. Among the characteristics you need to develop are accuracy, honesty, integrity, alertness, perceptiveness, punctuality, leadership, and creativity.

Develop your analytical ability—study your job and think of better ways to do it. Are there shortcuts you could use? Could a task be handled in less time or at less cost? Would a different division of labor help the office to operate more efficiently? Make suggestions for improvements, offer to take an additional responsibility, and take courses or engage in other activity to expand your knowledge and increase your skills.

When you have done something concrete to substantiate that you've earned a promotion, document your accomplishments and discuss the prospects for advancement with your superiors (or the personnel director). Even if you are aiming only for an increase in salary, use a similar strategy: take steps to prove your worth, document them, and present your request to your boss.

Resignations

Some people go to great lengths to avoid change and will live with a lower salary and an unappealing job simply to maintain the status quo. But many others are willing to put up with the trauma of not only moving from one job to another but moving from one part of the country to another. They do this to receive a higher salary, a more interesting or more challenging job, a position that will serve as a better steppingstone toward some ultimate goal, or merely because they're bored and want to do something different or live somewhere else.

Although you may discuss your desire for change with your boss, once the decision to resign has been made, you should write a letter of resignation. Include the following points:

1. Open with a statement that you are resigning your position as (job title) with (name of company) effective (desired date). Be certain you are complying with company regulations concerning how much notice is required.

2. Explain your reason for leaving: for example, to accept a position that will enable you to apply certain skills, training, or education.

3. Express appreciation to your boss and the company for previous opportunities and assistance.

Unless your circumstances are unusual, do not give notice or reveal your intentions to leave until the prospective position is confirmed. Even after everything is definite, continue to perform responsibly until you leave and avoid discussions comparing the new job (or company) with the old one, and do not cast adverse reflections on your former employer at any time—remember, you may need more recommendations one day.

If you are the employer losing an employee, wish the person well and do not take the departure personally. You, too, may decide to accept another opportunity if it arises. Work out an agreeable departure date with the employee and don't hesitate to ask him or her to help find and interview a replacement.

Firing

When you are fired. If this happens, it may not come as a surprise. Perhaps you have been unable to resolve a conflict with your boss or other coworkers, or perhaps there is another obvious reason. But if you don't know, ask why. You are entitled to an explanation, and the information may alert you to mistakes you have made that can be avoided in the future.

If you don't want to leave, ask if you can have a hearing to appeal your case. But if you prefer to go, accept the decision but ask about the terms of severance (severance pay, date, other available benefits). Keep in mind that unemployment benefits will be lost if you are discharged (fired) *with cause* or if you resign *without good cause.* (Since these distinctions are important in regard to your qualification for benefits, you may want to have your local unemployment office give their interpretation to you.) Generally, for example, it serves no purpose to ask to be fired, since the unemployment-insurance program considers this, in effect, a "constructive quit." For this reason, some employees ask an employer if they can be laid off instead, in order to qualify for benefits. But an employer who agrees to this practice is not helping the unemployment-insurance program.

Discuss an acceptable announcement to explain your departure to coworkers and to prospective employers. Inquire whether the company will accept a letter of resignation. Above all, do not act or speak out of anger or resentment either then or later. Make the departure as agreeable as possible and try to look upon it as a learning experience that will help you perform better in a new position.

When you must fire someone. Before you tell the employee your decision, reconsider one final time whether this is the wisest solution. Does the employee merely need further training? Could he or she be transferred to another office? If financial constraints are the cause, is there another alternative such as a temporary leave of absence until the cash flow improves? Have you given the person sufficient opportunity to improve? Have you clearly documented your warnings over a reasonable period? Once you are certain that the employee must be fired, call a meeting and get right to the point.

1. Tell the person why you have reached this decision, and do not make excuses or apologies or in any way appear to be indecisive or unsure that you are doing the right thing.

2. State your case calmly and unemotionally, using the documentation you have been developing over a reasonable period.

3. Do not engage in a debate or respond to emotional accusations. Simply state that you're sorry the employee feels that way and focus the discussion on severance conditions.

4. If you believe the employee will persist in a debate, hold the meeting outside the office so you can leave when desired.

5. Do not cast reflections on the employee after the firing or attempt to stop the person from working out a new professional life elsewhere.

6. Offer to accept a letter of resignation from the employee and work out an agreeable announcement to coworkers and outsiders.

Interviewing

Your boss may ask you to help interview candidates for the job you are leaving. Often there are likely candidates within the company. If not, consider whether you should use employment agencies, school placement offices, unemployment bureaus, or newspaper/magazine ads. You also may receive suggestions from associates or other outside contacts, or your personnel department may have material on file from previous applicants.

Schedule as many appointments as possible immediately. When applicants arrive, make them feel comfortable and make the atmosphere appear relaxed and congenial. If your company does not already have a written job description and material on company policies and procedures, compile a description of each and have photocopies available for applicants to review. If certain skills such as word processing are needed, give the applicant a standard test or one you have prepared for this purpose. Encourage applicants to volunteer information but also have a written list of questions to ask and use the list to guide the discussion. Follow the same procedure with each applicant and ask the same questions so that you can compare results later. When applicants leave, thank them and indicate when someone will notify them about a decision or in regard to further interviews. After each interview, give your boss a typed summary of the results.

HUMAN RELATIONS PROBLEMS

Not everyone will approach the workplace in a spirit of cooperation and sensitivity to the needs and feelings of others. When problems do occur, you need to know how to handle them, always aiming to nip them in the bud before they become unmanageable.

Gossip

Few things do as much damage as gossip. Original comments, perhaps even made in jest, are sometimes unrecognizable by the time they make the rounds of the grapevine. The way you handle any rumor or remark that fits this category is a test of your ability to deal with human relations problems.

First, choose your words carefully so that you do not unwittingly contribute to the rumor mill. For instance, if there is a female advertising manager (Ms. Breck) who meets (lunch, cocktails, and so on) regularly with a male marketing manager (Mr. Dobbs) and someone asks to see Ms. Breck, don't say, "She's probably out with Mr. Dobbs; they see a lot of each other." By the end of the day the office will be buzzing about the affair they're having. Instead simply say, "I believe she has a business meeting with the marketing manager."

Second, if someone else starts gossiping, offer an explanation that kills the gossip if you can; otherwise, refuse to participate or carry it further. For instance, if someone asks if you knew that Ms. Breck and Mr. Dobbs were having an affair, you might say, "Oh, it's nothing like that. The advertising manager always has to meet regularly with the sales and marketing managers. They wouldn't be able to do their jobs otherwise. But it's strictly business." If you don't have such information available, you could say, "I'm not aware of anything like that, so I certainly wouldn't want to start such a rumor. In any case, it's none of our business."

Third, if you can't stop others from gossiping, and if it is harming someone so that you are reluctant simply to ignore it, you might let the victim know in case he or she wants to take steps to discourage it. Ms. Breck, for example, might want to confine future advertising-marketing meetings to the office or company conference room or take along a third party such as her secretary, perhaps on the pretense of needing notes or minutes taken. The pleasure that the gossips derive from creating a torrid affair out of innocent business conferences would soon be dashed.

Office Politics

Teamwork, cooperation, thoughtfulness—these things are all necessary and admirable components of good human relations practices. But they do not mean that you cannot or should not devise honest and intelligent strategy to succeed or that you cannot or should not openly campaign to advance your career. Although some tactics are clearly destructive and go beyond the bounds of acceptable behavior anywhere, other strategy is clearly legitimate and necessary to improve your position. The following are examples of legitimate maneuvers:

1. Send your boss a memo summary of accomplishments whenever you finish an assignment or project.

2. Send your boss selected copies of pertinent external and internal correspondence to make your activity known, and keep copies of all communications for possible later verification of your actions.

3. Put in writing your requests or directives to uncooperative or ineffectual persons or departments, and retain copies in order to verify that any related inaction or other failure is not attributed to you.

4. Seek ways to become more visible, for example, chairing a committee or addressing a conference.

5. Volunteer for special assignments and extracurricular projects.

6. Document your accomplishments as part of your campaign for a raise or promotion.

7. Protect yourself from competitors by making your activity known so that others cannot claim credit for your work.

8. Identify sources of power in your firm so that you can go to the right people for recognition and requests.

9. Use incentives (praise, benefits, and so on) to motivate others to help you reach your goals.

10. Aggressively pursue an ongoing program of self-education to remain well informed and to be prepared for unexpected moves in any direction.

11. Be alert to outside activity such as a merger that may change the stability of your job and your goals.

12. Be flexible when situations require it while also having the courage to defend a position that you believe is right and essential.

13. Know your limitations and weaknesses and work at self-improvement while being alert to competitors who may take advantage of your areas of vulnerability.

14. Recognize when you have exhausted your resources

or your potential and when it is time to walk away or move on.

The dark side of office politics is the one that gives all of it a bad name. Ruthless people will use deception, lies, blackmail, and almost anything else to achieve their goals. When you are competing with such people, it is especially important to keep everyone openly informed of every decision you make and every act you perform. It's difficult for someone to distort something when your activity is highly visible.

When fictions (rumors) are created to handicap you, you again need to make your personal and professional activity so visible that the rumors will quickly wash out. For instance, if someone starts a rumor that you drink too much, take pains to lunch with others and be the one who stops with one drink or skips it altogether because you "have a lot of work waiting at the office." In other words, plan effective counterstrategy for every attempt to sabotage your position. Do not expect a problem to go away if competitors are bent on undermining your position. Sometimes one has to turn the tables on an adversary. *Strategy* is the password in office politics in more ways than one.

Personal Problems

Experts ask not whether you have any personal problems (who doesn't?) but whether you bring them to work; that is, do they influence your effectiveness and productivity in the office? One might also ask whether they affect your coworkers in any way. The other side of the coin is whether the personal problems of your coworkers affect you.

When you have a problem. The list of potential personal problems is endless. Some of the common ones are marital difficulties, drug dependency, and financial pressures. If you could quickly and simply solve such problems on your own, and if you wanted to solve them, you presumably would do so, and that would be the end of it.

But if they remain unsolved, it no doubt means that you haven't been able to cope with them successfully or haven't been motivated sufficiently to try.

Problems left unsolved tend to fester and grow, and they take their toll on one's health and energy. Mentally, they distract one; emotionally, they drain one. The resulting behavior begins to have an impact on others too, although some people mistakenly believe that their problems are private and need not concern others.

The only realistic course is to solve the problems if you want to succeed professionally as well as personally. Therefore, you may need to take advantage of outside professional services: marriage counselors, financial-planning consultants, doctors, ministers, and so on. Since it's not likely that such a personal problem will go away by itself, you really have everything to gain and nothing to lose by making a solution your first priority.

When others have problems. Although the steps to take in solving your own problems may seem clear, the steps to take in helping a coworker solve personal problems are less obvious. Generally, if a coworker has a serious problem that is affecting you and others at work, you have a right to recommend that the person seek professional help. You may not have to suggest it, in fact; the employee may ask for your help. In that case, make it clear that you are not a qualified physician or a minister or a psychologist. Instead, offer to find the name, address, and phone number of a reliable expert. Be supportive and encouraging, but do not be misled by coworkers who have no intention of solving their problems and merely want to dupe someone into covering for their errors and tardiness at work.

If someone refuses to take positive steps to solve a problem and is clearly jeopardizing the company through poor performance, deceitful actions, and so on, you can justifiably speak to your boss about it. You definitely should do this if your own work is threatened and there is danger that you may be blamed for someone else's mistakes.

If the employee reports to you, take steps on your

own. Call the person in, point out the adverse impact on his or her performance (as well as that of others), and give the person an opportunity to take prompt steps to rectify the situation. If the employee refuses, you have cause to fire him or her. Since circumstances vary greatly, you will have to use your own judgment in each case. But as a general rule, your responsibility is to the company, and therefore you cannot justifiably tolerate ineffective, unproductive work habits, regardless of your sympathy for the cause.

Sexual Harassment

Physical sexual advances, verbal pressures or requests for sexual favors, and other sexually oriented behavior that is not wanted by someone constitutes sexual harassment—and it is illegal. A common form of pressure is the offer of something such as job security or a promotion in return for sexual favors; the implication is that these things will be denied if one does not comply. In some cases the threat is less explicit, but the persistent advances create stress and anxiety in the victim.

Regardless of the form of harassment, it must not be tolerated. Try to put a stop to it at the first sign of unwanted attention. Indicate that you *never* get involved with people at work and that you feel extremely uncomfortable in this situation and want to continue your association on a strictly business basis. If the attention ceases, forget it and don't mention it again to anyone. But if the unwanted advances continue, other steps are necessary.

Be certain that you are not doing something to invite the advances (flirting, wearing sexually enticing clothing, using sexually provocative language). If you are guilty of any of those things, change your habits immediately. Keep a written record (date, place, and so on) of any comments or actions that are unwanted and what you did to discourage them. If you are unable to discourage the advances, tell your boss; if he or she is the guilty party, go to your boss's superior. If this does not help and you work for a large company, ask the personnel director to file a complaint with the Equal Employment Opportunity

Commission. If you do not have a personnel office, you can file the complaint on your own.

For your own protection, keep your family informed of these events and make certain that coworkers understand that you are an unwilling victim, not a willing participant, in any verbal or physical encounters. If you believe you are in physical danger and cannot count on assistance from a superior in your firm, go to the police; also consult an attorney if you need further representation. In all cases, respond promptly and firmly in the beginning and *do not submit* to threats and other forms of intimidation. Remember that sexual harassment is a crime, and if you look around, you will find numerous friends, coworkers, and professional organizations ready and eager to support you.

Employee Grievances

When you are responsible for an office or department with one or more employees, be prepared to deal with employee complaints and dissatisfaction. Do not assume that employees always complain or that there's a disgruntled employee in every office and that none of this should be taken seriously. Rather, use this type of problem as a means to monitor the morale of your staff and the success of your office practices.

If you use employee grievances to your advantage, you will want to *invite*, not ignore, complaints. By accepting this process, you can control it. For example, you can eliminate a certain amount of dissatisfaction merely by inviting suggestions and maintaining an open-door policy. Let employees know their thoughts, feelings, and recommendations are important. No one can then accuse you of not caring or listening. More important, you have a lot to gain from this approach. You may receive some very good ideas that will boost morale, lower employee turnover, increase efficiency and productivity, and enhance your own image in the eyes of your office staff.

It won't be enough to listen to grievances and then forget them. If complaints are justified or suggestions are good, take steps to solve the problem or make a needed change. If you believe the process of hearing all of these complaints and ideas will place too great a demand on your time, suggest that your company set up a grievance committee or appoint someone to hear complaints. Otherwise, set a certain time each week when you will meet with employees; that should eliminate any danger of people continually running in and out of your office every day. Consider your schedule and the needs of your office before deciding upon your specific plan—but do *something*. Employee grievances cannot and should not be ignored.

Money Matters

We live in a society where it is commonplace to borrow money. But a problem arises when one coworker wants to borrow from another. If you are in need of money, go to a bank or find another legitimate source of financing. Do not expect fellow employees to be your private bankers. Nothing puts a strain on a relationship as fast as borrowing and lending. If someone asks you for money, politely decline, saying that you simply have no available funds for lending. If you can recommend a bank or other lending agency, do so.

Some financial needs are far less pressing. Perhaps you accidentally left your wallet with cash, checkbook, and credit cards at home and you happen to have a very important luncheon date that day. Under such circumstances, it is acceptable to ask a coworker for an overnight loan of enough to pay for the lunch. But be certain to return the money immediately the following morning. You might want to include a thoughtful little gift such as flowers or a bottle of wine when returning the money. In general, use discretion in money matters, and as a general rule, when it comes to borrowing and lending, don't.

CHAPTER THREE

Following Proper Meeting Procedure

The word *meeting* is applied to all sorts of business assemblies or contacts—whether face to face, by telephone, or by video—between two or more persons. Very large organized meetings held in special facilities with a planned program are commonly called conferences or conventions. But formal or informal, internal or external, the meeting is a popular means of dealing with issues that are common to the participants.

Meetings are used to inform, to educate, to persuade, to sell, or to do anything else of interest or value to the meeting organizers and the participants. Although some people think that meetings are overused and are a time-consuming way to accomplish something, others believe that they can learn more and accomplish more in a face-to-face situation. Either way, meetings (both traditional and electronic) are clearly here to stay and sometimes even appear to be the great American pastime.

Since anyone can call a meeting for practically any purpose, the types of meetings are numerous and varied. Some of the more familiar types are the informal staff (or other internal) meeting, the dinner meeting, the directors' meeting, the stockholders' meeting, and the formal conference (including seminar, workshop, and convention). Although the size, agenda or program, degree of formality, and other characteristics may vary greatly from one type of meeting to another, a few practical guidelines apply in nearly all cases:

1. Have an agenda (or program) prepared in sufficient time to send participants a copy. That way everyone can

come prepared rather than waste precious meeting time in preparatory matters.

2. Have a meeting chairman (or appoint one) who is skilled in conducting and managing meetings. This will avoid time-wasting chaos and uncontrolled discussions that continually stray off course.

3. Arrange well in advance for facilities (conference room, hotel, and so on) and equipment (e.g., audiovisual) suitable for the size of the meeting and the types of presentations that are scheduled.

4. Rehearse if necessary to establish timing, movement, and other activity and to handle introductions and other program requirements smoothly and professionally.

5. Arrange well in advance for effective, knowledgeable speakers when the program calls for special addresses.

6. Control speaking time—whether planned or spontaneous—strictly, even to the point of using a timer, buzzer, or any other means to halt long-winded commentators who might otherwise throw the proceedings off schedule.

7. Arrange for minutes to be taken according to legal requirements or any other needs. (When appropriate, send brief summaries of the minutes to persons who could not attend, particularly if committee or other assignments were made during the meeting.)

8. Follow the rules of parliamentary procedure (study *Robert's Rules of Order*—Part I, "Rules of Order," and Part II, "Organization and Conduct of Businesses").

9. Bring to the meeting a well-organized meeting folder with a copy of the agenda, pertinent reports and other documents, a seating chart (if appropriate), pens and pencils, paper, paper clips, and anything else you might need.

10. Leave instructions for office personnel, for example, how to handle incoming calls for participants.

11. Make provisions for refreshments to be served (or provide for self-service) if desired so that a minimum of delay and distraction occurs during breaks.

12. Follow the rules of business etiquette (proper dress, courteous behavior, and so on).

STAFF MEETINGS

Staff and other informal meetings occur frequently, sometimes daily. The purpose may be to brief everyone on current activity, to discuss a special project, to decide something—virtually anything. A secretary may hold a ten-minute conference with an assistant to discuss problems and work assignments. An executive may hold a Monday-morning staff meeting to discuss ongoing business, new projects, and other issues. A committee chairman may call a committee meeting to vote on pending business matters. These and other forms of communication provide a means for participants to exchange ideas and reach decisions.

Preparations

The person calling the meeting should send participants a meeting notice and agenda, arrange for a meeting room, and prepare to conduct the meeting.

Notice. The notice for an informal meeting may be no more than a memo ("Could you meet me in my office at 10:30 A.M., Tuesday, June 9, to discuss the Eddings account?") or a telephone call followed by a reminder memo. Most informal meetings will be held in the office of the person calling the meeting or in a conference room. However, a junior executive should not ask a senior executive to come to his or her office. The meeting should take place in a conference room if senior personnel are invited. Morning hours are usually preferred since people are most attentive and productive in the earlier hours of the working day. Certain times such as the eve of a holiday or Friday afternoon, when people are eager to go home, are considered the worst times for a meeting.

Agenda. A single-topic meeting will not require an agenda, but a general meeting to discuss various topics should follow a specified order of business. An informal meeting, however, will not likely include the formal committee reports, reading of the minutes, and other business that would characterize a formal directors' meeting or a stockholders' meeting. But the person conducting an informal meeting should have a written plan, or order of topics, to guide the discussion among the participants and should begin and end the meeting on time. If a number of topics are to be discussed, participants should receive a copy of the informal list or an agenda along with the meeting notice or shortly thereafter.

The Meeting

Even a small meeting of two or three people should be conducted properly. Seating must be arranged with writing space, proper lighting, pencils and paper, ashtrays, water and glasses, a table with refreshments for self-service (optional), and copies of required documents pertinent to schedule topics of discussion. Seating at a conference table follows traditional etiquette, with senior personnel at the head of the table. The chair, or person calling the meeting, guides the discussion, sets the time for breaks, and controls wandering conversations. Although strict parliamentary procedure is not followed in an informal meeting, the person in charge should handle discussion, voting (if any), and other matters in an orderly manner. See DINNER MEETINGS for arrangements when a meal is provided. See also DIRECTORS' MEETINGS, The Meeting, *Parliamentary procedure*.

Teleconferences and videoconferences. When some participants of a meeting are in another location, telephone or videoconferences will save travel costs and related time. To arrange a conference call ask the long-distance operator to connect you with the conference operator and give her the names and numbers of people to be connected simultaneously at a desired time (alert participants by memo in advance so that everyone will be standing by at the selected time). Each connection on the conference line is treated as a separate person-to-person call in billing. (See also in chapter 10, Other Systems and Equipment, *Teleconferencing; Videoconferencing.*)

Videoconferences enable one to see as well as talk with other participants. An entire room of people, in fact, within the camera's view, could be involved. Presentations can be made to an entire group with this method in much the same way that television viewers can all watch a speaker on a commercial television program. Although videoconferencing is expensive and not yet widely used, some businesses believe the travel and time costs that they would otherwise incur make it worth considering. Ask for quotes from services in your area, and compare systems available for rental, lease, or purchase.

Minutes. If minutes (or informal notes) are required, the office secretary or some other staff member should take them. A written record is a good idea in any meeting that involves voting or other important decision-making activity. A seating chart is helpful to the person taking minutes if some participants are not familiar. Other material that should be available to the recorder includes a copy of the agenda, special reports, pertinent correspondence, and any other material that may be discussed.

Although notes of an informal meeting need not follow the prescribed order of a formal meeting, such as a stockholders' meeting, they should specify the meeting date and time, type of meeting, who attended, items discussed, motions made and seconded, voting results, any other pertinent activity, and time of adjournment.

Type the minutes double-spaced. Center a heading in all capitals consisting of the name of the group and type of meeting, for example:

SALES DEPARTMENT
FROMME MANUFACTURING COMPANY
NOVEMBER 5, 1987, STAFF MEETING

At the top of the page underneath the heading list the date, hour, place, presiding officer, and type of meeting. List attendees next if the meeting is small; otherwise, include a general statement such as "Twenty-five members of the sales staff were present." Use subheads (in all capitals) such as "MANAGER'S REPORT" and "ADJOURNMENT." Type signature lines at the bottom of the page for the group's secretary (if any) and the person chairing the meeting. Attach copies of reports and other documents discussed at the meeting. (See also the information on typing minutes in this chapter under DIRECTORS' MEETINGS.)

DINNER MEETINGS

Meetings that take place during lunch or dinner require special preparations. Some dinner meetings are very large, with hundreds in attendance. For example, lunch, dinner, and even a special banquet are commonly part of the program at large conferences. However, the small, local dinner meeting is the most familiar.

How often you hold such a meeting depends upon your budget and whether the attendance list includes important clients or officials who expect this treatment. Or the meeting may be part of another event such as an exhibit or workshop. Although a dinner meeting requires special preparations and cannot easily be thrown together on short notice, it is an appealing type of meeting that can be used to good advantage on special occasions.

Preparations

Invitations. Whether you send a traditional invitation or a regular meeting notice depends on the type of dinner meeting. If it is part of the program for a seminar, for example, the registration program should include dinner-meeting details, including date, time (both cocktails and dinner), place, guest speaker, and any other pertinent information. If you send an invitation (see chapter 1), specify the time for both cocktails and dinner (e.g., *Cocktails 7:30, Dinner 8:00*). Include a reply card or put *RSVP* on the invitation so that you can let the restaurant manager know how many guests must be served.

Mail the invitations for a local dinner three to five weeks in advance (as much as four to six months if there will be out-of-state guests).

Reservations. Reserve a room at a suitable restaurant, hotel, or other facility. A place close to the main airport is a thoughtful convenience if many guests will be arriving by airline. Work out a suitable menu with the restaurant representative, including head-table flowers and other needs. Use place cards for the head table (guest speakers, officers, and other important attendees) and assign other guests to a particular table but not to a specific place at the table. The chair sits at the center of the head table with the primary guest speaker on the right and the secondary speaker on the left, with other speakers alternating left and right. For other guests, women alternate with men and officials are seated by rank.

Speakers. Speakers are usually invited to address a meeting by business letter (see chapter 12). Although practices vary, it is common courtesy to meet speakers at the airport (and see about their return) and arrange for suitable hotel reservations. Compensation and payment for expenses of speakers are usually determined by company policy and the requirements of the guest (some persons will speak only for a certain fee and paid expenses). Present speakers with a written statement of special requirements: topic, maximum time allowed for the address, and so on.

The Meeting

As is true for any meeting, an agenda or order of business and a capable person to chair the meeting are needed to insure an orderly, successful progression. The chair should strictly control the time allowed for cocktails (half hour), the meal (one hour), the speeches (perhaps twenty-five minutes each), the committee reports (perhaps five to ten minutes each), and other business, which will vary depending on the type of meeting.

The chair must also be well prepared to introduce

speakers (using biographical data sheets collected in advance) and must study issues in advance in order to discuss them intelligently and make recommendations as needed. The secretary to the person chairing the meeting can help by gathering copies of pertinent correspondence, reports, and so on and setting up file folders with this material in logical order for the chair to refer to during the meeting.

If the meeting is formal, parliamentary procedure should be followed in discussing issues, calling for motions, and voting (refer to *Robert's Rules of Order*). Minutes should be taken by the meeting secretary (if any), an office secretary, or a stenographer (many hotels will make these arrangements for you).

The dress for an informal dinner meeting would be conservative business suits and business dressses. For a formal dinner meeting, the invitations will specify if black tie is required for men, which would mean that women would likely wear evening dresses (long skirts or other dressy attire). The meal itself should be treated like any dinner, and attendees should conduct themselves as if they were a guest in someone's home.

DIRECTORS' MEETINGS

A board of directors may be composed of inside directors and outside directors. Inside directors are usually important people within the corporation; outside directors may be heads of other organizations. Together they serve both the firm on whose board they sit and the firm's shareholders. Service on a board of directors is a mark of prestige and success. To the outside directors it can also be financially rewarding, depending on the fee paid to nonsalaried directors.

Preparations

Notice. Although the bylaws usually specify the time, place, and number of regular meetings to be held, special meetings may be called by the person(s) named in the bylaws (e.g., chairman of the board or president of the corporation). Notice must be given in writing according to the provisions in the bylaws regarding form of notice, date, and so on. Some corporations send notices on business letterhead; others use printed cards with blanks to fill in the date, time, and place of the meeting. Follow the wording specified in your bylaws or copy the wording of previous notices kept in the files.

Agenda. A formal agenda should be prepared by the corporate secretary and mailed to the other directors in advance, thereby giving them time to prepare. Secretaries commonly invite the directors to suggest topics for the agenda before preparing the final copy. The type of topics and the order may vary depending on the corporation's business activity, but some or all of the following items may be used:

1. Call to order
2. Announcement of a quorum present (the bylaws will specify the number required to transact business)
3. Reading (by the corporate secretary) and correction and approval (by vote) of the minutes of the previous meeting
4. Reports of officers and committees (e.g., treasurer's report)
5. Old business
6. Declaration of dividend (if any)
7. New business
8. Nomination and election of new officers (when specified in the bylaws)
9. Announcements
10. Adjournment

Facilities. The bylaws will state where the meeting must be held; often, this is the corporation's boardroom. The secretary to the chief executive officer or an assistant should see that the boardroom is properly set up with pads, pencils, and pens at each place; ashtrays; and paper cups or glasses with a water carafe at each end of the table. Arrangements may also be made for refreshments to be catered or a self-service table set up in a foyer or in the hallway.

Seating is formal, with the chairman of the board at the head of the table and the corporate secretary to the left and the corporate president to the right. If special equipment (e.g., display charts, audiovisual aids) will be used, arrangements must be made in advance and everything assembled before the directors arrive. Depending on the location of outside directors, the office of the chair or the corporate secretary may offer to make hotel reservations for directors and pick them up at the airport. See DINNER MEETINGS for additional arrangements when a meal is to be provided.

The Meeting

The chair calls the meeting to order and conducts it formally according to parliamentary procedure.

Parliamentary procedure. The various rules provide for the transaction of business through motions. Someone who wants a vote taken on some issue addresses the chair ("Madam Chairman, I'm Jane Littlefield"). After being recognized, the person begins his or her motion by stating, "I move that . . ." Someone else must second the motion (or it is lost) in order for it to be considered. After a second, the chair asks, "Is there any further discussion?" After discussion, depending on the formality and the preference, the chair asks for a vote by voice, show of hands, standing, roll call, ballot, mail or proxy, or general consent. Motions are ranked in order of importance, and those of highest precedence are considered first. A point of order calls attention to a violation of rules or proper procedure. It is the chair's responsibility to declare a motion (not a person) out of order. For full details on proper parliamentary procedure, consult *Robert's Rules of Order*.

Minutes. There should be a stenographer (often an office secretary) at the meeting to take official minutes. Procedures are sometimes tape-recorded as well. The person taking the minutes may want to use a blank sheet to record resolutions quickly and in an orderly manner; for example:

Resolution No. 1. Proposed by:_____

Seconded by:_____

Votes for:_____

Votes against:_____

The recorder should have handy a copy of all reports and other documents discussed, a list of the directors' names or a seating chart, and any other material that will help insure accuracy and completeness of the minutes. In typing the minutes, follow the style in the formal minute book. Often there is a heading such as the following:

MINUTES OF SPECIAL MEETING OF DIRECTORS XYZ CORPORATION

The first paragraph usually states the date, time, and place, as well as the presiding officer. The second paragraph mentions the roll call and who was present in person or by proxy (see STOCKHOLDERS' MEETINGS for a sample proxy). The third paragraph may verify that proper notice was given. The fourth paragraph may discuss the validation of proxies. Subsequent paragraphs detail the committee reports and old and new business, including resolutions and voting. The minutes close with a statement about adjournment and the signatures of the president and the secretary.

Words such as *Board of Directors* and *Corporation* are capitalized and *WHEREAS* and *RESOLVED* are written in all capitals. *That* is capitalized in *RESOLVED That*. Captions for different sections (*ROLL CALL, TREASURER'S REPORT*, and so on) are typed in all capitals and may be placed above the appropriate paragraphs or to the left in the margin. Errors of previous minutes are corrected by drawing a red line through the material and inserting the correct information between the lines. Large minute books may need a topic index similar to the index of a traditional book.

Meeting conduct. The chair guides the discussion following the prepared agenda. His or her office secretary and assistants should help collect a meeting file, perhaps consisting of several folders, with pertinent correspondence and reports organized for easy retrieval and reference during the meeting. The corporate secretary, who is responsible for the minutes, similarly must have all pertinent data ready for quick reference. The corporate secretary also arranges for payment of directors' fees (if any) and has checks drawn in advance so that payment can be made at the conclusion of the meeting.

Instructions must be given in advance to office personnel concerning urgent telephone calls and other emergency matters. Otherwise, the meeting should progress without interruptions.

STOCKHOLDERS' MEETINGS

Although directors' meetings are confined to board members and invited guests, stockholders' meetings are open to all who hold stock in the corporation. Holders of capital stock may vote each share in person or by proxy (see sample in the section The Meeting). Like directors' meetings, the meetings of stockholders may be regular ("general") or special ("called").

Preparations

Corporate secretaries are responsible for many of the preparations to hold a meeting of the stockholders. Both statutory provisions and corporate policy and regulations affect the steps that must be taken.

Notice. A meeting may be called by the persons specified in the bylaws. They notify the corporate secretary in writing, and the corporate secretary issues a notice or "call" to the stockholders. Type the call on business letterhead and follow the wording prescribed by the state statutes of corporation regulations (copies of previous calls will be in the files).

Upon receipt of the call by an authorized person, the corporate secretary prepares a notice, which is sent to all stockholders. It may be a postcard or other format and should specify the date, place, and time, as well as any other important details that are required according to the bylaws (such as the purpose of the meeting). Follow the required wording of your corporation (refer to previous file copies). Notices must be mailed a certain number of days before the meeting as stated in the bylaws. A proxy such as the following is enclosed (a quorum is determined by the number of voting shares available in person *or by proxy*).

PROXY

I hereby constitute (*name*), (*name*), and (*name*), who are officers or directors of the Corporation, or a majority of such of them as actually are present, to act for me in my stead and as my proxy at the (*meeting*) of the stockholders of (*company*), to be held in (*location*), on (*date*), at (*time*), and at any adjournment or adjournments thereof, with full power and authority to act for me in my behalf, with all powers that I, the undersigned, would possess if I were personally present.

Effective Date_____

Signed (stockholder)_____

Address_____

City_____State_____Zip Code_____

PLEASE BE CERTAIN TO INCLUDE YOUR ADDRESS AND SIGNATURE AND THE DATE OF SIGNING. THANK YOU.

Agenda. The agenda of a stockholders' meeting may include items not included at other meetings (see sample agenda in DIRECTORS' MEETINGS), for example:

Introduction of directors, officers, and special guests
Motion to accept transfer agent's affidavit regarding mailing of notice, proxies, and other material
Appointment of election inspectors
Ratification of auditors

Include all items required by law or policy of the corporation (refer to file copies of previous agendas). Directors and officers should receive an advance copy of the agenda in order to prepare for the meeting.

Facilities. The location of the meeting is determined by law and corporation policy. Experience and proxy returns are two guides to the number of stockholders who will attend such a meeting. Conference halls or auditoriums may be necessary for large meetings; ordinary board conference rooms may suffice for very small meetings.

Whether large or small, the meeting must be conducted within a certain period (although some meetings are adjourned until another date and/or time). Therefore, arrangements must be carefully designed to move people in and out in an efficient, orderly manner; to distribute reports and other printed material; to provide access to water and restrooms; to use properly operating visual and audio equipment and display materials; and to introduce guests and control speaking time. Proceedings of some annual meetings are transmitted by closed-circuit television to stockholders who cannot attend. Sometimes also corporations arrange special tours and other events for stockholders and their spouses. Many of the suggestions in DIRECTORS' MEETINGS are applicable to stockholders' meetings.

The Meeting

The order of business at a stockholders' meeting may dictate that, after the call to order by a presiding officer, a chair be elected who will then conduct the meeting, following proper meeting procedure (see DIRECTORS' MEETINGS, The Meeting, *Parliamentary procedure*). Depending on the requirements of the bylaws, strict parliamentary procedure may not be necessary at a stockholders' meeting, but the use of motions, voting, and other basic principles are usually necessary. Minutes must be formally recorded, however, according to strict legal requirements. (See DIRECTORS' MEETINGS, The Meeting, *Minutes*.)

The chair and the corporate secretary, as well as other directors and officers, should come prepared with carefully organized meeting folders containing copies of pertinent correspondence; reports; legal papers, including the certificate of incorporation and other corporate documents; and other material that may be needed during the meeting. Finally, the staff of the corporate secretary and the chair must be instructed how to deal with emergencies during the meeting.

CONFERENCES

Large meetings (annual conferences, conventions, and some seminars and workshops) consisting of members and guests of a sponsoring organization(s) require extensive planning and the assistance and involvement of many persons and service establishments (airlines, hotels, and so on). These meetings may last several days—sometimes longer in the case of trade shows and national and international exhibitions.

Although there may be one key individual such as the chair of the conference or the sponsoring organization's president, numerous specialty committees may be formed to handle budgeting, speaker invitations, the program preparation, registration, facilities, travel, special equipment, publicity, and exhibits. Representatives from hotels, airlines, car-rental agencies, and other service organizations are also active.

Preparations

Committees. Although each meeting may vary in the type and number of committees needed, most large gatherings will have some or all of the following committees: planning, budget, program, publicity, registration, facilities, meals and beverages, entertainment, equipment and supplies, and exhibits.

The *planning committee* will likely define the objective of the meeting and the theme, establish a preliminary budget, set dates, pick a tentative site, and form the other committees to deal with each activity.

The *budget committee*, probably including the organization's treasurer or budget officer, will prepare an overall conference budget, with allocations to each area of activity. It will monitor expenditures and refine figures as registration and other income projections are clarified. It will also check and pay bills and prepare whatever financial statements are required by the sponsoring organizations.

The *program committee* will select program topics; assign topics to various times during the meeting; select and invite speakers, session moderators, a keynote speaker, a banquet speaker, and any other person giving an address; prepare the copy for a program and related materials and work with the printer concerning production and mailing of the program package; and generally attend to any other program details.

The *publicity committee* will arrange for news releases, articles, radio and television announcements, press conferences, and any other form of communication to publicize the meeting.

The *registration committee* will process all advance registration forms and monies, setting up files, mailing acknowledgments, reporting receipts to the budget committee, reporting program session registration numbers to the program committee, and will handle incoming queries from prospective attendees. At the conference it will set up a door- or desk-registration and information booth where latecoming registrations are processed and printed proceedings and other material of the sponsoring organization are sold.

The *facilities committee* will work with hotel and transportation representatives to arrange for rooms in which to hold sessions, an area for desk registration and an information booth, rooms for meal and beverage service, a special banquet or reception room, overnight sleeping accommodations for guests, and any other facilities that are needed. Airlines and ground-transportation services will assist in transport matters and may, additionally, offer to contribute to the preparation (printing costs) of program materials in return for advertising benefits.

The *meals and beverage committee* will coordinate efforts with the facilities committee and with the hotel, convention center, or other facility. It will arrange for all breakfasts, lunches, dinners, coffee breaks, cocktails, and any other group service for attendees. Since attendance must be known in order to guarantee a certain number of guests at each meal, this committee will also work closely with the registration committee.

The *entertainment committee* will arrange for piano bars, dinner-dances, special performers, films, tours for attendees or spouses, theater tickets, and other extracurricular activity, scheduling events to avoid conflicts with the program sessions. Tickets and invitations will likely be printed in conjunction with the preparation of the program committee's program packet.

The *equipment and supplies committee* will coordinate efforts with the facilities committee and with the hotel. It will arrange for the rental of all special speaker's equipment (closed-circuit television, display boards, audiovisual aids, and so on), office equipment for staff use (typewriters, word processors, calculators, and so on), and miscellaneous supplies (paper and pencils for sessions and staff, word-processor diskettes, staplers, currency safe-deposit boxes, notebooks, and so on).

The *exhibits committee* will work coordinate efforts with the facilities committee and the registration committee. It will plan booth and other space, advise exhibitors of rules and regulations, and generally oversee the setup and maintenance of exhibits during the meeting.

Meeting Conduct

All of the essentials described in the earlier sections about other types of meetings apply here, such as monitoring the time allotted to each speaker, rehearsing introductions and movements to insure a smooth program, and following a proper order of business in any business meetings that are held during the conference.

Representatives of the sponsoring organization should work hard to insure that attendees have an enjoyable stay, are not made to wait for long periods, and are not accidentally left out of meals, sessions, or any other event for which they are registered. Attendees, too, should do their part to behave in a courteous and orderly manner. Dress at a large meeting may range from very casual at program sessions to black tie at a dinner-dance. Check the program material or inquire when you register if you are uncertain about dress, meeting procedures, or any other aspect of the conference.

RECORD
KEEPING

CHAPTER FOUR

Using Efficient Filing Systems

Correspondence, documents, and other material in an office must be classified, filed, and retrieved when needed. To do this in a minimum of time, with the least amount of effort, you need an efficient filing system, one that is appropriate for the type of material you have. If you have a variety of material, as most offices do, you will need more than one type of system.

In most offices file clerks and secretaries work with the files more than anyone else. But other office personnel should also be familiar with the system, so that material can be retrieved even in the absence of those most familiar with it. On the other hand, the files should *not* routinely be open to everyone. If they are, misfiles, lost material, security problems, and other difficulties will be inevitable.

Organizations do not always take filing as seriously as they should, and secretaries, in particular, rate it as one of the least desirable tasks. But since the processing and storage of paper is a major part of the activity in an office (or a department or the company in general), it is often an expensive aspect of activity. The wrong system can easily add to labor and storage costs. Legal implications, too, are of vital importance. State and federal regulations govern the period that certain records must be retained and thus affect not only decisions about what should be filed but how long it should be retained.

BASIC FILING SYSTEMS

A few basic systems (alphabetic, subject, geographic, and numeric) dominate the filing process, but many offices use some combination of these systems (e.g., alphanumeric) or less common systems (e.g., phonetic). A thorough evaluation of all aspects of records management is needed to make the right choice. This includes not only a determination of type of material, cost restraints, and legal requirements but of available space and access to mechanized or automated equipment. Experts also recommend simple systems (alphabetic or numeric) over more complex systems (subject or geographic); they also urge lateral or shelf filing (better visibility and minimum floor space) and wide application of color coding and any other technique that makes retrieval easier and reduces the likelihood of misfiles.

Alphabetic Files

One of the most common filing systems is the alphabetic system, traditionally used for classifying and filing by name (see also Subject Files). Most people feel comfortable with this system, primarily because the rules of alphabetization are learned early in life. However, there is usually more to the process than people realize (see INDEXING AND ALPHABETIZING).

Alphabetic files stored primarily in drawers, in boxes, or on shelves (as opposed to diskette or tape) require folders, labels, and guides. You may, for instance, have an alphabetical name file, with a separate folder for each name and a miscellaneous folder for occasional other names. Each folder would have a label with the name typed on it (use different-color labels when several persons have the same name). If additional folders are needed for one name, differentiate by adding the inclusive dates of material within each folder on the respective labels. Arrange the papers inside a folder by date, with the most recent date at the front.

Phonetic filing. This system is used when name files contain numerous surnames that sound alike but are spelled differently. The Soundex method, developed by Remington Rand, converts surnames to an alphanumeric code so that names with variant spellings such as Browne, Brown, and Broun will all be filed in the same place.

Subject Files

Subject files are also very common. Here material is classified by topic and is subdivided as often as needed. In other words, you may have a main heading on one folder, such as *CONTRACTS*, with various subheadings on other folders, such as *Commercial, Industrial,* and *Residential.* Main headings would be filed alphabetically throughout the entire file, with folders bearing subheadings filed alphabetically only behind the appropriate main heading; for example:

    CONTRACTS
    Commercial Contracts
    Industrial Contracts
    Residential Contracts
    FORECLOSURES
    Commercial Foreclosures
    Industrial Foreclosures
    Residential Foreclosures

A subject file may also be set up numerically (see Numeric Files) or with a combination called "subject-duplex." With this system a subject is assigned a number such as 500, and subheadings under this subject are given an auxiliary number such as 500.1. The main subject folders (e.g., 500, 600, and so on) are arranged numerically throughout the file, and folders with auxiliary numbers (e.g., 500.1, 500.2; 600.1, 600.2; and so on) are arranged numerically behind the appropriate main subject folder.

Any nonalphabetic system requires a separate alphabetical list of subjects, showing the topic names and numbers assigned to them. Often this cross-index file is prepared on three- by five-inch cards. Thus if you wanted to find a folder in the numerical file on the Patterson Project, you would look up "Patterson Project" in the alphabetical card file and might notice that it was assigned the auxiliary number 704.4 and is positioned behind a main folder—PROJECTS (700). In the main files, then, you would look for the guide and main folder, both labeled "700" and look at the folders with subtopics and sub-subtopics filed numerically behind that main folder, for example: 700–701, 701.1, 702, 703, 703.1, 703.2, 704, 704.1, 704.2, 704.3, *704.4*. Correspondence within a particular folder would be filed by date, with the most recent date in front. (See also Numeric Files.)

Headings in a subject file must be selected carefully and logically, or it can become difficult to find material later. Use nouns as much as possible. Keep a miscellaneous folder for material on various subjects that is not extensive enough for any topic to merit a separate folder. Use color coding of folders or tabs to help you locate material easily and to spot misfiles.

Geographic Files

Any type of business concerned with places—countries, regions, states, and so on—is likely to have a geographic file or a combination geographic-numeric file (similar to the subject-numeric file). The complexity of classification (number of subtopics) depends on the nature of the business. For instance, you may need to classify material first by region (e.g., Northwest) and then within the region break it down by state, next cities within the state, and finally customers within the cities. You may even need to break it down further into customers, type of business, and so on. However, in setting up any sales-account filing system, one should avoid making it unnecessarily complex.

Use the same supplies as in an alphabetic name file and a subject file—folders with tabs and guides with tabs. If you use an alphabetic rather than numerical arrangement, first file all main headings such as regions (*NORTHWEST*) alphabetically. Behind each main heading file first-level subheadings such as states (*Washington*) alphabetically, and behind that file the second-level subheadings such as cities (*Seattle*), and so on to the lowest-level subheadings such as firm (*Pierce Distributors*).

You will need an auxiliary card file with a geographic system. This file might list all customers alphabetically.

Thus to find "Pierce Distributors" in the main file, you would look under "P" in the alphabetical card file and on its card note that the folder is located in the *NORTHWEST* section of the files behind *Seattle* (which is filed back of the *Washington* State subsection). As usual, correspondence within a particular folder is filed by date, with the most recent date in the front of the file.

Numeric Files

Applications, insurance records, and a variety of other material all have identification numbers and are suitable for numeric filing. Although massive amounts of such material are often filed electronically (e.g., computer) or in reduced form (e.g., microfilm), when traditional paper files are also maintained, the numeric system (by itself or in combination with other systems) is preferred.

Consecutive numbering. Numbering files consecutively (1, 2, 3, and so on) is the easiest method to learn and set up, but it is not always the most practical as the files expand, since all new folders would continue to pile up at the end of the files.

Terminal-digit files. The terminal-digit system avoids the accumulation of all added folders at the end by dividing a number such as 324117 into units: 32-41-17. The last unit (17) is the principal one, the middle unit (41) is secondary, and the third (32) is last. So the number is filed as 17-41-32. By shifting the actual digits, incoming folders are scattered throughout the files, rather than all clustered at the end.

As with other systems, here, too, the arrangement of material in the files includes guides—such as a main guide *17* for all numbers having a primary digit of *17*—and folders with tabs bearing the full arrangement of digits: *17-41-32*. Color coding is useful in numeric files as well as in any other files, and the amount of subdivision depends on the type of material.

Digits may refer to location by drawer and folder. For instance, if an application had the number *324117, 17* might refer to the file drawer (or shelf), *41* might refer to the number of a folder containing applications, and *32* might mean the numerical order of application 324217 within folder 41. In other words, in file drawer 17 and folder 41 there would be a group of applications perhaps numbered 014117, 015117, . . . 324117.

Numerical files of any sort—straight numeric or a combination such as subject-numeric—must have an auxiliary card index. For example, if the number *324117* is the identifying number of a club-membership application for John Bryant, you would need an alphabetical card file of members' names. On the card for John Bryant you would note that his application is the thirty-second application in folder 41, which is located in drawer 17.

Chronological filing. Filing chronologically, or placing each item in a folder by date with the most recent date on top, might be considered a form of numerical filing. Sometimes in a small office, or when the date is the most important thing, a straight chronological file is appropriate. Often when the date is that important, it may be necessary to have follow-up or reminder date files as well as for things that must be repeated later or that may be unresolved later and require a reminder notice. See REMINDERS AND FOLLOW-UPS.

Decimal system. Numbers are used in the decimal filing system, which is based on the Dewey Decimal System. Used in some public libraries, this system classifies topics by sequential numbers (100, 200, and so on), with up to ten principal headings, and it lists subtopics by further subdivision of the ten main headings, for example: 100—110, 120, 130, 130.1, 130.2, . . . 190.9. See the list of Dewey Decimal numbers under RESEARCH in chapter 13.

MODERN EQUIPMENT AND SUPPLIES

Filing equipment today covers a wide range of containers and devices, some designed for manual filing and retrieval and others designed for mechanical or electronic filing and retrieval. Preferred styles and colors can be ordered from many manufacturers, enabling office designers to select files that fit the office decor and create a pleasant environment that enhances worker productivity. To cope with the space and handling problem—as well as the cost—of storing massive amounts of paper, some firms are reducing and transferring documents to microfilm or microfiche.

Modern supplies such as folders, guides, and labels are designed to make the process of filing, and especially retrieval, easier. Color coding is widely employed, and other supplies such as guide tabs are preprinted to save time or are removable for easy reorganization or expansion of the files. The principal considerations in selecting storage equipment and supplies are space, ease of filing and retrieval, speed of filing and retrieval, and cost of labor as well as equipment and supplies.

Filing Equipment

If you stop at an office-supply store and look at one of its catalogs, you will be amazed at the variety of available filing and storage devices—everything from the traditional file cabinet to the desktop index file to the latest computer-printout file, not to mention the large electronic storage and retrieval systems.

Selecting equipment is a problem when the choice seems unlimited, and each item seems to have merit at least for certain situations. Since space is a prime consideration in most cases, one first should review the existing files to determine whether old material should be removed and put into inactive storage either in appropriate storage containers or through a reduction process such as microfilming. Perhaps some material (brochures, catalogs, and so on) shouldn't be taking up file space and can be moved to a bookshelf or magazine rack. Photographs and other material may have heavy cardboard backing that could be removed, and some bulky documents such as maps or blueprints belong in a more suitable file or storage area. Some of the correspondence itself may be unnecessary. If there are three carbon copies of the same letter, consider whether one copy would be adequate with the name, date, and subject simply added to a cross-reference sheet in the other two cases. Most files contain more than they should, and careful reorganization periodically can sometimes save enough space to avoid adding more equipment and containers.

Traditional files. Few offices, particularly small offices, exist without the traditional *drawer-style filing cabinet*. With the movement away from legal-size paper, even in law offices in many jurisdictions, more of the drawer cabinets in the future may be letter size. *Shelf filing* is noted for ease of use (no drawer to open) and the visibility of the folders (enhanced with color coding). Some files are combination units such as both drawer and shelf. *Safety files* range from small fireproof boxes that fit in a desk drawer to large, room-size, controlled-entry safes. *Boxes* such as corrugated fiberboard and other storage boxes are often used when economy or inactive storage are principal factors.

Some files are designed especially for desk-top use. The simple *index-card box* is perhaps best known, although a variety of other products offer more features. One such product is the *rotary file*, in which small cards turn on a wheel. *Visible-card files* such as tray files, both manual pull-out and automated styles, where the cards lie flat, are noted for easy reference; other types of visible files include books with pockets for cards and traditional binders, or notebooks.

Modern files. The increasing use of computers in the office has led to a wide selection of *electronic-data-processing files*; for example: hanging printout racks, compartment organizers, diskette files, data binders, forms cabinets. The use of computers has also made electronic filing and retrieval more common.

Electronic filing itself refers to the transfer of data from computer memory onto an internal hard disk or onto small floppy disks, or diskettes, about the size of a phonograph record. When a hard copy (paper copy) is needed, the computer can retrieve the information on the disk and instruct the printer to print it on paper. Although this process is not suitable for filing massive amounts of data, it is sometimes used in individual offices as an additional means of record retention.

Electronic storage and retrieval commonly refers to the use of a computer to maintain an index that lists the physical location of files in a large, centralized filing department and the use of electronically controlled devices to transport files. Usually, there is a numerical keyboard by which an operator can enter the location of the file. A transportation device then automatically finds and physically moves the shelf or container in and out. These systems are essential for very large file rooms, with extensive activity, where it would be almost impossible to provide a staff to walk back and forth, searching for every folder.

Micrographics. The field of document miniaturization has offered one solution to the problem of space otherwise needed to store vast amounts of paper. The technology most often uses special cameras to reduce text and graphics to microimages on film. The two common microforms are film sheets (*microfiche*) and rolls of film (*microfilm*). These two forms can also be produced directly from computer-generated signals.

Microfilm (or microfiche) requires no more storage space than 35 mm camera film. The savings in filing space (and associated costs) are often coupled with savings in postage costs for firms that would otherwise have to mail bulky, heavy documents. With a *reader*, a machine that enlarges the microimages to normal size on a televisionlike screen, one can review any document when desired. A *reader-printer* will additionally print out one or more paper copies of the document.

Filing Supplies

The amazing variety of filing supplies equals that of filing containers and equipment. The supplies are intended not only to hold material of a certain size but to arrange it efficiently within a file and make it easier to locate it later.

Folders and labels. Traditional shelf and drawer files use letter- or legal-size folders. A familiar file folder is the manila folder with a top tab in various sizes such as straight cut, one-half cut, one-third cut, and one-fifth cut. Some tabs have numbers, letters, or dates printed on them; others are detachable clear plastic tabs, with removable inserts. Gummed and press-apply labels are available in many colors for color coding. You may want to stagger tabs left, middle, and right or use all right-position tabs and all left-position guides. Choose the arrangement that makes it easiest to locate material. Some folders are colored as well and available in manila stock, plastic, pressboard, and other material. Hanging-file folders that can't slide out of position are suspended on frames in a file drawer; interior folders are made to fit inside the hanging folder. Other folders are made to fit in binders and other notebooks; some are expandable pockets that, when full, resemble a small box with a foldover lid.

Guides. Pressboard or cardboard guides are used to divide groups of files. Like files, they may have printed numbers, letters, or data on the tabs, or the tabs may have an opening where you can insert your own label. Thus you might have a main guide with "A" on the tab, and within the A section of the files you might additionally have other subsection guides such as *Ac, Am,* and *As.* Folders would be grouped alphabetically behind the appropriate guides, for example:

Ac

Accounting International
Action Unlimited

Am

American Trust Co.
Amsterdam Manufacturing Co.
Amtrovich Lighting Fixtures

As
    Asterbrook Resort
    Astrophysics Research Center

Color-coded guides will help you locate various sections of the alphabet quickly. In fact, color coding can be used in many ways. You could, for instance, have all individual-name folders (or tabs) in yellow and miscellaneous folders (or tabs) in blue. Index cards of various sizes also come in different colors. The options in tabs are similar to the choices of tabs for folders and guides.

Label lettering. The labels for cabinets should be printed, not typed, in large letters readable from a distance. Do not use all capitals, because capitals are hard to read; also, do not underline. Folder and guide labels should be typed, using abbreviations and omitting punctuation whenever possible. Again, do not use all capital letters or underline. Center all headings in the visible space.

Cross-references. Use colored cross-reference sheets to distinguish them from other material in the files. A permanent cross-reference may consist of a colored guide or the back of an old folder, inserted among the regular folders, with a label such as this:

Morris, Fletcher, & Co.
See
Fletcher Morris & Co.

Use a different color to distinguish the cross-reference label from regular-folder or guide labels.

Out cards. To control material removed from the files, prepare *out cards*, a folder or guide of a color different from the file folders. It should have *OUT* printed on the tab and space ruled on the front to write the date of removal, description of material removed, expected return date, name of person removing the material, and additional remarks.

Insert the OUT card in the place where the folder was

before it was removed. You may also want to keep a desk file of charge-out slips—showing the date, who removed the material, and so on—to use as a reminder file. If a folder isn't returned when expected, you can then begin follow-up procedures.

INDEXING AND ALPHABETIZING

Preparing material to go into a filing system is just as important as selecting and installing the file containers and equipment.

1. Sort the papers that are ready for filing into logical categories (personal and business correspondence, documents, publications, and so on).

2. Within each category, arrange the material in the same subcategories that are used in the files. For example, if you have an alphabetical subject-file system, divide your correspondence and other material into the same subjects that are typed on the file-folder tabs, such as:

CONTRACTS
Commercial Contracts
Industrial Contracts
Residential Contracts

3. Scan each letter or document, select the appropriate main-folder heading and any folder subheading, and jot the headings down on the upper right corner of the material. Use erasable pencil or removable press-apply, slips of paper (sold in office-supply stores) on originals that should not be marred with writing. If you use a numeric system, note the appropriate numbers as well or any other information that is used in your file-classification system. If you have a simple alphabetic system, instead of writing the file-folder information on the material to be filed, you may be able simply to take a nonreproducible blue pencil and underline the key word(s) somewhere on the first page of the material. (Some offices will not permit any marking on originals.)

4. Immediately make up any necessary cross-reference sheets or cards.

5. Before you actually deposit the file material in the appropriate folder, mend torn papers with cellophane tape, remove cardboard backings and paper clips, and staple appropriate groups of papers together; discard envelopes only after you are certain that the correspondence or document already contains the correct mailing address and date of receipt.

The list of actual names or subjects that you choose from in classifying your correspondence and documents is determined earlier—when you open file folders and type the identifying labels for each guide and file-folder tab. In an alphabetical system, two sets of rules govern the order of the words in a name and the alphabetical order within the files: indexing rules and alphabetizing rules.

Basic Rules

Indexing, in regard to file preparation (as opposed to the indexing of a book, for example), refers to the arrangement of the words in a name on the tab labels. Certain widely accepted rules indicate which word you should type first. Only after the names are indexed in this way can you alphabetize them. You need to know these rules not only to be able to make up labels for new folders but to be able to find folders later when you are ready to file or need to retrieve your correspondence, documents, and other material.

All literate workers know that *a* comes before *b*, *b* before *c*, and so on. But not everyone knows the intricacies such as whether a hyphenated word is considered one word or two words in alphabetizing and whether abbreviations such as *St.* are alphabetized as *s-t* or as if they were spelled out as *S-a-i-n-t*. The following rules cover most situations. But no matter which rule you follow, *be consistent* in further uses.

Different rules indicate the procedure to follow in indexing and alphabetizing names of individuals, names of business firms and other commercial establishments, and names of institutions and governmental bodies. Two rules, however, apply in all three cases:

1. Alphabetize the indexed names *by unit*, first considering unit 1 words, then unit 2 words, next unit 3 words, and so on:

(1) Kosta   (2) Evans   (3) C.
(1) Kosta-Denton   (2) Estelle   (3) M.
(1) Madison   (2) Ross (&)   (3) Fields   (4) Ltd.

2. Add a cross-reference sheet or card whenever someone might look in more than one place for a name:

Kuo-feng, Mao. See Mao Kuo-feng.

Individuals. Follow these rules in indexing and alphabetizing names of persons and refer to the concluding alphabetical list for examples:

1. Transpose names (*Smith, Clarence*) except unfamiliar foreign names (*Mao Kuo-feng*), but add a cross-reference as shown for *Kuo-feng, Mao*, above.

2. Treat hyphenated names as a single word.

3. Alphabetize abbreviations such as *Ltd.* as if they were spelled out (*Limited*).

4. Treat names with prefixes such as *de* as a single word—(1) *Photography* (by) (2) *Tom* (3) *de Angelo*.

5. When two or more names are identical, include the address in determining alphabetical order: city first, state second, street third, direction fourth, and number fifth.

6. Place degrees or professional abbreviations such as *Ph.D.* and *CPA* in parentheses after the middle name (if any) or initial—(1) *Watts* (2) *J.* (3) *Henry* (CPA)—but disregard them in alphabetizing.

7. Place seniority titles (*Jr., Sr., II*, and *III*) in parentheses after the middle name or initial (if any), but disregard them in alphabetizing—(1) *Carson* (2) *Peter* (II). If there are two or more persons with that name (*Peter Carson II* and *III*), follow rule 5. *Note*: Some file departments prefer to retain seniority titles and use them as the next unit after the final middle name or initial.

8. When a title is given with only a first name (*Prince*

Charles), treat it as the first indexing unit. But when a title precedes a full name (*Dr. Arie N. Solomon*), place it in parentheses after the middle name or initial (if any)—(1) *Solomon* (2) *Arie* (3) *N.* (Dr.)—and disregard it in alphabetizing.

9. Treat *Mrs.* as an indexing unit when a woman is known only by her husband's full name—(1) *Oliverio* (2) *Mark* (3) *J.* (4) *Mrs.* Otherwise, place it with her husband's name in parentheses after the middle name or initial (if any)—(1) *Oliverio* (2) *Edna* (Mrs. Mark J. Oliverio)—and disregard it in alphabetizing.

Examples
(1) Archer   (2) Louise (Mrs. Joseph Nesbitt)
(1) Best   (2) Louis (III)   (3) Sacramento   (4) CA
(1) Best   (2) Louis (II)   (3) Trenton   (4) NJ
(1)Mao   (2) Kuo-feng
(1) Prince   (2) Andrew
(1) St. (Saint) Thomas-Weber   (2) Mary (Sr.)
(1) Sajek   (2) George   (3) O.
(1) Van Vleet   (2) T.   (3) M. (Jr.)

Names of businesses. Follow these rules in indexing and alphabetizing names of businesses and commercial establishments and refer to the concluding alphabetical list for examples:

1. Do not transpose business names—(1) *IBM* (2) *Corporation*—unless they include the name of an individual—(1) *Hill* (2) *Robert* (3) *P.* (4) *Inc.* Do not transpose a well-known individual's name used as a company name—(1) *Pierre* (2) *Cardin.*

2. Treat titles that are part of a business name as an indexing unit—(1) *Mr.* (2) *Clean.*

3. Treat firm endings such as *Inc.* as the last indexing unit in a name and alphabetize them as if they were spelled out (*Incorporated*).

4. When a hyphen in a name is used in place of a comma or the word *and*, treat the name as two words—(1) *McGraw* (2) *Hill.* Treat the name as one word when the two parts represent one person's surname—(1) *Stone-Milford* (2) *Rita* (and) (3) *Associates.*

5. Generally, ignore articles—(The) (1) *Graphics* (2) *Specialists*—conjunctions—(1) *Knowles* (and) (2) *Barton*—and prepositions—(1) *Lloyd's* (of) (2) *London*—in alphabetizing, but treat them as part of the name in foreign words—(1) *La France* (2) *Imports*.

6. Ignore accents (*Société*) in foreign words.

7. Treat compound geographical names that are not hyphenated as separate units—(1) *New* (2) *Jersey*—unless the first part is a foreign word (1) *Los Ángeles* (2) *Hotel*.

8. Treat words written variously as one or two words (*Midwest, Mid West*) as one indexing unit—(1) *Mid West* (2) *Distributors*.

9. Ignore an apostrophe and *s* after a name in alphabetizing—(1) *Mark*('s) (2) *Ski* (3) *Shop*. But keep the *s* when it is part of the name—(1) *Williams*(') (2) *Card* (3) *Shop*.

10. Treat each letter of an acronym as a separate unit—(1) *A* (2) *B* (3) *C*.

11. Treat trade names and coined names (*Just-4-U*) as a single unit—(1) *Just-4-U* (2) *Teen* (3) *Shop*.

12. Alphabetize numbers (*500*) as if they were spelled out—(1) *500* (Five Hundred) (2) *Club*.

13. When two or more names are identical, include the address in determining alphabetical order: city first, state second, street third, direction fourth, and number fifth.

Examples
(1) Boyce   (2) Jim (&)   (3) Associates
(1) Fern('s)   (2) Toyland
(1) Ferns (and)   (2) Things
(1) Littlefield   (2) Manufacturing   (3) Co.   (4) Inc.
(1) M   (2) C   (3) I   (4) Communications
(1) Marshall   (2) Fields
(1) Mr.   (2) T   (3) Sportswear
(1) Northwest   (2) Automotive   (3) Co.
(1) North West   (2) Industries
(1) San Francisco   (2) Harbor   (3) Patrol
(1) 22nd   (2) Street   (3) Coffee   (4) Shop
(1) Xavier('s)   (2) Lincoln   (3) NE   (4) Main
(1) Xavier('s)   (2) Lincoln   (3) NE   (4) Sixth

Institutions and government bodies. Follow these rules in indexing and alphabetizing names of institutions and governmental bodies and refer to the concluding alphabetical list for examples:

1. Do not transpose names of colleges and other institutions—(1) *Landmark* (2) *Agricultural* (3) *College*—unless the name begins with a common word—(1) *Illinois* (2) *University* (of).

2. Generally, ignore articles—(The) (1) *Scientific* (2) *Institute*—conjunctions—(1) *William* (and) (2) *Mary* (3) *College*—and prepositions—(1) *Rochester* (2) *University* (of)—in indexing and alphabetizing, but treat them as part of the name in foreign words—(1) *LaSalle* (2) *Vocational* (3) *School*.

3. Include addresses as indexing units when a well-known organization has numerous locations—(1) *Young* (2) *Men*('s) (3) *Christian* (4) *Association* (5) *Cleveland*.

4. Transpose names beginning with common words—(1) *Methodist* (2) *Church* (3) *First*.

5. When two or more names are identical, include the address in determining alphabetical order: city first, state second, street third, direction fourth, and number fifth.

6. The three units (1) *United* (2) *States* (3) *Government* precede the names of federal governmental organizations, and the descriptive word of the organization precedes the common word—(1) *United* (2) *States* (3) *Government* (4) *Labor* (5) *Department* (of).

7. Place the city name before general terms such as *board*—(1) *Orlando* (2) *City* (of) (3) *Education* (4) *Board* (of).

8. Place general foreign designations such as *republic* after the country name—(1) *Ireland* (2) *Republic* (of).

Examples
(1) Alcoholics (2) Anonymous (3) Denver
(1) Birmingham (AL) (2) City (of) (3) Highway (4) Department (of)
(1) Lutheran (2) Church (3) Second (4) Boston

(1) Lutheran   (2) Church   (3) Second   (4) Santa Fe
(1) New   (2) York   (3) Public   (4) Library
(The) (1) Palmer   (2) Institute (of)   (3) Dentistry
(1) Parsons   (2) College
(1) Texas   (2) University (of)
(1)United   (2) States   (3) Government   (4) Commerce   (5) Department (of)

REMINDERS AND FOLLOW-UPS

Busy people do not always remember office appointments, luncheon dates, deadlines for mailing certain material or for completing a project, and other commitments and obligations. A wise practice is to send brief reminders of approaching events or deadlines (see the sample follow-up and reminder letters in chapter 12).

If you are the one who has a deadline or appointment to remember, you should note the date on your calendar. Secretaries should note important dates on their own calendars and their boss's office and pocket calendars.

Calendars

Office-supply stores have a variety of calendars in various styles—notebooks, large desk pads, yearbooks, wall calendars, small pocket calendars, and others. Office personnel who have dates to remember need a desk calendar that stays in the office and a small pocket calendar to take along while out of the office.

Secretaries should keep a list of events and important dates that are repeated each year and put them on the calendars at the beginning of each year. Tax-payment dates, anniversaries, regular meetings, insurance-premium due dates, and annual holidays are among the recurring items to record each year.

A typed appointment list is another way that a secretary can remind an employer of special dates and activities. Secretaries should type such a list of appointments, meetings, and other scheduled activities each morning and place it on their boss's desk. Attach it to a file(s) if it involves material that the employer may want to review. As a reminder for future events, a four-week schedule can be typed on a weekly basis. It should list date, time, event, place, and special comments. Employers, in addition to using these measures, may want to call in their secretaries for a brief morning conference, at which time the secretaries can remind them of items scheduled for that day or coming soon.

Follow-up Files

Two common reminder and follow-up files are the folder-tickler system and the card-tickler system.

Folder-tickler system. Ordinary file folders are used for this system, but they are kept apart from the regular files. A separate folder (thirty-one in all) is maintained for each day of the month as well as one folder for each month itself.

Some offices group the thirty-one daily folders in the front and arrange the monthly folders behind them. Others prefer to set up the file in normal calendar order, with monthly folders filed from January through December and the thirty-one daily folders grouped behind whichever folder pertains to the current month. At the beginning of each month, then, you can simply remove the daily folders and reposition them behind the new current month's folder. Thus on May 1 you would take the thirty-one daily folders from behind the April folder and place them in numerical order behind the May folder.

Extra carbon copies (or photocopies) of correspondence as well as typed notes concerning something that will require a follow-up or reminder later can be dropped into the appropriate daily or monthly folder. For instance, suppose that on June 1 your employer sends a letter inviting three people to a June 22 luncheon and that he or she wants to mail a brief reminder letter confirming the date on June 14. Since the current month is June, you would simply drop a copy of the letter of invitation into the number 14 folder (which is already in position behind the general June folder). Since you will be checking the current day's folder each morning, on June 14 you will look into the folder labeled "14" and see a copy of the original letter of invitation, which will alert you to prepare a reminder.

As another example, assume that in June you type a letter from your employer to Joe Eddings giving him a deadline of August 1 for a report and decide that a follow-up letter should go out next month on July 15 inquiring about the status of the report and reminding him of the August 1 deadline. Since it is June when you type the original letter, you obviously will not file it in one of the current month's thirty-one daily folders. Instead, you will drop in the general "July" folder. On July 1 you will be moving the thirty-one daily folders from behind the June folder into their new position behind the July folder. At that time you will also remove everything from the general July folder and file each item in the appropriate daily folder. Thus the copy of the letter to Joe Eddings will be pulled out of the July folder on July 1 and dropped into the daily folder numbered "15" (for July 15). When July 15 arrives, you will look into folder 15 in the morning, see a copy of the original letter to Joe Eddings, and remember that it is time to send a follow-up letter.

Card-tickler system. The card system (often consisting of three- by five-inch or four- by six-inch cards) is similar, except you have no file folder in which to keep copies of correspondence or typed sheets. Instead, the correspondence is filed as usual in the regular files and the pertinent information is typed on an index card, which is filed behind a numbered (daily) guide or a guide labeled with one of the twelve months.

The arrangement of guides in the card file can be the same as for the file folders, for example, beginning with a guide for January, then one for February, and so on to December. The thirty-one numbered guides would be grouped back of the guide for the current month and would be moved from one month to another as time progresses.

Card files are less desirable than file folders for correspondence, but if you want to have only one follow-up file, and it should be a card file (to accommodate other items such as insurance premiums), you could proceed as follows: In the case of the luncheon invitation for which you want to send a reminder letter on June 14, you would file the carbon copy of the letter in the regular files and would instead type the pertinent information (date of letter, to whom sent, purpose, type of reminder or follow-up needed, date of follow-up, and so on) on an index card. Since the current month is June and you want to send the reminder on June 14, you would file the reminder card back of the guide labeled "14" (which is already in the June section of the card file).

In the case of a follow-up to Joe Eddings on July 15, you would type a card with the necessary reminder facts and file it back of the general "July" guide. On July 1 you would move the thirty-one daily guides from the June to the July section and at the same time pull out the July 14 tickler card from behind the general July guide and place it back of the daily guide labeled "14" in the July section.

Whereas folders are usually preferred for correspondence, tickler cards are more practical for reminders of matters such as the due dates of insurance premiums. For example, you wouldn't want to remove an insurance policy from safekeeping and drop it in a follow-up file folder; it is best to leave a policy where it is and simply type a reminder card for the tickler-card file.

CHAPTER FIVE

Keeping Books
and Records

Books of account and related records are kept for many reasons: to provide profit and loss operating data; to show activity within various segments of a firm; to provide information for tax purposes; to comply with federal, state, and local regulations; to have historical data for use in long-range planning; and generally to use as an ongoing management tool.

A certain amount of information must be kept in an orderly fashion to meet federal, state, and local regulations and to fulfill any additional corporate requirements. But organizations also keep books and records to help decision makers allocate resources, determine expenditures and pricing, and provide evidence concerning the success or failure of previous policies. The type of organization and the needs of its management—as well as legal and corporate requirements—will determine how many accounting records must be kept and how extensive they must be, how frequently financial statements are prepared and how detailed they must be, and what kinds of supporting documents will be required for each transaction and how they are processed and maintained. Most organizations whose books are audited will also be guided by the recommendations of the accounting firm that handles the auditing function for them. In fact, since auditors are largely concerned with verifying income and expenses, they will insist that every financial transaction in an organization not only be recorded but also be backed up with invoices or other proof that the transaction took place exactly as recorded in the books of account.

Computers have taken the drudgery out of many bookkeeping and accounting functions. Although they have not replaced adding machines, electronic calculators, or other common devices in many offices, a variety of computer software such as a spreadsheet analysis is designed to reduce repetitious work and perform complex, error-free calculations. Not only can journals and ledgers be maintained by computer, but financial statements, too, can be prepared in far less time without the risk of error by manual calculations and the tedious page-layout efforts that are necessary when one uses typewriter preparation. Small offices, however, still use many traditional bookkeeping methods as well as typewriter preparation of statements; many large organizations also retain some traditional accounting tools and procedures.

The principles of accounting in general and record keeping in particular are the same whether one prepares material manually or electronically. Therefore, office workers should become familiar with the proper check-writing and bookkeeping procedures, the preparation of financial statements, and other practices such as recording investment transactions.

CHECK WRITING

Certain people in an office are authorized to write checks. Some organizations have both regular and special checking accounts, and the secretary may be authorized to write checks on the special account (e.g., for miscellaneous office supplies), whereas the manager is authorized to write all other checks on the regular account. Often, except for the signature, the secretary prepares the regular checks too, fills out the check stubs, and presents the check to the manager for signing.

The person writing the checks must follow proper procedure and also take appropriate steps to safeguard the checkbook and related materials. The checkbook, bank statements, supply of blank checks, and other check-writing material should always be locked in a secure place when not being used.

Check-Writing Procedures

Check data. Write checks legibly in ink or type them, except for the signature, which should be handwritten in ink by the authorized person. Date the check the day it is written (do not postdate it). Write the payee's name in full but omit titles such as *Mr.* and *Dr.* Spell out the amount, beginning at the left margin and adding a single line across the blank space between the amount and the word *Dollars.* Do not leave room anywhere for someone to alter the figure on the left or right. (Check-writing machines that print the amount are a safeguard against alterations.)

Two hundred twenty-four and No/100 ------------Dollars

For amounts of less than one dollar, cross out the word *Dollars* and write, for example:

Only thirty-three cents --------------------------------~~Dollars~~

Add a note about the purpose of the check at the bottom (e.g., "To pay invoice 76081"). To void a check, write *Void* across both the check and the check stub and file the check numerically with the other cancelled checks when they arrive. Never sign blank checks, and never write a check to "Cash" until you are ready to cash it (anyone can cash a check made out this way).

The stub. Record the same information on the check stub as on the check. Depending on your bookkeeping system, you may also want to write other information on the stub such as the pertinent bookkeeping account number (refer to your company's chart of accounts, on which expense categories such as rent are given a number that must be followed in the books of account). To avoid overdrafts, keep a current balance recorded on the stub. It is illegal in most states to overdraw an account, and banks may impose a charge against a depositor when this happens.

Stop payments. Sometimes it is necessary to stop payment on checks (perhaps the payee lost it and you don't want someone else to find it and try to cash it). You may telephone the bank, giving the name of both the drawer and the payee, the check date, and the amount, and follow up with a confirming letter. Your bank's charge for a stop-payment order will appear on your next statement; be certain to deduct this amount from the current checkbook balance.

Electronic processing. Most checks can be processed by magnetic-ink-chararacter recognition (MICR). With the proper equipment, checks can be sorted as desired, and amounts that are printed in magnetic ink can be totaled and posted electronically to a customer's account. Some banks will also convert all cancelled checks to reduced form (e.g., microfilm) and store them for customers. When needed, a copy of the check can be printed out and mailed to the customer. The bank statement, then, is the customer's sole source of data in reconciling the statement each month.

Bank Statement

Both individuals and firms receive bank statements each month showing a list of deposits and checks written, the service charge (if any), and other items. On the back of each statement or separately enclosed with the statement is a blank form to use in reconciling the statement balance with the checkbook balance. By filling in the form you can determine whether your addition and subtraction in the checkbook has been accurate. If it has been, the balance shown in your checkbook should equal the ending balance on the bank statement plus any recent deposits not shown minus the total of outstanding checks. If the bank has made an error, you should report it immediately.

The statement for a savings account will vary depending upon the type of account. It may be a sheet of paper showing each deposit or withdrawal, interest added or paid out, and other pertinent information. A passbook account would have such information recorded in a small booklet that you would take with you each time you made a deposit.

Deposits

Deposits may be made by mail or in person. Coins should be placed in paper rolls and bills in bill wrappers, both supplied by the bank. Checks received should be endorsed properly, and a deposit slip should be filled out in full to accompany the endorsed checks and money orders, bills (arrange all to face the same way), and coins. The bookkeeper or someone else in your office must stamp or write "paid" on the file copy of the invoice that each check covers (also note the date paid and any other facts required for bookkeeping). Follow the required practices in your office for processing paid invoices and other material as the checks arrive. Put a check mark on each check or in some other way indicate that you have marked the proper material (e.g., invoice) paid *before* depositing the check in the bank.

Endorsements. Each check must be properly endorsed for the bank to accept it and credit it to your account. The three basic types of endorsement are blank, special, and restrictive. All endorsements should be written in ink or stamped on the back left end of the check. The payee's name in the endorsement must correspond exactly with the name on the face of the check. For example, if your bank account was in the name of James A. Fletcher and the check was written to Jim Fletcher, you would endorse it "Jim Fletcher" but write "James A. Fletcher" immediately underneath it.

A *blank endorsement* consists of the payee's signature on the back (remember that anyone may cash it then):

Kevin R. Anderson

A *specific endorsement* names the person to whom a

check is being transferred. For instance, Arnold Williams may want to sign his check over to Helena Monitelli:

Pay to the order of Helena Monitelli

Arnold Williams

When Helena Monitelli is ready to cash or deposit the check signed over to her, she will then sign her name beneath that of Arnold Williams.

A *restrictive endorsement* restricts the use of the funds on the check. It may, for example, specify that the funds are to be deposited (not received in cash) to an account in a particular bank. A check endorsed that way can be deposited only to the account specified. If you were depositing a check in the Wilcox Company account at First National Bank of Morristown, N.J., you would write, type, or rubber stamp the following endorsement:

Pay to the order of
FIRST NATIONAL BANK
OF MORRISTOWN, N.J.

For Deposit Only
The Wilcox Company

This form of endorsement is essential for deposits made by mail.

Supporting Documents

Supporting documents are forms of evidence that back up information on your check stub. It isn't sufficient merely to record the reason for writing a check and other data on the check stub. You might, for instance, write a check to Lee Dennison for $100 and note on the check stub that it is payment for art services. Without an invoice from Dennison marked "paid" with the date, corresponding check number, and so on, how can you prove that the $100 wasn't simply a gift at the company's expense? For each check written, some form of documentation must be added to the paid-bills file to prove that the expenditure was legitimate and authorized. If no invoice is available, a typed memo could be prepared describing the date of the art service, purpose, person who authorized it, and so on.

Supporting documents may be collected in a folder, placed in a special binder, or collected in any way that your office (and your auditors) find acceptable. Should an Internal Revenue Service audit ever take place, this material must be in proper order for the agent to use in comparing checks written with the supporting material proving the validity of the transactions.

Deposits, too, require supporting material. If you bill on a regular basis you probably have printed invoices that are numbered and ready for preparation by typewriter, computer, or other billing machine. If you must do follow-ups on overdue accounts, multiple-copy invoices are useful, so that a carbon copy can be removed every thirty days for mailing. As soon as the invoice is paid, the date and any other necessary information should be noted on it, including the initials of the person processing it, and it should be removed from the "billed" file and placed in the "paid" file. When the bookkeeper records deposits in the cash receipts journal and disbursements in the cash disbursements journal, supporting material should be available to back up each check received as well as each check written.

Petty Cash

Small expenses such as charges for a COD package are commonly paid out of a petty cash fund. The amount kept in a petty cash fund depends on your office needs. Twenty-five dollars may be sufficient, or you may need a hundred dollars.

Usually, a check is written to start or replenish a petty cash fund by making it payable to cash. The amount of cash received with this check is then placed in a cash register, cash box, or any other safe place in the office.

The person who is responsible for making payments from the cash fund should keep on hand a supply of petty cash vouchers (available at office-supply stores). Each time cash is removed, if no invoice or other document is available, a voucher should be filled out stating the date, payee, amount, purpose, and account (e.g., postage) to which the expenditure should be charged in bookkeeping. At the bottom of the form should be a line where the payee signs to indicate that payment was received and where an authorized individual signs to show that the expenditure was approved. The balance of the remaining cash in the account plus the sum of the vouchers should always equal the amount originally deposited in the fund. Petty cash books are also available at office-supply stores.

These books have columns that you can label "office supplies," "postage," and so on. Each time an expenditure is made, the date, explanation, and amount are recorded in the appropriate columns. A "miscellaneous" column can be added for items that don't fit another category.

To receive additional cash to replenish the fund, prepare a summary of cash payments made and attach vouchers, invoices, and other supporting material proving each expenditure. The statement should begin with the balance on hand the last time the fund was replenished, as shown in the sample petty cash statement below.

PETTY CASH STATEMENT
February 1 to 31, 19—

Balance on hand, February 1		$50.00
Expenditures		
Postage	$23.00	
COD payments	6.95	
Office supplies	14.35	
Coffee supply	3.70	
Total expenditures		$48.00
Balance on hand, February 28		$ 2.00

BOOKKEEPING

The accounting process includes analyzing, classifying, and summarizing financial transactions; recording the information; and interpreting the results. The recording step is known as bookkeeping. Although usually only bookkeepers, accountants, and other financial and accounting personnel are concerned with the actual recording operations, all office personnel can benefit from understanding the principles that govern this essential part of business activity.

Principles

All bookkeeping systems record changes that occur in an organization's *assets* (things of value that are owned), *liabilities* (debts), and *owner's equity* (what is left after paying all liabilities). In accounting, the fundamental equation is:

Assets = Liabilities + Owner's Equity

This means that:

Liabilities = Assets − Owner's Equity

and

Owner's Equity = Assets − Liabilities

Any change (increase or decrease) in one of the three elements of the accounting equation will be offset by another change. If you paid a bill, for example, you would have fewer debts (liabilities) but you would also have less cash (assets). Therefore, the change in liabilities causes a change in the assets as well in this case.

Double-entry bookkeeping. Since all transactions cause a dual change, both changes are recorded—hence the term *double-entry bookkeeping*. To record changes that occur, the bookkeeper must make debit (Dr.) and credit

(Cr.) entries on the columnar sheets in the books of account. As this T-account shows, debit amounts are always recorded on the left side and credit amounts always on the right:

ACCOUNT NAME

Debit	Credit

All of such accounts, grouped together, are known as a ledger.

Basic Records

The various books of account may be kept according to a cash or accrual basis of accounting. In *cash accounting* income is recorded at the time it is actually received, and expenses are recorded on the date bills are actually paid. In *accrual accounting* income and expenses are assigned to the particular period to which they apply regardless of the *date* that receipts were deposited or bills paid. With both methods the transactions must be recorded somewhere.

Large organizations may have formal books, whereas a small office may merely purchase bound or loose sheets of ruled paper with columns that will fit in any three-ring binder. The most simple form of professional activity may need only two journals—one in which to record income and another in which to record expenses. Other firms may use several journals such as cash, sales, and purchases journals and a general journal for all other transactions, as well as ledgers in which there are separate pages for each account—cash, office supplies, and so on.

The bookkeeper first records all transactions in the

journals. Figures from the journals are then posted to the ledger accounts. At the end of each month or accounting period a *trial balance* (list of all ledger-account balances) is prepared. Certain financial statements are also prepared periodically (see FINANCIAL STATEMENTS).

Journals. The various journals, such as the cash, sales, purchases, and general journals, are the books of original entry, the place where transactions are first recorded. Entries are made by date in the order in which they occur. As the sample general journal entries below show, one account is debited and another account is credited for the amount of each transaction. The narrow column of numbers next to the description column shows the account numbers (taken from the firm's chart of accounts). These numbers are usually entered at the time that figures are being transferred from the journal to the ledger. In the first entry, for example, the firm received $981.76 from Boylston Associates for consulting services. The bookkeeper therefore debited Cash (account 101) and credited Consulting Fees (account 314) for $981.76. Observe the following general rules in determining whether to debit or credit an item:

198–   General Journal   page 5

Jun 3	Cash	101	981 76	
	Consulting Fees	314		981 76
	Boylston Associates			
9	Miscellaneous Expense	521	18 00	
	Cash	101		18 00
	magazine subscription			
17	Office Supplies	141	228 00	
	Accounts Payable	201		228 00
	A & Z Office Supplies			
30	Telephone Expense	436	137 00	
	Cash	101		137 00
	phone bill			
Jul 1	Rent Expense	425	560 00	
	Cash	101		560 00
	July rent			
14	Office Supplies	141	99 69	
	Accounts Payable	201		99 69
	A & Z Office Supplies			
15	Cash	101	710 50	
	Advertising Fees	314		710 50
	The Evans Store		2789 95	2789 95

Debit entries: Increase assets and expense accounts and decrease capital, income, and liability accounts

Credit entries: Increase capital, income, and liability accounts and decrease assets and expense accounts

To verify your addition in the journal, total the debit and credit columns and pencil the totals at the bottom of the two columns (cross-footing). The total of debit entries in a journal *must* equal the total of credit entries, or an error has occurred.

The ledger. The books of final entry in accounting are called ledgers. Journal entries are transferred (posted) to the ledger accounts on a regular basis, even daily when the activity is heavy. Ledger accounts are listed each on a separate page with the corresponding account number, as shown in the sample ledger entries below. The bookkeeper

Cash   101

DATE	ITEMS	FOLIO		DEBITS	DATE	ITEMS	FOLIO		CREDITS
19—					19—				
Jun 3		5		951 76	Jun 9		5		18 00
Jul 5		5		710 50	30		5		137 00
				1 692 26	Jul 1		5		560 00
									715 00

Office Supplies   141

DATE	ITEMS	FOLIO		DEBITS	DATE	ITEMS	FOLIO		CREDITS
19—									
Jun 17		5		228 00					
Jul 14		5		99 69					
				327 69					

Accounts Payable   201

DATE	ITEMS	FOLIO		DEBITS	DATE	ITEMS	FOLIO		CREDITS
					19—				
					Jun 17		5		228 00
					Jul 14		5		99 69
									327 69

transfers debit and credit entries from the journal(s) to the debit and credit sides of the ledger accounts. The post-reference (folio) column next to the items column in the ledger is used to record the journal page from which the data has been transferred. After posting, the debit and credit entries in the ledger can be checked for accuracy against those in the journal by turning to the journal page noted next to the item columns.

Columns in the ledger should be totaled (footed) with the footings written in small figures beneath the last item. The difference between the debit and credit total of an account should be written in the item column on the side with the largest total (see the sample ledger Cash account).

Trial balance. Bookkeepers must regularly check the accuracy of their ledger postings. In some offices a specially written-out trial balance must be prepared as described below, but usually, essentially the same thing is done more easily and more quickly on an adding machine tape:

1. Foot the ledger columns (notice the position of the pencil totals in the sample ledger accounts).

2. Find the difference between the left (debit) and right (credit) ledger-account columns and write that figure in the item column on the side with the largest total. In the sample ledger Cash account, for example, the penciled balance of $977.26 is written on the left (debit) side since that side had the largest column total.

3. Make a list of all accounts and account numbers in numerical order and put the account balance in the proper column—debit or credit. For example, the balance of $977.26 shown in the sample ledger Cash account appears in the left (debit) column, so it would also be written in the left column of the trial balance.

4. Total the debit and credit columns of the trial balance and place a double rule after the total in each column.

Refer to the sample trial balance for the XYZ Company.

The fact that debits equal credits in the trial balance means that the ledger posting is correct.

XYZ Company
Trial Balance
June 30, 19—

Account Title	Account Number	Debit	Credit
Cash	111	$3,400.00	
Office Supplies	201	431.98	
Accounts Payable	214		$1,601.98
Rent Income	309		4,090.00
Salary Expense	500	1,860.00	
		$5,691.98	$5,691.98

Payroll

Although state and local requirements may vary concerning payroll and withholding taxes, federal regulations apply to all persons and firms that have employees. Generally, accurate records must be kept concerning all employees, and payroll taxes must be paid at specified times.

Records. Whereas large firms will likely use computers or special payroll-accounting machines to record hours, earnings, withholding taxes, and other payroll data, small firms frequently use standard payroll forms available in office-supply stores and make manual entries. Multiple-copy carbon or carbonless checks and pay slips are commonly used as well. The employer then retains one or more of the copies to serve as a payroll record for each employee. Employee-compensation cards (or sheets made to fit a binder) are available too. A payroll register, or book, is designed for recording information on all employees. Usually, firms maintain both individual employee-earnings cards and a general payroll register or book.

Standard employee forms show name, address, phone, social security number, pay rate, number of exemptions, hours worked, earnings, deductions (social security, federal income tax, state income tax, group insurance, and so on), and net pay. Payroll books have columns for essentially the same information except for personal data such as employee address, phone, and social security number. Instead of an individual sheet in the book for each employee, names of all employees are listed one after another on the same sheet.

Taxes. Employers must report and file all income taxes withheld, employee social security taxes withheld and the matching employer's share, and federal unemployment taxes (if the employer meets the stipulations).

To make deposits of payroll taxes, use the *Federal Tax Deposit Coupon*: form 8109. Depending on the amount of your liability, you may be required to make deposits on a quarterly or more frequent basis. Check the latest circular E (*The Employer's Tax Guide*) for details concerning the current amount of cumulative liability that determines when you must make a deposit. Any required deposits must be made to an authorized commercial bank or a Federal Reserve Bank.

Each year employers should check the current requirements for filing and tax computation stated in the instructions for federal form 940: *Employer's Annual Federal Unemployment Tax Return.* Those employers who paid a certain amount of wages or had one or more employees for part of one day or more during each of twenty calendar weeks are liable for this tax. Depending on the amount of your liability, you may be required to make deposits throughout the year (which are reported on the annual return when you pay any balance due). For full details, refer to federal circular E. Since rates and regulations change, request a new circular E and a new form 940 with instructions each year.

FINANCIAL STATEMENTS

Two of the most common financial statements are the profit and loss (income) statement and the balance sheet.

Both of these statements can be quickly and easily prepared at any time with electronic equipment. New data can be entered as it is available, and a revised statement is automatically computed and printed out according to the format instructions (spacing, indentation, number of columns, and so on) given to the computer. If the statements are prepared manually and typed, special care must be given to setup as well as to the collection of figures. With both manual and electronic preparation, the initial procedure is the same: one must check the account balances for the figures that are needed.

Profit and Loss Statement

A profit and loss, or income, statement is essential to decision making in business operations. It lists income and expenses and thereby shows profit or loss at the end of a certain period such as a month, quarter, or year. Since the information on it comes from the books of account, all journals and ledgers must be completely up to date.

A work sheet with numerous columns is typically used to organize the data that will be needed. Accounts are listed numerically on this sheet, and next to them are two trial balance columns (debit and credit). Next to the trial balance columns are two income statement columns (also debit and credit). Finally, next to the income columns are two balance sheet columns (also debit and credit). Copy the figures from the ledger into the trial balance columns (refer to the instructions mentioned earlier for preparing a trial balance). Then copy the figures pertaining to income and expenses from the trial balance columns to the income statement columns. Copy those pertaining to assets, liabilities, and owner's equity to the balance sheet columns. You then have the figures you need to prepare both statements.

A profit and loss statement can be typed on regular 8½- by 11-inch bond paper or on standard forms available in office supply stores. Some forms have several columns that show current figures and the figures for the same period a year ago or figures for the current period and for the year to date. Different types of businesses use different types of format and various degrees of detail and complexity.

Examine a copy of a previous statement in your files to determine length, accounts listed (e.g., operating expense), and a method of preparation (e.g., fill-in form, typewriter, computer). A simplified short form is shown below to illustrate standard spacing in typewriter preparation. Notice that account names are indented several spaces from the general categories of "Income" and "Expenses." Totals are indented several spaces more than the line immediately above. A double rule signifies the final figure and the end of the statement.

ABC Company, Inc
Profit and Loss Statement
For the Month Ending February 28, 19—

Income:		
Net sales	$365,000	
Dividends	2,109	
Total income		$367.109
Expenses:		
Cost of goods sold	$102,714	
Selling expenses	92,613	
Operating expenses	51,977	
Interest expenses	70	
Total expenses		$247,374
Net income		$119,735

Balance Sheet

A balance sheet shows a firm's financial status on a certain date such as the end of a month, quarter, or year. In the example shown in this chapter assets are listed on the left and liabilities on the right, with both sides ending on the same line across from each other. The sum of the two columns must be equal (in balance), or there is an error.

List assets in the order of liquidity with current assets first and fixed assets last. List first those liabilities that mature first (current) and last those that mature last (long term). Except for changing the order of items, the balance sheet basically summarizes the ledger accounts.

Follow the example of preparation for a profit and loss statement and here, too, prepare a work sheet first. Again list the accounts in numerical order and after that make the first two columns of figures (debit and credit) the trial balance columns. The next two (debit and credit) will be the income statement columns, and the last two will be the balance sheet columns. The left of the two columns in each case is always the debit column and the right is always the credit column. Copy the figures from the trial balance column into the income and balance sheet columns: income and expense figures into the income statement columns; assets, liabilities, and owner's equity into the balance sheet columns. You then have the list of account names and balances ready for compiling the balance sheet.

An abbreviated balance sheet is included below to illustrate layout, indentation, and spacing. Indent names of accounts several spaces more than main headings such as "Liabilities." Indent subtotals such as "Total liabilities" several spaces more than the line above. End both

Jones Interior Designs
Balance Sheet
December 31, 19—

Assets		Liabilities & Owner's Equity	
Cash	$ 700	Liabilities:	
Accounts receivable	3,200	Notes payable	$54,000
Land	15,000	Accounts payable	1,221
Buildings	65,000	Total liabilities	$55,221
Office equipment	2,900	Owner's Equity:	
		John Jones, Capital	$31,579
Total assets	$86,800	Total liab. & o.e.	$86,800

columns (assets on the left and liabilities and owner's equity on the right) on the same line and place a double rule under the column totals.

INVESTMENTS

The records for extensive holdings of a firm are handled by specialists in the financial or accounting office. Individuals and their secretaries, however, maintain their own records. In either case, some files are mandatory to account for securities owned and ongoing transactions. Such records are especially vital in preparing tax returns.

Common Investments

Securities traded through one of the principal exchanges or available directly from an investment company offer opportunities for investment. Stocks and bonds are the common forms of this type of investment. *Bonds* are issued by corporations and are usually secured by a mortgage. The amounts are typically multiples of $1,000, or $5,000, less often $100 or $500. *Stocks* are shares that represent ownership in a company. Preferred stock has preferential treatment over common stock in claims and payment of dividends. *Mutual funds* are portions of the shares of securities purchased by an investment company. Savings accounts, money market funds, and other institutional accounts also offer opportunities for investment.

Record Keeping

Maintenance of securities transactions and holdings often falls to the office secretary or someone on the administrative staff. Those responsible must keep a separate record of each security owned, with all records filed in alphabetical order. At the top of the card or sheet, this record should identify the security, the exchange traded on (e.g., New York Stock Exchange), the broker, and the location of the certificate (e.g., safe-deposit box).

Other information is usually typed as column headings across the page:

Purchases
Number of shares
Kind of security
Certificate number
Purchase date
Price per share
Broker's commission
Total purchase price

Sales
Number of shares
Kind of security
Certificate number
Sale date
Price per share
Total sale price
Broker's commission
Taxes and other charges
Capital gain or loss (short term and long term)
Balance of shares owned

You can divide your page into two halves with purchases information and the respective columns on top and sales information and the respective columns on the bottom. Or you can combine the two sets of columns all across the top of the sheet, adding an additional column preceding the Purchase/Sale Date column for type of transaction (where you will record either *P* for a purchase or *S* for a sale).

A separate list of all securities owned should also be maintained. This sheet should have columns to show the name, number of shares or face value (bonds), maturity date, purchase price, total cost, and current market value. You may use separate sheets for stocks, bonds, investment (mutual) funds, and other forms of investment or divide the sheet into four sections if there are only a few items per section. At the bottom, total the purchase-price column and the current-market-value column.

A file of all broker's trade advices and statements

should also be kept. These statements are often letter size or smaller and can be filed in a regular file folder. They may also be kept in a binder or any other suitable container. The certificates themselves should be kept in a fire- and theft-proof safe-deposit box or other locked security container. If securities are scattered in various locations, you may want to add a code to the list of securities you type showing where they are (H = home; SD = safe-deposit box, and so on).

Interest- and dividend-income records are necessary to show income received that must be reported on tax returns. Again, use a card or sheet and state the period covered at the top. Column headings might include name of security, date (of interest or dividend) received, amount received, and annual total received.

Keep all records current. Record security transactions as soon as they occur, and record dividend and interest income as soon as it comes in. At the end of the year copies of all of these records, or a summary of the pertinent facts and figures, should be made available to the tax preparer.

WORD
PROCESSING

CHAPTER SIX

Using the Typewriter

Text processing is a major activity in most offices. Large organizations often have typing pools to handle a substantial portion of the work, although some of the typing is still handled in individual offices. Word processors and computers with word processing software now handle a lot of the text processing in organizations nationwide (see chapter 7). But the typewriter (electric and electronic) occupies a stable place in the industry, and in general, good typing skills are mandatory for clerical and secretarial personnel.

EQUIPMENT AND SUPPLIES

The principal choice in typewriters today is between the electric and electronic models. The choice of supplies, such as ribbons and correction materials, depends on the type of machine one has.

Electronic Typewriters

The electronic typewriter appears to be the direction of the future. By 1984 sales of electronic machines had already surpassed those of electric models. The fundamental difference between conventional and electronic models is that electromechanical machines use numerous mechanically driven parts, whereas electronic models have fewer parts (hence less breakage) and function through microprocessor controls. In addition, conventional machines have no memory, display, or automated functions. As the cost of electronic models declines and their superior capabilities become more widely known, they will become even more popular and more widely used.

Electronic typewriters were introduced in 1978 and since then have advanced technologically to compete successfully not only with electric typewriters but, in many cases, with the more expensive word processors and computers. The features of electronic machines vary from one model to another, but some or all of the following capabilities are present.

1. *Memory* features enable users to store a certain amount of text that can be recalled later. *Document memory* retains a specified number of pages (e.g., eight to ten). With *phrase memory*, common phrases can be entered and called up later with one or two keystrokes instead of retyping the entire phrase each time. *Multiple-line memory* means that you can recall and correct more than one line at a time. A *stored-format* feature provides a means to store instructions such as margins and tab settings and then repeat the instructions later simply by pressing one or two keys. *Diskette storage*, similar to that of a computer, is an add-on feature of high-level machines.

2. A *display* feature lets you look at one line (or more) of text before it is committed to paper. Some advanced models even have a full-size add-on monitor (such as that used with a computer) for viewing an entire page of text.

3. *Search and replace* refers to the ability of the machine to locate a word or phrase wherever it occurs within a document and then automatically change it as you specify.

4. *Delete* and *insert* capabilities enable you to remove text or move it to another place in the same or a different document.

5. *Automatic format* capabilities provide for features such as automatic centering and automatic decimal alignment with a single keystroke. Other format features that can be easily specified are bold-face type, automatic underscoring, preselected line spacing, and multiple-column layout across a page.

6. *Automatic carrier return* means that the machine decides when it is time to begin the next line.

7. With *automatic paper feed* the machine automatically moves the paper on each page to any line you specify (e.g., six lines down) as the first line of type.

8. A *spell-checker* is an internal dictionary that can be activated so that the machine will find typos and automatically correct them as one specifies throughout the document.

All of these features—and many more (memory protection, pitch selection, right-margin justification, hyphenation, and so on)—amount to less work for the user, faster and easier production (up to 50 percent increase in performance), more accurate and attractive results, and generally more efficient office operations. Business analysts predict that in the coming decade electronic typewriters will be used primarily in secretarial-administrative work stations in large companies but will also be widely used throughout small-and medium-size firms.

Typewriter supplies. For quality work, carbon film ribbons are preferred over fabric ribbons. Multistrike ribbons give more impressions than single-strike ribbons. Various typefaces are available for machines (e.g., Selectric) that use interchangeable elements. Daisywheels for electronic machines come in a variety of type faces and can be changed at will. For other important typing materials, see Correction Supplies.

Carbon Copies

Typing paper. Good-quality stationery is usually 25 percent, 75 percent, or 100 percent cotton content, of twenty-pound weight or higher, and comes in a white, cream, or conservative pastel color. Paper for all other stationery and for miscellaneous text production (e.g., reports) is commonly a sixteen- or twenty-pound sulphite bond. These bond papers are given numbers (usually, No. 1, No. 4, and No. 5) that indicate brightness and opacity, with the best being No. 1. The best grade (No.

1) would likely be used for stationery, and the poorer grades (No. 4 and No. 5) might be used for copying, duplicating, and routine text typing.

Onionskin and copy paper. Whereas an economical bond paper of sixteen- or twenty-pound weight is commonly used with plain-paper copiers, lighter-weight paper (onionskin) is necessary for carbon copies, usually seven-or nine-pound weight, smooth or cockle finish. Various colors (yellow, green, and so on) are available for color-coded file systems.

Like stationery, carbon-copy paper is available in cotton rag (usually 25 or 100 percent) or a sulphite bond. Up to fifteen copies can be made using a glazed, lightweight onionskin; unglazed paper, however, will erase better. *Copysets* are thin papers to which the carbon paper is attached on one end. *Carbonless paper* is a treated paper that will make duplicates without any need for a sheet of carbon paper between the copies.

When carbon sheets are used, they should be selected on the basis of both the number of copies that can be made and durability. Lightweight carbon paper will yield one to ten copies; medium weight, one to five copies; heavy weight, one to two copies; and film or plastic, one to ten copies. Solvent-coated carbon papers usually last longer and give cleaner impressions than wax carbon papers.

Typing on carbon papers. Adjust your machine for the number of copies you are making. Use carbon paper with a corner cut to make it easier to grasp the typing paper and separate the carbon sheets when you're finished. Always place a steel eraser guard or celluloid shield behind the original when you erase something. Otherwise, any pressure or erasing will make a black smudge on the onionskin copies.

If the corrected letters on some carbon copies are too faint, set your typewriter on the stencil position, retype the correction, and then reset it again to normal to resume typing. Try using a sheet of heavier paper at the back of the carbon pack to prevent the tree-branch effect caused by creasing of paper with use. To type only on the carbon copies, insert a sheet on top of the original and then type normally. You can also set the machine to stencil and omit the extra top sheet, although this setting may nevertheless leave a faint impression of each letter on the original.

Correction Supplies

If you have an electronic typewriter, you will be able to correct errors before they are printed on paper (although some typists nevertheless prefer to print out a draft for proofreading). If you have a self-correcting electric typewriter, you will need correction supplies but not for the original copies. Instead, you will use the correctable ribbon cassette or the correction tape that fits in your particular model. This self-correcting mechanism "lifts" the incorrect letters from the paper. A self-correcting bond paper is also available for use with self-correcting typewriters to improve the correction "lift-off" process.

For your carbon copies, however, you will still need an eraser or correction fluid to blot out the error. If your typewriter does not have a self-correcting mechanism, you will need either an eraser, coated correction paper, press-apply tape, correction fluid (different colors are available to match your stationery), or a combination of these supplies.

A white, press-apply tape comes in narrow stripes that you press onto the paper and on which you type the correction. But the tape is very obvious and should not be used on final copies. A good eraser often leaves the least evidence of a correction, although most typists prefer the convenience of correction fluid to blot out the error or coated correction paper that whitens the incorrect letters on the page so that the correct letters can be typed over them.

Some correction materials are especially suited for stencils and masters. A white eraser, for instance, is made especially to remove carbon-ribbon errors from certain reproduction masters. A special fluid is used to coat errors on stencils. First lift off the outside film (if any) and then burnish (rub) the error smooth with a paper clip. Always use the right correction material for your stencil or master, or the correction will show as a blemish when copies are reproduced.

PRACTICES AND PROCEDURES

Most offices have established practices and procedures. Your office, for instance, may require that all letters be typed in the simplified style (see chapter 12), that all reports be typed double-spaced on twenty-pound No. 1 sulfite bond (see chapter 13), that you make three carbon copies or photocopies of all letters and two photocopies of all reports, that all transcription of dictated material (see DICTATION AND TRANSCRIPTION) be completed by noon each day, and so on.

General office requirements are usually straightforward. It's the things that are left up to you that cause the problems. How many spaces do you leave after a colon? Do you align roman numerals on the left or right? How do you type a paragraph sign when your typewriter keyboard doesn't have that symbol? How do you evenly insert a dozen sheets of carbon paper and onionskin into the typewriter? Fortunately, various rules and techniques have been established to help solve the many problems that arise every day in the life of a typist or secretary.

Standard Rules

Your typewritten material will look much more professional if you follow traditional rules for proper spacing around punctuation marks, for improvising to make special signs and symbols not on your keyboard, and for typing numbers and fractions.

Spacing with punctuation. Insert no space or one or two spaces around punctuation as follows:

No space: Between a word and the punctuation following it (*Look out!*)

Before or after a dash, or two hyphens (*the best style—full block*)

Before or after a hyphen (*color-coded files*)

Between quotation marks and the copy enclosed (*"The result is obvious."*)

Between parentheses or brackets and the copy enclosed (*[1987]*)

Before or after the periods within a single-unit abbreviation of letters (*a.m.*)

Before or after the periods within a traditional state abbreviation of letters (*N.Y.*)

Before an apostrophe that ends a word or falls in the middle (*Williamses'*)

After an apostrophe that begins a word as in a single quote (*"He said 'yes, I agree.' "*)

One space: After a period ending an abbreviation (*Ph.D. candidate*)

After a period in the initials of a person's name (*B. A. Smith*)

After a comma (*pens, pencils, and paper*)

After a semicolon (*today's mail; therefore*)

Before and after "X", meaning "by" (*4" × 6"*)

Two spaces: After any punctuation ending a sentence (*Please call me tomorrow. Thank you.*)

After a colon (*the following: bills, receipts, and statements*)

After a period following letters or figures introducing items in a list (*1. typing, 2. dictation*)

Making special signs and symbols. Your typewriter may not have all of the signs and symbols you need. Many of them can be made by combining other keys that you do have and striking one letter or number over another. The following are ten signs and symbols that can be realistically duplicated by using a combination of standard characters:

⊬	Plus	Type a hyphen over an apostrophe or a hyphen over a diagonal.

=	Equals	Type a hyphen, backspace, and turning the platen slightly, type it again.
÷	Division	Type a colon over a hyphen.
f	Pound Sterling	Type an *f* over *t* or *f* over *L*.
ç	Cedilla	Type a comma over a *c*.
!	Exclamation point	Type an apostrophe over a period.
¶	Paragraph	Type a *P* over *l*.
§	Section	Type a small *s*, backspace, move the platen slightly forward, and type the *s* again.
⎣ ⎦	Brackets	Combine underscores and the diagonal, moving up a line to make the top part of the bracket.
⎡	Caret	Combine a diagonal and an underscore one line up.

Typing numbers and fractions. In nontechnical text spell out the numbers one through ninety-nine as well as all large round numbers (one hundred, two thousand, thirty-five hundred)—except in paragraphs where there are large uneven numbers (*67 men and 107 women*). In technical material spell out only the numbers one through ten—except in paragraphs having higher numerals (*14 men and 9 women*).

Fractions should be hyphenated when they are used as one word (*two-thirds*) but when either the numerator or denominator already has a hyphen, omit the additional hyphen (*four eighty-sevenths*).

Roman numerals are typed in all capitals and are most often aligned on the left. Arabic numerals are always aligned on the right and, if they include decimals, should be aligned at the decimal point:

I	7,621	14.70
II	9	6.00
III	132	191.85

Special Techniques

Some tasks such as chain-feeding small cards are relatively easy when you use certain techniques and timesaving measures. If you have an electronic typewriter, some tasks (e.g., centering) are handled automatically. But if your machine doesn't have all of the latest features, the following suggestions will help you simplify some otherwise difficult tasks.

Organization. Before you begin any typing job, organize your materials. If you need to look up an address, do it before you start typing. If you are almost out of paper, replenish the supply before you start. Interruptions affect your pace and lead to errors.

Type at a steady pace and use an even touch. Rushing beyond your effective speed will cause errors that in the end will take more time to correct. Adjust your chair to the proper height for you to avoid back strain and fatigue, and arrange paper, correction supplies, and other materials so that you do not have to make inconvenient moves or reaches during a typing session.

After you finish each page, proofread it before you remove it from the machine. It's always more difficult to realign paper to make a correction later, especially when there are carbon copies involved (see Correction Supplies).

Centering. Two types of centering are important: centering the paper in the machine and centering headings and other material on the page. To center your paper in the machine, align the middle of the paper with the middle of the scale on your typewriter and then move the left paper guide against the left edge of the paper.

If you have an electronic typewriter, it will center headings automatically. Without this feature, first find the center of the page (or the midpoint between the left and right margin settings). Presumably, you have set the left paper guide as described in the preceding paragraph so that the center of your paper always aligns with the center point on the typewriter scale. Then simply back-space once for every two letters. To center text on a page vertically, move the platen forward to line 33 (letter-size paper). Then turn it back once for every two lines you will type.

Cards and labels. Small, odd-sized items such as cards or labels can often be chain-fed into the typewriter. To do a lot in succession, feed from the front of the platen. Put one card in and then feed it backward until you see a three-fourths-inch margin on the top. Insert the next card until the bottom is held secure by the first card. Continue feeding cards from the front, inserting each one until it is held in place by the preceding card. They will come out and pile up in the same order that you inserted them.

To type small, narrow labels, fold a sheet of paper horizontally to make a shallow pocket. Insert the sheet so that the folded edge is up. Then turn the platen until you see the pocket at the front. Insert the labels in the pocket and feed all of the material back until it appears where you can type on it.

Envelopes. You can chain-feed envelopes the same way that you feed small cards (described above). If a wide flap makes the typing ragged, open the flaps and feed them from the back, inserting each envelope between the previous one and the paper table. You can still chain-feed three at a time this way. The other alternative is to make a pocket by folding a sheet of paper, inserting the folded end, and rolling it through until you can see an inch of it above the front scale. Then insert the envelope back of the folded paper at the front of the roller. Turn the roller back to bring the envelope into typing position. As you remove each envelope, the folded paper remains in place to insert another envelope behind it.

Forms. Typing a form with one or more carbon copies requires careful alignment. First hold the copies up to the light to align them. Then insert the originals without the carbon paper. Use the procedure described in *Carbon packs*, below, to insert the sheets of carbon paper. Use the variable line spacer to have the descenders (tails of *y*, *p*, and so on) rest on the printed lines of the form. If you want to be able to check alignment of the copies from time to time, stick pins through the entire pack— carbon paper and all—in various places. Later you can insert the pins to see if all copies are still aligned.

Subscripts and superscripts. To type raised footnote numbers or subscripts and superscripts in chemical formulas and mathematical equations, turn the platen slightly and type the character. If your machine has a line-retainer lever, you can roll the platen to any point and then return to precisely the previous position.

Vertical lines. Although the trend is to avoid vertical lines in tables, some material may require both horizontal and vertical rules. For a horizontal rule, you can lock the shift key and use the underscore. Or you can lock the shift key, set the machine to "stencil," and put a pen or pencil into the fork of the ribbon guide, moving the carriage across the paper. To make a vertical line you should release the platen for variable spacing and then roll it while holding a pen or pencil in the fork of the ribbon guide. As the paper rolls up or down the pen or pencil will make a vertical line where the ribbon guide is positioned.

Carbon packs. To insert a bulky pack, first align the paper sheets without the carbon paper and insert them until the paper rollers get a grip. Then slip in the carbon sheets one at a time, carbon side toward you. If you have a small pack you can align them all under the flap of an envelope or into the pocket of a folded sheet of paper, inserting the entire group all together. Always use the paper-release lever to get the pack into position more easily.

Stencils and masters. Mimeograph stencils and paper offset-press masters have lines (which don't show in reproduction) on them to show you the area in which to type. For a stencil, set your machine for stencil typing and clean the typewriter keys. Follow the instructions regarding insertion of a cushion sheet, special correction fluid, and so on. Handle the stencil with care to avoid tearing or smudging. Set the impression control on your typewriter to medium and type normally.

You also need to clean the type before preparing a paper offset master. You can use either an offset ribbon or a standard carbon ribbon to type a master. (Some manufacturers recommend that you use a backing sheet with a carbon ribbon.) Insert the master into the typewriter carefully; set the impression control on low and type normally.

Corrections

Although you can correct errors with an electronic machine before the type appears on paper, you must proofread and correct errors afterward with other typewriters. Materials and supplies for making corrections were described earlier in the section Correction Supplies. Even with the proper correction supplies, however, certain types of corrections require special techniques.

Carbon copies. To erase errors on carbon copies, place a plastic card or an index card on top of the carbon paper and erase the copies one at a time, moving the card from front to back. (Place a card behind the original to erase it.) If the retyped word(s) is too faint on the carbon copies, switch to the stencil position and retype it.

Stencils and masters. For stencil corrections, lift off the film (if any) from the stencil sheet and burnish the error with a paper clip. Apply the fluid and let it dry before retyping. For paper master corrections, use a white followed by an orange offset eraser.

Bound pages. When pages are bound at the top, insert a blank sheet in the typewriter and roll the platen until it extends about an inch. Insert the unbound edge of the page you want to correct between the blank sheet and the platen. Roll the platen toward you until the typewriter grips the page to be corrected. Adjust the position and make the correction.

Bottom or edge of a page. Feed the page backward until the bottom edge is free, make the correction, and return to the previous position. Use the line-retainer lever so that when you return to the former position, the alignment will be correct.

DICTATION AND TRANSCRIPTION

Dictating and transcribing the dictation are two routine activities in most offices. Some people write out everything (letters, reports, and so on) in longhand, and a typist or secretary types the material from this handwritten source. But most people dictate in person, with a stenographer or secretary taking the dictation, or by machine. Machine dictation and transcription has dominated the field in recent years and is replacing shorthand in many offices.

Dictation

Not everyone is comfortable talking into a machine, but a little practice usually removes any initial apprehension. The advantages of machine dictation are so overwhelming that even the most reluctant users are drawn to the process. The most obvious advantage is that you can dictate while away from the office—in a car, on a plane, in a hotel room, or anywhere else—at any time of the day you choose.

Equipment. Dictation equipment can be classified as portable machines, desktop machines, small work-group systems, and central systems. The *portable machines* are small units that will fit in a briefcase or even in a pocket. A *desktop unit* is small enough to occupy a small area on a desk but sufficient for heavy use, with additional features such as integration with telephone answering systems. The *small work-group system* integrates desktop and telephone-answering capabilities among a number of persons who share secretarial support (rather than each person having a separate unit or system). The *central-dictation system* is a large system that serves an entire organization. Usually, it is connected to the phone system and may be integrated with other departments and functions such as word processing, electronic mail, and voice-data communications.

Depending on your needs and the type of equipment you or your company has, you may be able to dictate from out of town by telephone at any hour and have the material automatically recorded and waiting when your office opens, ready for transcription while you are still out of town. Such features enable one to make optimum use of dictating equipment, and one of the most important considerations in selecting equipment is its compatibility with other dictation and word-processing equipment throughout the firm. If the machines cannot be integrated, a valuable feature—and cost-saving advantage—will be lost.

Media. The media used by various machines and systems are discrete or endless loop. *Discrete* media, suitable for portables and desktop units, may be a removable belt, disk, standard cassette, microcassette, or minicassette. *Endless-loop* tape, used in small work-group or central systems, is used over and over without being removed from the machine (a timesaving feature and safeguard against loss or theft). Endless-loop dictation is thus transmitted electronically without one having to stop to remove a cassette, belt, or disk and physically transport it to the transcriber.

Techniques. Practice is the key to successful dictation. Once you have learned how to speak clearly at an even pace, you will be able to use virtually any equipment with ease. If more than one person in your organization provides dictation, you will probably start off by stating your name, department, identifying number (if any), date, time, kind of document, and special instructions (format, number of carbon copies, priority, and so on).

Indicate periods and any special punctuation desired. Otherwise, let your voice (e.g., pauses) indicate commas and other breaks within a sentence. Spell out proper names (*Smith, Smythe; Brown, Browne*; and so on). Also spell out unusual terms and acronyms, and in technical areas, specify if any mathematical or other symbols (e.g., %) are to be used rather than spelled-out forms (*percent*).

When one letter might be confused with another such as *f* and *s*, clarify it (*"s" as in "Sam"*). Speak directly into the mouthpiece and avoid turning your head while talking. Do not raise or lower your voice but stay at an even, moderate level. Also do not speak so fast that you muffle and slur words or the transcriber will have trouble keeping up with the material.

The most frequent complaints of transcribers are that dictators do not enunciate clearly and often speak excessively fast or slowly. Another complaint is that dictators do not clarify words and letters that are difficult to understand or are unfamiliar. It is important to remember, too, that the usual efficiencies provided with dictation equipment are cancelled out when transcribers must waste a lot of time searching for zip codes or other information that the dictator could easily have provided but didn't.

Transcription

The way that you transcribe dictation depends in part upon whether you are working with shorthand notes or machine dictation. When your employer dictates to you in person, you will be concerned with two steps: taking the dictation (shorthand) and transcribing it.

Shorthand. Keep pencils (No. 2 lead) sharpened at all times (check your supply the first thing each morning), since you may be called in for dictation at any moment. (Some secretaries take all notes in pen, since ink is easier to read, and keep their pencils as backup in case the pen runs dry.) Check your shorthand notebook each morning, and take an extra blank notebook along in case you run out during a dictation session. If you have more than one boss, use different-colored notebooks for each one. Other supplies you will need are a pen(s), a red pencil to mark interruptions and instructions, paper clips to clip pages together, and rubber bands to tie off pages that are completed. Attach the paper clips and rubber bands to the notebook so that you don't forget them. Also take along a calendar and files or documents that you or your boss may want to refer to during dictation.

If your employer doesn't begin by stating the required format and other instructions, ask about style, number of copies needed, priority of the material, addresses, and any other special instructions. Place your notebook on a desk if possible or anywhere else that is comfortable and where you can easily flip the completed pages. Bring along other work (e.g., proofreading) in case your boss is interrupted. Be certain to have someone monitor the telephone and take messages while you are in a session.

Don't hesitate to ask your boss to repeat anything or slow down if you cannot keep up. Date the pages at the bottom in red (easier to see when flipping through them). Spell out unfamiliar terms, names, addresses, and so on. Start a new page for each new item and leave extra pages blank for long material that will likely have additions or revisions later. You may want to use only one column of the ntoebook (left column if you are right-handed) for the dictation and leave the other column blank for later use in making corrections, additions, and other changes.

If you are taking dictation by telephone, read it all back to the dictator. If you are taking dictation at the typewriter, find out the length of the material first and then type it like a draft without worrying about punctuation until later. (Some experienced typists are able to type many dictated pieces as originals without first preparing an initial draft.) Reread any dictation (in person, telephone, typewriter) immediately afterward, while it is fresh in your mind, and clarify spelling, punctuation, and other unfinished business right away. After you finish typing each letter or document, draw a diagonal line through the corresponding notes in your shorthand notebook.

Machine transcription. As soon as possible, become familiar with your transcribing equipment. Some machines have features such as an indicator tape by which you can judge the length of a letter or other material. Otherwise, you have to listen to the material before judging the length. In some cases you may have to type a rough draft first and then type the final version later. With experience, though, you will become adept at judging length and be able to set margins and center letters and other material on a page perfectly the first time around.

Before beginning transcription, collect the necessary tools and materials and organize them on your desk—paper, corrections supplies, addresses, and so on. Listen to the dictation and follow the special instructions at the beginning of each item. Note which items are priority. After you finish each belt, disk, or tape, draw a line through the identification strip. (If there is no strip, you can make up your own list on a sheet or index card and check off each item as it is finished.)

Be certain that your machine is operating properly at all times. Most belts, tapes, and disks are easy to insert and remove from a transcription unit. In addition to putting in and taking out the medium your machine uses (unless it is an endless-loop system), you will be adjusting volume, speed, and so on. A foot or hand control will enable you to stop and start the dictation at any point while you are typing. Other controls enable you to go backward or forward to various items or positions within a particular item. If your office reuses the belts, disks, or tapes, determine whether you should save any portion of the dictation and be certain to mark anything to be saved (on the identification strip or on a separate record) before you return it to your boss for reuse with more dictation.

Always proofread your typed copy before you erase anything. (Some offices require that nothing be erased until the typed copy has been approved and mailed.) Use the same care in proofreading that you would use for any other typed material. Double-check addresses, dates, statistics, and other facts. In addition, be certain that the material is dated the day you transcribe it, not the day your employer dictated it, unless told otherwise. In conjunction with this, watch for references in the material to "yesterday" or "tomorrow" or something else that would be inconsistent with the date of transcription. Most employers expect their secretaries to make ordinary grammatical corrections and to change minor errors in dates, figures, and so on. If you have any doubts about the extent of the corrections you should make, ask your boss to clarify this point.

CHAPTER SEVEN

Using Word Processors and Computers

Typewritten documents are primarily produced by electric and electronic typewriters (see chapter 6), automated typewriters (e.g., magnetic tape), and electronic text-editing machines (e.g., word processors and computers). Word processors are dedicated computers; that is, they are designed primarily for text production, whereas computers are designed to handle a variety of tasks such as word processing, mathematical computations, and inventory maintenance. With the word processing software (the instructions that direct the computer), a multipurpose computer will function like a dedicated word processor, and with the right software, a word processor can perform other functions, such as billing.

Generally, therefore, the term *word processing* refers to the preparation of typewritten material by any means, but in a narrower sense it refers to the text preparation, or text editing, done by either word processors or computers. In the same sense, the term *word processor* is used generally to refer to both the dedicated word processing machines and the multipurpose computers that run word processing software.

Enhanced productivity is one of the principal benefits that word processing users seek. Organizations that must turn out vast amounts of typed material could not manage in today's fast-paced business world without the speed and advanced capabilities of electronic communication. The speed and ability to simplify repetitive and otherwise cumbersome tasks sets word processing systems apart from even electronic typewriters. It is clear how large organizations or any firm that is heavily involved in information processing must have the increased productivity of a word processing system. But even individual owners can benefit from the timesaving features and special capabilities of word processors. Time is money in the working world for both individuals and large corporations.

One of the most annoying aspects of word processing is the lack of standardization in equipment and software. Just as a part for one make of car will not necessarily fit on another car, so the word-processing software for one machine will not necessarily run on another. Everything else differs as well from one manufacturer to another. You may become familiar with an IBM keyboard at home and have to work with a Wang keyboard in the office. Perhaps you were first taught how to use the Wordstar word processing software and now you have to learn how to use Microsoft Word. As a result of the many differences in equipment and software, the learning process never ends for many people. However, everything is much easier if you have a general understanding of the basic types of word processing systems (e.g., stand alone), the basic equipment (e.g., keyboard), and the basic media (e.g., diskette).

WORD PROCESSING SYSTEMS

Since magnetic-card and magnetic-tape typewriters are considered nearly obsolete (they lack more advanced processing features such as a video-display screen), the word processing systems that receive the most attention are the stand-alone systems and the larger shared systems.

Stand-Alone Systems

The term *stand-alone system* describes a word processor that can function by itself apart from any other system or part of a system. Technically, an electronic typewriter and a magnetic-card or magnetic-tape typewriter would fit this category since both are independent systems that are operated by one person. But the full-fledged stand-alone system has other components, such as a display screen and a printer. It also has permanent storage capacity, which the typical electronic typewriter, for example, lacks.

Physically, the electronic and the magnetic-card and magnetic-tape typewriters look like a large version of any typewriter. Although the full-fledged stand-alone system has a typewriterlike keyboard too, the resemblance changes after that. It also has various other components such as a central processor, disk drives, a storage device, a video-display screen, a printer, and other optional equipment such as a telecommunications interface.

Since the term *stand-alone system* refers only to an independent system, not to a specific size of system, a wide variety of word processors fits in this category. The smallest portable computer on the market today is technically a stand-alone system, although it is commonly classified as a "portable" or "portable PC" (personal computer) in the popular and trade press. Similarly, a very large computer would qualify as a stand-alone system if it operates with only one workstation and one printer and is independent of other systems. Among the general public, the most familiar system is the personal computer, a collection of desktop components that can be used at home, at school, or in the office.

Size and processing capacity, therefore, may vary greatly among stand-alone systems, but to qualify as this type of system, each must have its own memory and own computing ability. Nevertheless, one stand-alone system can communicate with another system if the proper interface (connection) is established. More often, though, when this type of communication is used, it is through one of the shared systems.

Shared Systems

Large organizations often have shared systems, whereby individual terminals (e.g., keyboard and video-display screen) are connected to a large central computing source.

Shared-logic and shared-resource systems. When individual workstations have no memory or intelligence of their own (dumb terminals), and all must be connected to a central processing unit (CPU), the arrangement is often called a "shared-logic" system (i.e., the terminals share a central "logic" source). But when an individual workstation connected to a CPU has not only a keyboard and display but also some memory and its own processing unit, the arrangement is often called a "shared-resource" or "distributed-resource" system. An advantage to this type of system is that if something happens to the central logic unit, the individual workstations can use their own memory and processing capability to continue working.

Organizations use shared systems for several reasons. Less overall space is needed, the CPU is never or rarely idle (more efficient use), the per-unit cost is less for individual workstations (although the overall cost may be higher). Also, a cluster type of arrangement gives a firm more flexibility, since peripherals can be added where needed and in the number needed. If more workstations are needed in remote parts of a building, they can easily be added. If a lot of printers are needed but only a few keyboards, that arrangement is also easy to set up. More material can be stored since the large CPU will have hard-disk storage, which has greater capacity than the diskettes often used in stand-alone systems (see BASIC EQUIPMENT). Since information is stored by the central unit and all workstations have access to it, several people can work on the same document at the same time.

The main problem with shared systems is that each one may have to wait from time to time depending on how many other workstations are using the CPU or central printer(s). If the CPU is overburdened at certain times, it will respond less efficiently, and users may find that editing time is greater than it would be with one operator using one complete stand-alone system in each workstation. Also, with a breakdown in a shared-logic system, all workstations must wait until the CPU is repaired, since they have no logic of their own. Security, too, is more of a problem with a central logic and memory. Unless operators have passwords to protect their confidential documents, any other operator using the central storage can retrieve someone else's material.

Time-sharing. Some workstations share a large mainframe computer by telecommunications. Operators in virtually any location linked by telephone lines can access the central computing source and process information the same as one would do in a shared-logic or distributed-logic system. The difference is that the time-share users are tapping into the central computer long distance. The CPU in a time-sharing system is usually owned by one organization and "time" is sold to the various users outside of the organization. Since delays are inevitable with this type of system, it is less suitable for ongoing word-processing activities than it would be for other miscellaneous work.

Future Systems

Smaller size is one of the most noticeable changes that will be evident in the future. Experts predict that massive amounts of information will be stored on equipment no larger than a credit card. Also, networks will be emphasized, with more independent workstations linked in a network by which information is readily and easily exchanged. Systems will have the ability to expand with ease, and controls of document production will be enhanced (e.g., spell-checkers will be expanded to include grammatical improvements). Word processors are expected to occupy an important position in the ongoing computer revolution, and the impact will be felt in all organizations and in all departments as the proliferation of electronic operations affects training and other functions.

The widespread use of personal computers has already influenced trends. In the future the PC will thrive to the extent that it will be designed to handle networking activities and will function equally as a stand-alone system and a workstation integrated with other operations. To be cost effective, PCs may be required to use mainframe storage, and to be suitable for wide applicability in the future, they must be designed for heavy use and must be technologically state-of-the-art systems (e.g., designed for voice-data applications and other innovations).

BASIC EQUIPMENT

With the drive to reduce the size of computers, some of the components such as the central processing unit and the storage device that you use in a workstation or those that are part of your PC package may be different in the future. At present any differences in equipment reflect manufacturer design variations, type of equipment (e.g., portable), and number of components at the workstation (shared logic versus shared resource). The increasing use of the PC as a workstation is also a factor. Large organizations, however, will continue to have a larger central computer to handle a substantial amount of processing and storage in spite of the popularity of desktop units with their own computing and storage capabilities.

Specialists operate central computer rooms, and employees in general are not required to know the intricate operations of a mainframe. But most office workers today and certainly those in the future should be familiar with the basic equipment of a personal desktop or workstation word processor or computer. A familiarity with the components and their use (see OPERATING PROCEDURES) will help you feel much more at home in the computer age.

Hardware

The hardware of a word processing system is the equipment—the keyboard, the video-display terminal, and so on. Both the stand-alone dedicated word processor and the microcomputer that has word processing capabilities have the same equipment configuration. Therefore, either way, if you are going to handle word processing with an intelligent stand-alone system (having its own logic), you will likely have a central processing unit, a video-display screen, a keyboard, a magnetic storage device, and a printer. If you are working at a dumb workstation that is linked to a large mainframe, you may have only a keyboard and video-display screen.

Keyboard. Anyone who has ever typed on a typewriter considers the keyboard to be the one familiar component in a word processing configuration. The keyboard may be a lot thinner (if it is detachable), and it has more keys than an electric typewriter, but if you know how to use a typewriter keyboard, you can easily start typing on a word processor or computer keyboard. Both are arranged in the basic QWERTY format. But some keys are unnecessary with a word processor (e.g., margin-release key), whereas extra keys are needed to perform special editing functions.

The keyboard you use may be permanently attached to the cabinet that contains the CPU and the screen, or it may be a thin, lightweight, separate component attached to the terminal only by a cable. Detachable keyboards can be moved around as far as the cable will reach and can even be held on your lap. Since the equipment of one manufacturer differs from that of another, there is no standard word-processing keyboard, just as there is no standard video-display screen or printer. Each time you change equipment, you will likely have to learn how to use the new components. However, knowing the fundamentals will shorten the learning time and simplify the process in the future. (Refer to the Model Keyboard for an example of one design having a separate numeric keypad as well as a separate cursor keypad.)

Word processing is achieved not only by typing on the alphabetical part of the keyboard (the part that looks like that of any electric typewriter) but also by pressing keys that represent instructions. A key often labeled "Del," for example, would delete any word(s) you select if you press it (see OPERATING PROCEDURES). Although there is a "return" key, usually in the same position as the typewriter return key, you don't need it to start each new line. Instead, you set the left and right margins where you want them, and the machine automatically moves to the next line each time the typing reaches the right margin. The return key is used instead if you want

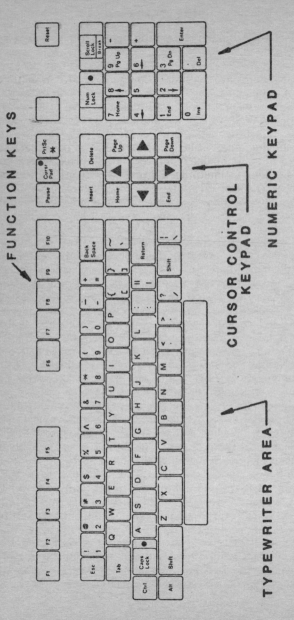

FUNCTION KEYS

TYPEWRITER AREA

CURSOR CONTROL KEYPAD

NUMERIC KEYPAD

Source: Key Tronic Corporation. *KB5151 Operator's Manual*, copyright © 1986, Key Tronic Corporation. Reprinted with permission.

to start a new line or paragraph before reaching the right margin.

Your keyboard may have a separate group of ten numbered keys known as the "numeric keypad." Sometimes these keys double as a cursor pad. Cursor keys move a tiny mark, sometimes a small rectangle, that appears as a bright highlight on the video-display screen. Cursor keys move this little mark up, down, and sideways on the screen to enable you to position it on top of a character that you want to delete or to mark a place where you want to insert something. By pressing other keys you can keep highlighting characters, words, lines, paragraphs, or even pages. With some software, if you were to highlight an entire paragraph and then press the "delete" key, that paragraph would disappear from the screen.

Various keys on the cursor pad are known as "editing" keys. They enable you to delete copy, insert copy, move copy, and so on. Some of them will move copy up or down on the screen (called "scrolling"). Perhaps you have just typed ten pages and now want to look at page five on the screen. By pressing a certain key you can cause the previous pages to keep appearing until the one you want to see is on the screen. By pressing other keys, depending on your software capability, you may be able to type the number of the page you want to see and it will automatically appear in the screen. Editing keys give typists a versatility that isn't possible with an ordinary typewriter. A popular alternative to using editing keys, however, is to use a "mouse," a little hand-held object that moves the tiny cursor around the screen. It has buttons on it that you press to delete, insert, and so on (instead of pressing keys on the cursor pad).

Other special-function keys provide for storage or printing. If you want to save the ten pages you typed (which you saw on the screen while typing), you can press certain keys to transfer the material to permanent storage on small floppy diskettes or on a higher-capacity hard disk (see Media). If your equipment is connected to a large central computer, the copy will probably go into the central storage device. If you then decide to print out the material onto paper, you press other keys that activate the printer, which automatically "types" the copy onto paper so that it looks the same as any typed page.

Depending on the word processing program you are using (see Software), you may have a *spell-checker*—an automatic proofreading capability that is activated by inserting the proper diskette and pressing the designated keys. Other special keys are programmable. For instance, if a certain paragraph is going to be used over and over, you can type it once and thereafter simply press one of the programmable keys rather than retype the entire paragraph each time.

Because word processing equipment offers users such a variety of functions, and numerous instructions are specified by pressing keys, it can be difficult to remember all of the combinations of keys for the different tasks. As a typing aid, you can purchase *templates*—plastic forms that usually fit around the edge of the keyboard and on which many of the various instructions are printed (e.g., how to switch to italic) along with a list of the keys to press for each one. With a template you don't have to memorize all of the instructions and keys, nor do you have to stop typing frequently to page through your instruction manual or review displayed menus.

Video-display screen. The most common televisionlike screen on which you see the words you type is known variously as the video-display screen, the cathode-ray tube (CRT), the video-display terminal (VDT), the video terminal (VT), the display, the monitor, or simply the screen. The shape of the video-display screen may vary slightly, as may the color of the case (usually light color), just as televisions differ somewhat in shape and color. But the key difference is in the color of the typed words and background that appears on the screen—green on a black background, amber on black, and so on.

Full-size screens are ten to twelve inches (measured diagonally); small, or partial, screens (used in compact portables) are only about half as large. The full-size screen will usually display up to twenty-four lines of type up to eighty characters wide. Most desktop PCs have about a twenty-four-line display capacity. Some larger workstation CRTs have a full-page screen that displays the equivalent of a letter-size typed page, or sixty-six lines, eighty characters wide. Since the ability to see as much of your typed page as possible is clearly advantageous, you can easily understand the difference between having a limited electronic-typewriter display (a line or two) and much greater display of a stand-alone dedicated word processor or computer, even a small portable computer.

The color of the screen is significant in terms of clarity and the likelihood of eyestrain. A popular color combination is green letters on a black background. Some persons, however, believe that there is less eyestrain with amber letters on a black background. Some screens display only white on black, whereas others, with full graphics capability, display in vivid multicolors. Some screens, no matter what color, have a better resolution than others. Anyone who is involved in word processing must be concerned with clarity and any other factor that will prevent eyestrain. Since the glare from lights or windows can be a problem, some users purchase antiglare screens that attach to the display portion of the terminal and cut glare in much the same way that sunglasses keep out sunlight. Also, eyeglasses with a photo-blue coating are sometimes used to reduce glare.

The principal use of the monitor is to observe the typing and editing before it is printed on paper. There you can watch words being deleted, or inserted, or moved around; parapraphs being indented; and so on. You can watch the tiny movable cursor highlight words as you maneuver it across the screen by pressing cursor direction keys or moving around a hand-held mouse. With some systems, what you see (on the screen) is what you get (when it is printed out on paper). With others, the printed version may look very different from what you see on the screen. Perhaps your equipment shows everything on the screen single-spaced, even though you have entered instructions to double-space and the printed version will, therefore, be doubled-spaced.

The word processing program you use will determine what appears on your screen and how it looks. You may, for instance, see the outline of a box (window), and each word you type will appear on the screen within that outline. Beneath the window may be something called a *menu*, which is a list of commands such as "Print." Beneath that you may have a message line, where important messages will appear from time to time such as "Disk is full." Another line beneath the message line may be the status line, which gives you information about the document you are typing such as the name of the diskette file where the document is stored.

Central processing unit. The brain of a word processing configuration is the CPU. This unit uses something called a "microchip," which makes it possible to perform certain tasks such as word processing. In other words, the CPU is a control unit. Nothing else is possible without it.

The speed at which the CPU performs is measured in bits (binary digits). For example, a 32-bit unit usually works faster than a 16-bit unit, which in turn works faster than an 8-bit unit. Eight bits, meanwhile, equal 1 byte (character or space) and 1K (kilobytes) refers to a thousand bytes. Therefore, if you have a desktop computer with a memory of 64K, it has 64,000 bytes. If you assume that a typed, double-spaced, letter-size page of a text has perhaps 2,000 characters, or 2,000 bytes, or 2K, you can judge how many pages a particular size of memory will accommodate (64K would accommodate 32 pages).

The two kinds of memory in a computer are random-access memory (RAM) and read-only memory (ROM). *ROM* is the information put into the equipment by the manufacturer. The CPU can "read" it, but you can't change it. *RAM*, on the other hand, is open memory. It's a capacity, and you can input information, take it out, or change it as you wish—up to the limits defined by the capacity. ROM is permanent, but RAM vanishes as soon as you turn off the computer. That's why you have to transfer anything you want to keep to a diskette or hard disk (see media) *before* you shut off the computer, or you will lose everything in the RAM memory.

Two or more types of software packages are necessary

for word processing. First, an *operating-system package* is needed to direct the various devices such as the printer, and second, a *word processing package* is needed to enable you to do things such as type and edit a document. Other software may be needed or at least desired for functions such as proofreading (see Software).

Depending on your equipment and its capacity, you may be able to establish an interface with various telecommunications devices, such as answering services. Electronic mail (see chapter 8) depends on such a linkage. By using the telephone lines and a device called a *modem* (modulator-demodulator) connected to your CPU, you can access various electronic libraries (databases) as described in chapter 13. Such interfaces with other equipment and other operations are an important part of the overall communications network in many organizations.

Printer. The typed copy that you see on your screen and that you can store permanently on disks or tapes can be printed out in hard-copy form (e.g., on stationery or other paper). The equipment used for this consists of a printer and a device to feed the paper into it.

A variety of printers are available differing not only in speed and special features but in quality of the printed word. The matter of quality is especially significant since the images of some printers are not suitable for correspondence and other important material where appearance of the typed page is important. Speed is also a major concern in organizations that must produce huge amounts of typed material each day. Printers are also distinguished according to method of type. *Impact printers* strike the paper like a typewriter. *Nonimpact printers* transfer the type onto the paper by another method.

Many *letter-quality printers* use ribbons like a typewriter. They also produce clean, sharp letters, although often at a slower speed than some other printers. Printers that use a *daisy wheel* (a somewhat flat daisy-shaped type element) are popular in word processing operations. Since they are usually noisy, however, it is sometimes necessary to use an enclosed stand to muffle the sound.

Dot-matrix printers form letters out of tiny dots. Although quality has improved in newer models, the older ones produced images too coarse for many users. Since these printers are much faster (and less expensive) than many letter-quality machines, they can be used in operations such as billing where image quality is less important. *Ink-jet printers* also form images from dots, but the quality is better than that of dot-matrix printers. *Laser printers* that use a laser light process to form images are expensive but will produce good-quality images at high speed. Other printers are the high-volume *line printer*; the *thermal printer*, which uses heat-sensitive paper; and the *electrostatic printer*, which sends electrical charges to the paper that in turn attracts the carbon particles forming the letters.

Printers act and look like a typewriter except that they have no keyboard (some models have the option of attaching a keyboard to convert the printer into a typewriter). They have other parts, however, including various controls for printing and spacing. Many have features such as pitch selection and storage of text fed from the computer (until the machine is ready to type it out). Some will pause while you check something or change a ribbon and then resume typing. Some will also print out multiple copies of each page, depending on your software. Features vary depending upon the manufacturer, price range, and so on.

For the printer to type sheets of text, the paper has to be inserted into the machine. There are several ways to do this. You could manually insert each sheet, although that would become tiresome if you needed more than a few pages. Two popular devices for feeding the paper automatically are the sheet feeder and the tractor feeder. The *sheet feeder* is a device mounted on top of a printer where you can stack sheets of paper that will automatically be fed into the printer. You could stack sheets of business letterhead or envelopes in the feeder, for instance, or any other paper you choose.

A *tractor feeder* is also mounted on the printer, but you have to use continuous-form paper—paper with bands of feed holes on each side by which the tractors pull the paper through the machine. Afterward each sheet must be torn apart from the other sheets at the top and bottom, and the side bands must be pulled off each sheet. Since some continuous-form paper may be of lower quality and may leave a ragged edge where it is torn apart, you should check a sample before purchasing a large supply.

Media

Information that is temporarily held in RAM while you are typing and editing can be saved, or transferred to permanent magnetic storage. The medium on which the information is stored is usually a disk or tape. External memory also can be a physical device (e.g., punched paper tape and punched computer cards) or an electrical form of storage (e.g., electrical charges in the integrated circuits of personal computing systems and home video games). But the common storage systems today are magnetic.

Tapes are distributed in cassette form, and disks may be either small 3½-, 5¼-, or 8-inch Mylar circles (like a small phonograph record), a separate larger-capacity hard disk, or a built-in larger-capacity Winchester disk (a sealed hard disk). Disks require a disk drive, devices with heads that read and write across the disk surface. Permanent metal hard disks spin at a much faster rate and have a great deal more space to record information. The diskettes (also called floppy disks or minidisks) are put into and taken out of the disk-drive device and are filed elsewhere (again, like phonograph records) when not in use. "Video disk" refers to a storage medium primarily used with home-entertainment systems. In this case, images are stored as a picture rather than as a code. Some authorities predict greater use of this process in business as well.

Care and Maintenance

Both equipment and the media are subject to damage and normal wear. Although computers and word processors must be cleaned internally and repaired by qualified service personnel, you can contribute to lower repair costs by protecting your equipment and magnetic disks from excessive heat or cold and extremes in humidity, from direct sunlight, and from physical jarring and static buildup. Keep the equipment exterior free of dust and keep the disk-drive heads cleaned by using a head-cleaning diskette periodically. Surge-protection devices can be purchased to prevent electrical jolts to the equipment and possible loss of data from storms or other power fluctuations. Always keep magnets away from both equipment and diskettes.

You can protect your diskettes by handling and inserting them carefully (don't touch the magnetic surface) and keeping them in dust-free files. The type of diskettes you purchase can make a difference too. Some have lifetime guarantees; others of poorer quality have a short life. (Be certain to purchase the diskette that fits your machine. Like typewriter ribbons, diskettes vary according to the equipment.)

Security. If you work with confidential material, your options for protection depend on the type of system you have. If your material is filed on removable tape or disks, you need a lock-proof storage file kept in an inaccessible place. Some firms can physically lock a diskette in the machine itself. If you use central mainframe storage or have a built-in hard disk in your stand-alone system, you need to protect the information you type from others who have access to the same central storage or who could simply sit down at your workstation and retrieve data from your hard disk.

One method of protection when you use a hard disk or central storage in a shared computer is to have a system of passwords or personal identification. In other words, the file containing your information cannot be called up until the user first types the proper password or identification data. To discourage carelessness, some firms also hold the one who prepares the file under a certain password accountable for the protection of it. Although these problems of security may seem more acute than those with noncomputer protection, the protection of confidential material has always been a concern for organizations; electronic files simply require a different means of thwarting misuse of equipment and theft of sensitive data.

Software

The programs, or instructions, that tell the computer what to do are known as the software, as opposed to the hardware, or the equipment. The special-purpose programs such as word processing or accounts receivable are the software packages that one can purchase on diskettes or tapes for use in performing a specific type of work.

Although there are many word processing software packages to choose from, not every program will run on every machine. Some programs are written exclusively for particular equipment such as Apple or IBM. Other programs (e.g., Wordstar) may be available for more than one manufacturer's product, but you still must purchase the one written to run on your equipment. Thus you can buy Wordstar for both Apple and IBM, but you cannot run the one for Apple on the IBM equipment. Most of the current word-processing programs sell within a range of fifty to five hundred dollars.

The program or systems software activates the computer, instructs it to do certain things, and gets it ready to accept special-purpose programs such as word processing. The special-purpose software lets you perform specific tasks such as editing and formatting. All of these programs are available on tape or, more commonly, diskette. Written by specialists, some of the programs are updated and upgraded from time to time, with new, usually more powerful, versions available to purchasers of the previous version at a lower cost than the full retail price.

Although the full capabilities of word processing software vary, you can basically use it to enter (type) a document, change it (edit), print it out, and file it on a magnetic disk or tape. Some of the specific functions you can perform, often merely by pressing one or two keys, include automatic formatting (margins, tabs, and so on), centering, inserting copy, deleting copy, moving copy, searching, paginating, and proofreading. Some of the common operations made possible with word processing software are described in OPERATING PROCEDURES.

OPERATING PROCEDURES

Since software packages differ, it is impossible to specify precisely how to accomplish a certain function such as moving a paragraph from one document to another. But you can gain a head start in learning the basics of word processing by becoming famiiliar with some of the things that various packages can accomplish as well as learning routine steps such as how to get a program started and how to shut down the equipment when you are finished.

Preparations

You will have a lot of instruction books (documentation) that come with your equipment and software to help you. Unfortunately, a great deal of the documentation is confusing and inadequate. Experienced users will tell you that they had to learn many things through trial and error, sometimes even making a discovery by unintentionally hitting a wrong key. In other cases the instructions were clear but the users ignored them. One is advised, for example, to save material frequently (i.e., transfer it from temporary RAM to permanent storage on a disk) and to make backup copies of diskettes. But some persons take this advice only after losing many hours of typing because something such as a power outage has wiped out the copy from RAM before they have saved it. Or perhaps they have accidentally lost or destroyed a diskette with forty pages of typing and hadn't bothered to make a backup copy. Such minor disasters soon impress upon one the importance of following instructions and heeding such warnings.

To prepare for a typing session you need to have your source copy, blank cassettes or diskettes (if you don't have a hard disk or share the storage of a large central computer), and tools such as a felt-tip pen for writing file names on the diskette label (a hard pen or any type of pencil might damage the diskette). Most microcomputer users transfer the information from their operating-system diskette onto their word processing software diskette. To start then, they can simply insert the one combined diskette into the left disk drive, if you have a dual-drive system. After inserting the diskette and turning on the computer, the operating system is activated. Then by typing the proper instructions, the word processing program also begins. After inserting a blank diskette—or another one you want to continue working on—into the right disk drive, you are ready to begin.

If you are starting a new document separate from any previous file, you will have to pick a name. No document can be filed or retrieved without such an identifying label. Follow your software instructions for creating a file and naming documents. If you want to work on a file you created previously, you will type the name of the file and by pressing the proper keys "call it out" (have it appear on the screen).

Formatting

With a new document, one of the first things you may want to do is set up the format (paragraph indentation, space between lines, and so on) so that the computer can automatically follow your instructions as you type. Depending on your software, you may be able to see on the screen how spacing, margins, and other format elements will look in the printed version.

Type of formats. Word processing software commonly has three types of formats: character (e.g., bold, italic, or normal), paragraphs (e.g., indentation, space between lines, and space between paragraphs), and page (e.g., overall appearance, such as page margins, position of running heads and page numbers, pitch, and number of columns). With some software you can store all of these instructions and use them over and over simply by pressing one or two keys each time. You may be able to specify measurements in inches, centimeters, points, pitch, or lines.

Formats for special elements. By following your software instructions you can format special text such as footnotes and tables. If your program has a multiple-window option you can divide your screen in two or more parts and prepare general text in one window and work on something such as a table or footnotes in another window. Thus you do not have to scroll (move from one line or page to another) to the end of a document to read or revise such elements.

Tables, which may have many columns of data, make use of tab settings. Often the software has a ruler that appears at the top of the screen to show specifically where the tab settings fall on the page. Tabs can be easily cleared and reset. Some software will automatically align all columns at the decimal place so that you can type the columns at each tab setting no matter where the decimal falls and merely press a key afterward to realign each column at the decimal points.

Entering Text

To enter text, just begin typing. If you have done your formatting in advance, you already have established the margins, spacing, tab settings, and so on. Using what is called a wrap feature, your machine will automatically decide when to begin each new line. Do not press the return key as you would do with an electric typewriter. But when you want to start a new paragraph or add extra blank lines, you must use this key. If you decide to change the margins later, the machine will automatically decide again where each line should end and make the changes in every line throughout the document.

You can start a new page at any time or reformat a particular page or paragraph. If you need to look at an earlier page you can use a "page-up" or "page-down" cursor key or pick one of the "up" or "down" cursor keys that lets you scroll line by line backwards or forwards in the text. As you use these keys different lines will appear on your screen.

Saving text. Users have different systems for deciding when to save what they have typed. Some press the "save" key about every five pages; others save the material every fifteen minutes. If a power failure, power surge, or some other problem occurs then, they won't have a huge amount to redo. With most software, each time you save something, the material from the previous time becomes a backup file. For example, assume that you have created a file called MN06. Each time thereafter that you press the "save" key you will have two documents on your disk: the most recently saved MN06.DOC (*DOC* means document) and the previous copy, which becomes a backup and is automatically labeled something such as MN06.BAK. If later your diskette is getting full and you need a little more space, you can always delete the earlier version now labeled MN06.BAK. (A message may appear on your screen to warn you when your document disk or the systems-program disk is full.)

Revisions

The ease of making revisions is what sets computers and dedicated word processors apart from either electric or electronic typewriters. Not only do a wide variety of instruction keys enable you to make almost any change quickly and easily, but also a screen that displays a large portion of every page helps you to visualize the results of your changes. Revising or editing a document may sometimes mean no more than changing a word or comma here and there. On other occasions it may even mean moving large blocks of copy, changing a lot of format specifications, and practically rewriting every sentence. Whereas you would have to redo every page with a typewriter, you can simply type the correction with a computer or word processor and let the machine automatically adjust each page throughout the entire document.

Moving text. Depending on your software, you can

delete text by backspacing, which wipes out characters one at a time, or by using the "delete" key. For example, to pick the word(s) you want to delete, you might move the cursor and press the appropriate key to highlight that word(s). Then you would press the "delete" key. With some software, material that you delete is held in temporary storage, so if you want to use the material you have just deleted somewhere else, you can move the cursor to the point where you want to use it and press the "insert" key. The deleted material will automatically reappear in the new position. Since words and phrases can be stored, you can recall and reuse something without retyping it each time.

Using a mouse. The results are the same in moving text whether you move the cursor around the screen by pressing directional cursor keys or by moving around a hand-held mouse. A mouse is usually rolled around a level surface such as your desk. As it moves left, right, up, or down, the cursor on the screen moves in the same direction. Thus you can maneuver the tiny cursor highlight to a word you want to delete by moving the mouse on your desk. After highlighting the word to be deleted, you press the appropriate button on the mouse. Some persons can edit faster with a mouse. Others insist that when they lift their hands from the keyboard to pick up and move the mouse, the interruption causes them to make an error when they try to reposition their hands and resume typing.

Adjusting page breaks. With some software you can adjust the page breaks before the text is printed by pressing the "print" key and next the "repaginate" key. The machine then shows you where it has ended each page and asks you to confirm the choice. If you want to end the page somewhere else you can move the cursor to the line you prefer and the machine will automatically change the page ending to your preference.

Other editing functions. Numerous other editing options are available. Some keys, for example, will enable you to type over another line. A *search and replace function* will find the word(s) you indicate wherever it appears in your document and replace it with the new word you specify. A *help command* will cause instructions to appear on the screen itself so that you don't have to leave the keyboard to page through your documentation books. A *library spell* command will introduce a proofreading function whereby errors are displayed on the screen and you are asked if you want to type the correct version or ignore the error. If you want to correct it, the proper spelling will be substituted wherever the error appears. A *merge command* will merge two separately prepared documents so that they print as if they are one. Some or all of these editing functions—and often more—are available with word processing software, depending on the particular program you choose and your equipment. The more powerful the software, the more editing tasks you can perform. (Guides to available software are in bookstores, and computer magazines regularly review software packages.)

Printing

Before you press the "print" key, you are given an opportunity to make important decisions. For example, do you want to print the entire document, certain pages, or various blocks of copy? How many copies do you want? Do you want to continue working on another document while the printer is printing out the one you specify? After printing has started, you may see something you don't like as the first page appears. Keyboards usually have an "escape" key with which you can stop whatever is in progress. Some have a "pause" key with which you can halt the printing long enough to examine something, and if it looks satisfactory, you can then press another key to resume the printing. (For more information, see Hardware, *Printer*.)

Shutdown. At the end of a day or the end of your printing session, when you are ready to stop word processing, you need to shut down the equipment. The most important thing to remember is that when you turn off the CPU, anything that you typed will be lost if you left it temporarily in RAM and did not save it, that is, transfer it to a disk. With some software, when you stop working and press the "quit" or other designated key, a message on the screen will ask if you want to save or lose your work. If you respond "yes," that you want to save it, the material will be transferred to permanent storage on your document disk (e.g., a diskette or hard disk).

Making backup copies. After quitting, when something called a "prompt" appears on the now blank screen, you can make a backup copy of your document disk. Follow your operating-system instructions for one or two disk drives. Be certain to insert the completed disk in the right drive of a dual-drive system. When the copy procedure is finished (it takes only seconds to copy a diskette), you can remove both diskettes, label them with a felt-tip pen, and file them vertically in a diskette file box. You are then ready to shut off the printer, the video-display screen, and the CPU and disk drives.

MESSAGE
TRANSMISSION

CHAPTER EIGHT

Processing Mail

The volume of mail going in and out of offices keeps increasing in spite of the wider use of telecommunications (see chapter 10) and various forms of automatic message transmission (see ELECTRONIC MAIL and chapter 9). Conventional mail includes not only a heavy flow of correspondence but also a massive amount of other material such as bills, statements, advertisements, newspapers, magazines and books, and a variety of merchandise and supplies.

The U.S. Postal Service and numerous local, national, and international private delivery services physically transport a constant flow of mail by way of complex networks of ground, air, and water transportation. Whereas some things such as merchandise have to be moved physically from one place to another, other mail such as correspondence can be sent another way. Electronic mail eliminates this need to transport paper or other material physically between the source and the destination. But it has been advancing slowly. There is no indication that the use of conventional mail will be significantly reduced in the foreseeable future, and in fact, in the short term the volume of conventional mail is likely to increase even more.

CONVENTIONAL MAIL

The handling of conventional mail includes processing both incoming and outgoing mail. Whenever mail comes into an office, it has to be opened, sorted, and processed (first answered or routed and eventually filed). When it goes out of an office, it has to be proofread (if it's a typed document), signed, assembled, folded, inserted in an envelope or mailing carton, addressed, and stamped or metered according to postal service or private delivery regulations. There is clearly a lot of handling involved in conventional-mail procedures.

Incoming Mail

A large organization usually has a mail department that receives and distributes the mail to the office addressees. A smaller organization may receive the mail in each office, where a secretary or another employee is responsible for the opening, sorting, and distribution procedures.

Opening. You will probably sort the mail twice to make the opening task more efficient—once before opening it and again after opening it. When the mail arrives, separate letters in envelopes from the tied and taped packages and then collect newspapers and periodicals together. In a large mail room bins or trays are often used to facilitate the sorting of mail by department or office. A messenger then delivers each group to the respective departments or offices. However, procedures differ from one organization to another. Some large mail rooms, for example, open all mail (except letters marked "Confidential" or "Personal") with an automatic mail opener. In other cases the material is distributed unopened to each office.

If you are opening the mail for your office, and you accidentally tear a letter, mend it with transparent tape before sending it on. But never open private correspondence marked "Personal" or "Confidential." If you open such a letter accidentally, tape it shut and on the outside write "Sorry, opened by mistake" with your initials. If any of the mail is not yours or for your office, cross out the incorrect address and write the correct address on the envelope (if you know it). Write "Not at this address" on the face of the envelope and put it back in the mail.

Remember, however, that only first-class mail is forwarded without applying additional postage.

Check each envelope for enclosures and attach the envelope or mailing label to any material that otherwise has no return address. Write a note on any letter if it mentions an enclosure that is not there. Also keep envelopes for checks and important documents if the postmark differs from the check date. Mailing dates are important in some cases. Mark the date and time on each piece of mail, using a pen, rubber stamp, or a time-stamping machine.

Sorting. Now that the mail has been opened, you can take the sorting process a step further. Divide letters into stacks for each addressee, with urgent messages on top. Paper-clip large enclosures behind the letters and small ones in front of them. Similarly, divide packages and newspapers or periodicals into stacks according to addressee.

Find out if your boss and others to whom you distribute the mail want to have junk mail discarded. If they do, always be certain that you are not destroying something useful. Perhaps the announcement of a conference looks like just another piece of advertising, but your boss may want to have someone from the office attend that event. Or the flyer you receive about a new dictating unit may be something your boss has been eager to learn about. As a general rule, it's better to risk saving something that appears unimportant than to risk discarding something important.

Processing. After you have opened and sorted the mail, a few more steps are necessary. Your employer may expect you to read and annotate the mail. Presumably, you scanned each letter during the sorting process to decide who should really answer it. For instance, someone may write to the president of the firm for routine information. You certainly wouldn't bother the president with an inquiry that you or someone else could easily handle. Perhaps the inquiry should go to your boss but you notice that it first requires some routine research. In that case you may want to set the letter aside (if it isn't urgent) for the moment while you collect the facts or pull something from the files that your employer will need to compose a reply.

In regard to annotating the mail, your boss will tell you whether he or she merely wants key phrases underlined or whether you should prepare an actual digest of the mail—short paragraph summaries of the contents. To annotate the mail, underline only in a nonreproducible blue pencil. Some employers prefer yellow marking pens or something else, but remember that most colors will show if you later must make a photocopy of the material. (Some offices will not permit any marking on original letters.) If you need to write comments, attach self-adhesive, removable slips of paper (available from office-supply stores).

Mail records are important in many offices, particularly when executives are often away on business. This is a record of each important item received (but not junk mail, bills, orders, or such routine items). A ruled sheet in a notebook can serve this purpose. At the top of each page, make column headings such as Date Received, Time Received, Description, From, To Whom Sent, Mail Notations (e.g., Special Delivery), Action to Be Taken, and Follow-up Date. Such a mail record is necessary in some businesses to keep track of important information. It is always useful when your boss travels a lot and you need such summaries in front of you while discussing office matters by telephone or when you need a daily digest of activity to photocopy and mail to your boss while he or she is away.

Some mail must be routed to others in your organization. Possibly it should have gone to them in the first place and was merely sent to your office in error. Perhaps your office always decides which employee handles various tasks, and the incoming mail is always routed accordingly. Or perhaps you or your boss wants others to receive a copy of certain material even if one of you will handle the actual reply.

Office-supply stores have printed routing slips, but you may prefer to type and photocopy your own. Two basic types of slips are used. One is used when you are sending something to one person; another is used when material is to be passed from person to person, eventually returning to your office. In the latter case, each person who receives the material initials and dates the routing slip and then puts it back into the inneroffice envelope to be delivered to the next person. For example, if general manager Jim Bates wants three of his departmental managers to see something, you might attach a slip with the following information, put it in an inneroffice envelope, and place it in your Out box for a company messenger to pick it up and deliver it to the first name on the list:

Please route to	Initials	Date
Harold Shackle	HS	4/9
Edna Unta	EU	4/10
Donna Simpson		
Jim Bates		
File		

In this example, Harold Schakle and Edna Unta have read the material, but Donna Simpson still has to read it. After she is finished, it will be returned to the general manager, Jim Bates. After he has taken final action, it will be ready for filing.

But assume that the general manager simply wants to send the material to one person and ask that person to read it and then return it. It may be his policy to issue instructions or give routine assignments this way. You might, then, attach an action-requested slip with the following information and send it to the appropriate person:

FROM THE OFFICE OF JIM BATES
( ) Please reply.
( ) Please prepare a reply for my signature.
( ) Please send me background information.
( ) Please discuss with_____.
(✓) Please note and return.
( ) _____.
Thank you.

If you make up your own slips, you can design them and

word them to fit the type of needs your office usually has. Even with a slip attached, you may have to jot other instructions on the material being routed or on the routing slip. Perhaps you are sending an inquiry letter to someone else for reply but you have already taken care of something. Write "Done," the date, and your initials in the margin of the inquiry letter next to the paragraph or sentence pertaining to the matter you have already handled.

Outgoing Mail

The size of your organization will determine the procedure for handling outgoing mail. If you work for a large company, the mail room will likely collect your mail and seal and meter it, although you will be responsible for proofreading typed documents, attaching enclosures, and all other preliminary processing. If you work for a small organization, you may be in charge of proofreading outgoing typed material, seeing that correspondence is signed, assembling the items to go into each envelope or mailing carton, folding and inserting them, sealing them, applying the postage stamps or meter tape, and even delivering some of the letters and packages to the post office.

Proofreading. Before you can even consider the steps in mailing a typed document or letter, you must proofread it. Although you should proofread pages even before removing them from your typewriter or use a spell-checker (if you have one) with computer or word processor preparation, you also should review a letter or document before putting it in an envelope. You may have missed an error earlier, and spell-checkers could miss something. For instance, if you typed "the" when you meant "then," a straight dictionary spell-checker would not identify "the" as an error. But if you typed "htem" for "them," it would pick it up as a typo.

Check correspondence and other material one final time for appearance as well as errors. Does the typed page(s) look attractive? Is it clean (no smudges or correction blemishes)? Is anything missing? Review the chapters about writing in this book, especially chapters 11 and

12 and the discussion of proofreading in chapter 13. See also chapters 6 (typing) and 7 (word processing).

Signing. Most of us have received letters that someone forgot to sign or have sent letters that we forgot to sign. Sometimes this happens because the person in charge of processing the mail doesn't check each letter or check to see if it is signed. The only safe procedure is to check every piece of outgoing mail, one at a time, and immediately set aside any unsigned material.

Keep a "signatures" folder on the desk or table where you prepare the material for mailing and put each unsigned piece into it. Return the unsigned material right away to the appropriate persons and indicate if anything is urgent and must be signed and mailed immediately. Otherwise, the signer may want to wait for a more convenient time. Also separate letters that the signer dictated and those that someone else wrote for the signer.

You can present the letters to be signed with or without the envelopes, but always remove the carbon copies. Some secretaries insert the flap of the envelope over the top of the letter. Others submit the letter right away and, while waiting for it to be signed, type the envelope from the address on the carbon copy. (Do not file carbon copies until the letter is signed since there may be last-minute changes.)

Processing. After a letter has been signed you are ready to go through the steps of assembly, folding, inserting, and so on. When you assemble the contents for each envelope or package, check again that any letter is signed and that all enclosures are included and arranged in the order mentioned at the bottom of the letter by the enclosure notation (see chapter 12). Compare the inside address with the envelope address or mailing-label address. They should be the same.

Look for late changes your boss may have made that necessitate retyping the letter. It may be more than a handwritten postscript that must be added (typed) to the file copies, or it may be a more extensive correction or revision. Check whether the envelope address has been typed so that the post office can sort the envelope automatically by optical-character reader (see chapter 12). After you have examined everything and corrected any errors, divide the mail into categories (correspondence, bills, and so on) before folding and inserting it.

Standard letters (8½ by 11 inches) mailed in standard envelopes (nos. 9 or 10) are folded in thirds, with the second fold leaving a small edge (1/16 inch) at the top. Insert the folded letter so that the narrow edge is on top in the envelope and so that the reader can remove it and have the letter facing with the typed side forward, right side up. To insert a standard letter in a smaller envelope (no. 6), fold it almost in half with a quarter-inch top edge showing, and then fold the half-size folded sheet in thirds, again with a narrow edge showing, this time on the right. Always insert letters with the protruding edge on top. If you use window envelopes, be certain to fold the letter so that the panel with the inside address is facing to the outside and is inserted in the envelope with the address to the front of the envelope.

Enclosures should be folded along with the letters when they are about the same size—large enclosures behind the letter and smaller ones stapled to the front of the letter. But if there are various odd-sized enclosures, fold them together apart from the letter, clip or staple them together, and slip them into the last fold of the letter so that the person removing the letter will pull out the enclosures at the same time. (Since post office equipment can be damaged by processing mail prepared with paper clips, it is better to staple items whenever possible. If paper clips are used, the material must be inserted in the envelope so that the paper clip is at the bottom where it will not jam in the postal equipment.) Coins and other objects that cannot be clipped or stapled must be taped to a card or sealed in an extra small envelope.

Some enclosures are so large and bulky that a large mailing envelope must be used. For example, you may want to send a booklet with your letter. Depending on the urgency and your postage budget, you may want to put everything in a single large envelope and apply first-class to all of it. You can also affix a small sealed envelope with the letter to a large unsealed mailing envelope. In that case, apply first-class postage to the small envelope with the letter and third-class postage to the large envelope with the booklet. You could also simply send each item separately, the letter by first-class mail and the booklet by third-class mail. With any parcel, you may enclose a letter, provided that you state "Letter Enclosed" on the package and pay additional first-class postage for the letter.

Mail clerks and others who handle mail frequently become very skilled at inserting items rapidly when many envelopes are involved (mass mailings, however, would be processed with folding and inserting machines). If you have a lot of similar enclosures (perhaps a brochure to go into each envelope) but do not use automated folding and inserting equipment, open the flaps of several envelopes and arrange them in a row, each one slightly overlapping the other. While holding them stationery with one hand, slide enclosures in, one after another, using your free hand. But do not try this when the enclosures differ, since you could easily slide the wrong enclosure into one of the envelopes. If you don't have a postage meter that automatically moistens and seals each envelope, you can use a sponge to moisten groups of envelopes with their flaps turned up in the same position used for rapid inserting.

The mail room. Your firm may have a large, fully equipped mail room with addressing equipment; sorting bins; large collating, folding, and inserting machines; electronic scales and postal meters; and various other mechanical and automated equipment. Or you may simply have a corner of your office with a scale, a postage meter or box of stamps, a sponge for moistening envelopes, and a manual letter opener. Regardless of the size of your mail operation, keep current postal regulations and rates on hand. If the volume of mail warrants it, purchase copies of the *Domestic Mail Manual* and the *International Mail Manual* from the Superintendent of Documents in Washington, D.C. Pick up free guides at your local post office too, and ask to be put on the list to receive the free newsletter *Memo to Mailers* (U.S. Postal Service, P.O. Box 1, Linwood, N.J. 08221-0001).

Modern equipment is a money saver as well as a time saver. Not only will electronic scales calculate postage precisely and meters apply precisely the correct amount of postage, thereby eliminating waste, some of the modern electronic equipment will also provide an accounting function, keeping a record of expenses for you. Since you in essence purchase postage in advance with a meter, having it set for a certain amount, you have an immediate check on postage used by watching the register. Some offices maintain an account at the post office for which meter postage expenses are deducted. You can also apply for an imprint permit and have indicia printed on your envelopes for bulk mailings. No postage or postal meter tapes need to be applied then. The cost of the mailing can also be deducted from an account maintained at your local post office. However, permit-imprint mail, regardless of class, must be sorted by the mailer, which involves added time and labor costs.

Bulk mailings require more than sorting. They involve envelope addressing on a large scale, too large for someone to type every envelope. Some offices with small mailings type a master sheet of labels and photocopy additional sheets of labels for further mailings. Computers and magnetic-tape typewriters can also maintain address lists and print out address labels or envelopes.

For very large mailings, some firms use an outside service to maintain their lists, simply sending in address changes as they occur. Other organizations with large mail departments purchase their own computers, automated typewriters, or special addressing machines that use cards or metal plates, which are filed alphabetically or numerically. The quality of the addresses imprinted on the envelopes or labels varies according to the type of equipment used. An envelope addressed by computer or automatic typewriter looks as if it is individually typed, but some addressing machines make fuzzy images or, after repeated use, faint images.

Convenience is as important as economy in some firms. In other words, it may cost more to have one's own addressing and mailing equipment, rather than use an outside service, but the greater control and convenience of handling everything under one roof seems worth it. Other organizations may believe it is more trouble than it is worth or too costly in terms of equipment, space, and labor and training costs.

With rising postage costs and greater volume, many organizations are concerned with economy above all else and are concerned most with day-to-day savings. For instance, you can cut costs by combining mailings to the same person, by sending nonurgent bulky material third class or in reduced form such as microfilm (see chapter 4). Documents and messages can also be transmitted by facsimile or telex (see chapter 9) or by electronic mail (see ELECTRONIC MAIL). Perhaps some heavy enclosures could be omitted. Or perhaps a phone call would cost less than a letter. Some special services that cost additional postage (e.g., express or special delivery) have little or no effect on delivery time over weekends or holidays when offices are closed. For bulk mailers, updating and cleaning up their mailing lists periodically can save a great deal of postage otherwise wasted on incorrect or obsolete addresses. Most persons who seriously examine their mailing practices discover a surprising amount of waste and can soon apply potential cost-cutting strategies.

DELIVERY SERVICES

You have many choices today when it comes to sending correspondence and other documents. Electronic mail (see ELECTRONIC MAIL), facsimile (chapter 9), and telex (chapter 9) are examples of transmission without actually transporting the physical material between two points. But even when you choose to send the letter or document itself you have many choices. The U.S. Postal Service remains the leading carrier of mail, but an ever-increasing number of private delivery services (local, national, and international) are providing high-volume, competitive service.

To make a choice you need to compare charges, speed, and convenience. Pick up current domestic and international mail pamphlets and charts at your local post office, and use the Yellow Pages to find the addresses and telephone numbers of private delivery services serving your area. Call to write to them for the latest information. Since some delivery services update their service brochures and rate charts several times a year, request new information periodically throughout the year.

Postal Service

Although everyone in business is familiar with the U.S. Postal Service, not everyone knows the many rules and regulations for domestic and international mail. Serious mailers usually purchase the large, detailed *Domestic Mail Manual* and *International Mail Manual*. With both manuals you receive sheets of revisions throughout the year. You can also request free brochures and pamphlets, but the information is limited and revised copies are not automatically sent to you. Since the rules and regulations for domestic mail are very different from those for international mail, you need information in both areas if you mail outside the United States.

Domestic mail. The Postal Service classifies mail as domestic if it goes within, among, and between the fifty states, its territories and possessions, the areas comprising the former Panama Canal Zone, and the army-air force (APO) and navy (FPO) post offices, as well as mail to the United Nations in New York. (A list of approved two-letter postal abbreviations is given in the reference section at the end of the book.)

The Postal Service has a helpful brochure titled "Secretarial Addressing" that shows the basic format to follow in addressing an envelope so that it can be sorted with automatic equipment (see chapter 12 for a sample address that meets postal requirements). Whereas use of the recommended format is optional, other regulations are not. You must, for instance, follow the proper format for *indicias* (imprints on envelopes in the place where postage is normally applied). Applications must be filed for use of postage meters, mailing by precancelled stamps, and so on. To obtain a license to use a postage meter you must submit an application (Form 3601-A).

Other regulations pertain to size: all mailing pieces must be 0.007 inch thick, and pieces that are a quarter-inch or less must be rectangular, 3½ or more inches high, and 5 or more inches long. Some regulations are not well known, such as the provision concerning green-border envelopes: any envelope or card with a green border will be charged postage equivalent to the first-class rate. Many of the regulations pertain to the five basic classes of mail:

1. *Express mail* for domestic use is a high-speed delivery service available in three categories: Express Mail Same Day Airport Service is provided between designated airport mail facilities; Express Mail Custom Designed Service is available only on a scheduled basis between designated postal facilities or other designated locations; Express Mail Next Day Service is available at designated retail postal facilities for overnight service to designated areas. Offices in small towns, therefore, may not be in a designated mailing area for complete express service (ask at your local post office if you can send or receive Express Mail within the time frame indicated for designated areas).

2. *First-class mail* includes anything sent at the first-class rate unless it fails to meet size, weight, or safety requirements of the aircraft on which it is transported. Some things *must* be mailed at the first-class rate, such as an original letter or a statement of account. The categories are single letters not exceeding twelve ounces (over twelve ounces, it becomes zone-rated priority mail), postal cards (Postal Service) and postcards (commercial), presort first class and carrier-route first class (both reduced rates for presorted mail), and zip + 4 first class (a nonpresorted reduced rate). Ask at your post office for details on preparing presorted first-class mail and presorted carrier-route first-class mail. The first-class weight limit is seventy pounds (except to APOs and FPOs), and combined length and girth may not exceed 108 inches. First-class

mail, which is guaranteed to be delivered by the third day in most cases, can be insured, registered, or certified and can be sent special delivery.

3. *Second-class mail* includes newspapers and other periodicals that meet the requirements of the Postal Service (e.g., issued at least four times a year). Qualified nonprofit organizations may be able to mail at a special nonprofit rate. Unlike first-class mail, second-class mail is not guaranteed to be delivered within a certain time. Before mailing at the second-class rate, publishers must complete an application (Form 3501). In addition, publishers must maintain certain records (number of copies printed, distribution, and so on) and make them available to the Postal Service as required. All postage must be prepared before mailings will be dispatched. "Return Postage Guaranteed" must be printed on the outside to have undelivered copies returned. Ask your local post office about mandatory sacking in the various categories (firm, five-digit, three-digit, state, and mixed states). There are no physical limitations, except the minimum sizes for first-class mail apply (see no. 1).

4. *Third-class mail* consists of matter that is not mailed first class or second class and weighs less than sixteen ounces. This includes circulars, printed (not original) letters, and printed (not original typewritten) matter. Although one usually seals third-class mail, it may be opened for postal inspection. Third-class bulk mail is a reduced-rate category for presorted mail. Application for a permit to mail at bulk rates is made on Form 3624. Different requirements apply depending on whther it is carrier-route presort, five-digit presort, or basic presort. Nonprofit organizations may apply for special bulk rates. As with fourth-class mail, with third-class mail also there is no guaranteed delivery within a specific time. Minimum-size standards are the same as those for first-class mail (see no. 1). Although there is no maximum size for single-piece third-class mail, carrier-route presort mail must not be more than ¾ inch thick, 11½ inches high, and 13½ inches long.

5. *Fourth-class mail* is everything not mailed as first class or second class that weighs more than sixteen ounces

(except special or library rates). Parcel post rates are based on zones, like priority-mail rates. Fourth-class mail includes a number of categories: parcel post, bulk parcel post, bound printed matter, bulk bound printed matter, special fourth-class, special fourth-class presort, and library. (You must file an application to mail at the reduced bulk or presort rates.) Special regulations and different rates apply in each category. Certain books (as well as films, printed music, and recordings) fall into the special-fourth-class-rate category whereas books mailed by a publisher or a distributor to a library fall into the library-rate category. Fourth-class parcels must not weigh more than seventy pounds or exceed 108 inches combined girth and length (like first-class mail).

For an additional fee the Postal Service provides a number of special mail services for domestic mail:

1. *Registered mail*, available for material with first-class postage, provides added protection. In addition, you can insure the registered package (up to twenty-five thousand dollars), send it COD, and request a return receipt. The letter or package must be completely sealed with paper or cloth tape (glazed tape should not be used).

2. *Certified mail* provides proof of mailing and a record of delivery, but no insurance is provided (use registered mail if insurance is desired). Like registered mail, certified mail is available only for first-class mail.

3. *Insured mail* provides insurance (up to five hundred dollars liability) for third- and fourth-class matter when mailed at the first-class rate or the third- or fourth-class rate, except when restrictions apply (e.g., a parcel so fragile that it cannot be safely mailed). Insured first-class mail is forwarded and returned free, but postage must be guaranteed in the case of third- and fourth-class mail.

4. *Collect-on-delivery mail (COD)* enables one to send an article and collect payment and postage costs (not exceeding five hundred dollars) from the addressee upon delivery. The fee is then returned to the mailer by postal money order. First-, third-, and fourth-class mail may be sent COD.

5. *Special handling* is available for third- and fourth-class mail, including insured and COD mail. It provides preferential handling (e.g, for live poultry) but does not provide for special delivery.

6. *Business-reply mail* enables mailers to receive first-class mail from customers by guaranteeing payment of the postage. Application for a permit is made on Form 3614 and must be renewed annually. The appropriate legend (e.g., BUSINESS REPLY MAIL) must appear above the address in capital letters at least ³⁄₁₆ inch high. Beneath that must be the permit number and a "Postage Will Be Paid by" endorsement. Paper envelopes must be twenty-pound weight, and various size and weight restrictions apply to the types of envelopes, self-mailers, cards, labels, and so on. (Inquire at your local post office.)

7. *Money orders* can be purchased from any post office for amounts up to seven hundred dollars.

8. *Stamps* for special purposes are issued from time to time through the Postal Service.

9. *Other services* include the sale of savings bonds, general delivery (when you don't have an address), special delivery, and post office box numbers.

International mail. Different rules and regulations apply to mail sent to other countries. Not only do the requirements differ from domestic mail in general, but individual countries have their own requirements, so mail prepared for one country might not be suitable for another.

Addressing is important in international mail. At least the entire right half of the address side of the envelope, package, or card should be reserved for the destination address, postage, labels, and postal notations. The bottom line of the address must show only the country name (except in the case of Canada) typed or printed in all capital letters. For parcels the address should also be written on a separate slip of paper and enclosed in the package.

There are three categories of international mail: postal union, parcel post, and Express Mail International Service. Inquire at your local post office for rates and weight and size limits for each category per country and fill out the proper customs forms at the time of mailing.

1. *Postal union mail* is governed by the regulations of the Convention of the Universal Postal Union and includes LC (letters and cards)—letters, letter packages, postal cards and postcards, and aerogrammes—and AO (other articles)—regular printed matter, books and sheet music, publishers' periodicals, matter for the blind, and small packets. *Letters and letter packages* are items with original handwritten or typed messages. Write "LETTER" or "LETTRE" on the address side of the package. *Postal cards and postcards* are single cards sent without an envelope. A folded card, however, must be sent in an envelope. *Aerogrammes* are air letter sheets that are folded to form an envelope and are then sealed.

Printed matter is material produced by some means other than handwriting or typewriting. It includes regular matter and other (books, sheet music, and publishers' periodicals). *Matter for the blind* consists of books, tapes, and so on intended solely for the blind. *Small packets* consists of small quantities of merchandise, commercial samples, and documents that don't qualify as current and personal correspondence.

2. *Parcel post*, like domestic parcel post, consists of packages of merchandise and material that do not include handwritten or typewritten current and personal correspondence. But the parcel may include an invoice or out-of-date file correspondence.

3. *Express Mail International* is a high-speed class of mail exchanged with forty-nine countries through mutual agreements. It offers one- to two-day delivery. The two types of service are Custom Designed and On Demand. *Custom Designed Service* may be picked up from any address or mailed at designated postal facilities. *On Demand Service* is available at designated facilities for non-scheduled expedited service to certain countries. Insurance is available for both services.

A number of special services are available at extra cost with international mail, the same as with domestic mail.

1. *Registered mail* provides extra protection and a mailing receipt as well as a delivery record on file at the destination post office. Indemnity limits vary per country (up to $20.40, but Canada has a $200 limit).

2. *Certificate of mailing* provides evidence of mailing but no delivery receipt.

3. *Insurance* is available only for parcel post and only to certain countries.

4. *Special handling* provides preferential handling for surface parcel post, printed matter, matter for the blind, and small packets between the post office where mailed to the office of dispatch but not from there to the foreign country.

5. *Special delivery* is offered in certain countries according to the local regulations. It is available only for postal union mail and only in specified countries.

6. *INTELPOST* uses facsimile to send exact black-and-white copies of original documents to twenty-seven countries with window pickup within one hour after transmission, same-day delivery in metropolitan areas, and next-day delivery elsewhere. Customers with compatible facsimile machines can dial in to the system from their own offices.

7. *ISAL (International Surface Air Lift)* is a fast bulk-mail system for publications, advertising mail, catalogs, and other printed material to sixty-eight countries. Delivery is usually seven to fourteen days from shipment.

8. *International priority air mail*, available anywhere except Canada, saves one day on delivery by bypassing domestic sorting and processing. Mail must be sorted, and the Postal Service provides sacks, labels, and tags.

9. *Air mail* provides four- to seven-day delivery of letters and other mail worldwide.

10. *Other services. International money orders* enable one to transfer funds to certain countries. *International reply coupons* are used to prepay a reply from someone. The receiver may take them to a postal facility in that particular country and exchange them for postage.

Because of the complexity of international regulations, you should review a current *International Mail Manual* or ask for instructions from your local post office concerning customs, filing claims, and so on.

Private Delivery Services

Competing with the U.S. Postal Service for a share of your mail are the international, national, and local private delivery services such as United Parcel Service and Federal Express. Most of these companies are devoted exclusively to the delivery of shipments, but other organizations, such as bus lines, airlines, and messenger services, also provide package delivery as an additional service. Since all of these companies are private concerns, there is no uniformity in rate schedules, size and weight restrictions, delivery networks, or services. Whereas first-class mail in the U.S. Postal Service means the same thing in any post office, something such as next-day air service may mean different things in private companies in terms of rates and regulations. To determine the differences you have to contact the companies that serve your area and compare services and prices.

Federal Express, for instance, provides domestic and international service. Domestic services include Zapmail (two-hour delivery), Priority 1 (10:30 A.M. next business day), Courier-Pak Overnight Envelope (10:30 A.M. next business day), Overnight Tube (10:30 A.M. next business day), Overnight Box (10:30 A.M. next business day), and Standard Air (one- to two-day service). United Parcel Service offers Next Day Air and 2nd Day Air delivery options as well as full ground-transportation services. Emery advertises that it will ship virtually any size virtually anywhere, next day. Other delivery services offer similar options.

Pickup and delivery are offered by companies that specialize in this service (but usually not by bus lines and other companies for which package delivery is a secondary activity). Or you may deliver your packages to a local office if one is available. Many of the companies provide free kits containing mailing envelopes and boxes. Usually, you can open an account with the service and receive a bill on a monthly basis.

Some companies provide not only ground and air transportation but also electronic mail, facsimile transmission, and other high-speed message-transmission services. They may offer the service and use their own equipment and facilities or simply handle Western Union or other messages as an intermediary and ship through one of the other private delivery services.

Fast delivery services are convenient but often expensive. If you have an urgent shipment, it is no doubt worth an additional charge to insure delivery on time. But extra services are sometimes purchased needlessly. A package that would normally take two to three days to arrive if mailed on Friday does not need overnight service if it must wait at the destination anyway until offices open again on Monday.

Shipments should be planned carefully after comparing the various private delivery options as well as the possibilities with the U.S. Postal Service. (See also ELECTRONIC MAIL and chapters 9 and 10 for other options.) To make this comparison you could compile a list of possible services—overnight delivery, two-day delivery, and so on—and across from or under each heading identify the organizations in your area that provide such services, their rates in each category, and any other pertinent data (e.g., pickup and delivery schedule).

ELECTRONIC MAIL

Electronic mail (E-mail) is a fast means of exchanging information by creating a message on a computer terminal or word processor and sending it to another terminal electronically, generally by using the telephone lines. The type of material that can be sent is essentially whatever can be prepared by computer or word processor: letters, reports, graphics, and so on. (Facsimile and telex transmission are also sometimes considered in the category of electronic mail. For more on message transmission by such other means, see chapter 9.)

With the trend to develop the integrated office, electronic mail has been gaining in popularity, but it is considered a relatively recent addition to the corporate workplace. Even now, there are mixed feelings about the near future of electronic mail. Lack of compatible equipment has kept many potential users from exchanging messages. Lack of interest among some potential users has been evident as well.

Since one can exchange this type of mail only between terminals, the success depends upon whether customers, clients, suppliers, and others are also prepared to use it. If the principal organizations do not use it, those who do want to make use of it are severely restricted. The number of subscribers to electronic-mail services, in fact, has not been increasing as fast recently as it was around 1984. But proponents believe that E-mail is effective and efficient and that its growth will continue.

Electronic-Mail Systems

The E-mail systems in use today are still evolving, but there are now and will continue to be both private and public systems.

Private systems. Private E-mail systems are those for which you set up your own hardware and software. Companies that want to achieve total integration of all functions (computer and word processing operations, facsimile transmission, telex, and other messaging) find an advantage in making their equipment more productive and expanding their messaging capabilities. But installation costs are high when companies do not already have the necessary hardware. For those who do have required equipment, savings in copying, long-distance delivery, and other traditional costs are realized more rapidly.

Most E-mail systems transmit messages to computer "mailboxes," which are really files in the computer that accept and hold messages. The system may be centralized (a number of terminals linked to a large central computer) or a network (various independent terminals that transmit and receive messages on their own).

Facsimile (see chapter 9), or fax, is the simplest form of electronic mail, whereby exact copies of material are transmitted from one location to another. These machines, however, have no editing capability, and the message goes only from one machine to another. With computer-based electronic mail, multiple users can access the same message.

A *node-to-node stand-alone electronic-mail system* refers to an independent messaging computer that can communicate with another compatible computer. A modem and telephone are used to reach the receiving computer. An *integrated system* is one that links the mail function to word processing, voice-data transmission, and other functions in a company. Not all communicating computers use the telephone lines to exchange messages. A *local-area network (LAN)*, for example, is a network of computers that are wired to one another.

Voice-mail systems, like electronic-mail systems, can transmit, receive, and store messages; both can be accessed from almost any telephone in the world. But a voice system requires manual intervention to transcribe a message on paper whereas a computer-based electronic-mail system can print out a hard copy when desired. Industry analysts predict that voice mail and electronic mail will be integrated in the future and that electronic mail will ultimately become voice mail.

Public systems. Public data networks offer third parties access to large databases. This type of service acts as a clearinghouse for the electronic messages of subscribers. One of the most familiar electronic-mail services is MCI Mail. Such service organizations usually offer hard-copy (paper) mail as well as other miscellaneous services. Through something known as a switching technique, subscribers to certain data networks can access the network through a telephone number and then reach another computer if it is part of the network. Charges and ease of use differ from one service to another, and potential subscribers should request information including current rates, types of service, and instructions on use of the service.

Procedures

Although organizations set up their own systems and subscribers offer their own array of services—all of which differ—there are nevertheless some common threads in the use of electronic mail.

1. With a computer terminal or a communicating word processor, you can create a message of any length at any time of the day and send it to another terminal over the telephone lines. (Refer to chapter 7 for further information on the use of computers and word processors.) The precise configuration—independent stand-alone computers, terminals connected to a mainframe, time-shared arrangements, and so on—may vary.

2. If you use a service, you will follow the particular service's instructions for accessing its network. By typing the proper words and codes you can learn if there are messages waiting. Through some services you may be able to receive preliminary information such as who sent the message, how long it is, when it was sent, and so forth. You can then read the mail, store it again until later, or immediately create replies. With some systems you are informed as soon as a new message arrives in your electronic mailbox (often by a beep). But you can retrieve the messages at any time (using the telephone lines) from a remote location, just as the people who receive the electronic messages that you send may not be waiting at the destination precisely at the time you send the messages but will receive them later when they are ready to check their "mailboxes."

3. Since you create the messages you want to send on a computer or comunicating word processor keyboard, you can edit them, send them to others for review, receive their suggestions, edit them some more, and continue to revise them as you wish. You can make your own hard copy at your own terminal. (Some subscriber services will mail a hard copy of messages or send mailgrams or telegrams. Options vary depending on the service.)

4. With most subscriber services you must type the name and address (for paper mail) of the recipient (it must be another subscriber) and other required codes or

information. Editing with E-mail software is much more limited than with word processing software, but some can be done. Many programs have an on-screen "help" command, in addition to the accompanying software-instruction guide, to get you through the more complex steps of sending and receiving messages.

5. Messages are sometimes classified according to access by others. For example, with a *private electronic "mailbox,"* only the designated recipients can read their own mail. With a *bulletin-board system*, messages are available for all users to read. Passwords are commonly used as a security measure in electronic mail, but some systems have no security measures. Users need to consider their requirements very carefully before installing a private system or subscribing to a particular service.

6. A variety of E-mail software programs is available (or you can design your own program). Compare each program's requirements (e.g., amount of RAM your computer must have) and other features (e.g., maximum number of users).

7. E-mail software programs have numerous features such as password security, deferred delivery, message-waiting indicators, and concurrent operations with other functions such as word processing.

The future. Although it is likely that E-mail in the future will change, along with other technology (e.g., voice-data integration), one aspect will continue to characterize it. It is clearly a step toward a paperless office, and even though a completely electronic world is hard for most people to imagine, a partially electronic system of communications is clearly a reality today. To heavy users the postal system is already obsolete, but it seems most likely that, rather than disappear, paper-delivery services will simply incorporate electronic communications into their operations. But the failure of some efforts in this direction and the continuing paper explosion suggest that for now office workers should remain fully in touch with the use of both traditional paper-mail delivery and the various forms of electronic-mail transmission.

CHAPTER NINE

Transmitting Messages

Whereas electronic mail (chapter 8) often refers to the use of computers to send and receive messages electronically, other forms of message transmission use facsimile machines and teleprinters to send and receive messages. Like computer technology, this technology is changing almost daily in various ways: New, more advanced equipment is being introduced; service networks are expanding both in number of subscribers and variety of services offered; and large companies are linking their own computer, word processor, telex, facsimile, and other capabilities to form a more efficient and productive integrated office. Smaller firms may have some of these capabilities in house but still find it more practical and economical to rely on outside service organizations for sending certain messages.

FACSIMILE TRANSMISSION

One of the most useful machines in the modern office is the facsimile, or fax, which is also one of the oldest forms of office technology. The name "facsimile" refers to a process whereby exact copies of documents with words or graphics can be sent over the telephone lines to another terminal virtually anywhere in the world that the telephone lines reach. The document that is transmitted is reproduced as an exact copy on a receiving machine at the destination. To some users, facsimile is actually a form of electronic mail.

Equipment and Supplies

Equipment. Fax machines, which look like compact copiers, are usually classified according to four groups of machines designated by the Consultative Committee for International Telephone and Telegraph. Member countries have established standards of design and operation of the machines that allow for compatibility among brands. Generally, fax machines are operated by placing a document in a tray or around a cylinder. The document is then scanned and light and dark areas are converted into signals that can be sent over the telephone lines to a compatible machine at the receiving terminal. To send the message you then dial the appropriate telephone number and push the transmit button. The term *fax transceiver* refers to a machine that can both send and receive documents. Individual fax machines differ not only in features but according to group classification.

GROUP I. Most of these machines, primarily dating from the early 1970s, were manufactured before the committee developed compatibility standards. They use an analog device, a slower process whereby information is scanned and transformed into a continuous-wave form, with speeds of four to six minutes a page.

GROUP II. These machines, built after 1976, are faster. However, they also use the slower analog technique and transmit at two to three minutes a page.

GROUP III. These machines use a much faster digital technique in which messages are converted to code and transmitted at speeds of twenty seconds to a minute a page.

GROUP IV. These machines are still being developed. They will use a digital technique and will transmit a page in seconds.

The older and slower analog machines are disappearing and will no doubt eventually be replaced entirely by the faster Group III and Group IV digital machines. Usually, digital equipment costs more but transmission costs are less.

As a result of other technological improvements, the newer machines can be programmed to store data and have it sent automatically at a time of one's choice, even if the machine is unattended. Group IV machines will use public data networks, which are limited as yet, and this will in turn restrict the use of the new generation machines. Group III machines, therefore, will likely predominate for a while since they still use voice-grade telephone lines.

The Group III machines, standardized in 1980, are still relatively new and are the most popular. Not only are they considerably faster than the earlier generation machines, making them more cost effective, but they have other features, such as automatic feed and cut, unattended operation, programmable capability, document reduction, and telephone-line or satellite transmission.

Advantages and disadvantages. Fax machines are generally viewed as convenient, simple to use, and capable of low-cost operations. All that is needed is a telephone, since the unit has its own scanner and printer. Because they are so simple to operate, no special training is required, and they can even be programmed to send and receive when no one is around. Moreover, they can transmit graphics as well as typed or handwritten material, unlike telex, for example, which is limited to text. Such documents can be sent in minutes or even seconds, compared to the overnight or longer delivery by conventional postal or courier service. The cost of a page sent by fax is usually less than the cost of a first-class letter and much less than overnight express or a long-distance telephone call.

But fax machines can transmit only what is already prepared. In other words, you must first prepare the document on a typewriter, computer, or word processor; perhaps cut and paste on the graphics; and do whatever editing is necessary—all before taking the final product to the fax machine. Experts, however, predict that the simplicity, convenience, and economy of fax insure its future in the working world, particularly since the integration of facsimile with computers and voice mail is already on the horizon.

Fax supplies. Fax paper is not compatible to the degree that fax machines are or that other paper such as computer paper is. That is, the paper used in different fax machines is usually not interchangeable. Most fax machines use thermal printing, although some firms are moving to lasers, and much of the thermal paper has been produced in Japan especially for each brand of fax equipment. Alternatives, though, are available from some U.S. suppliers, many of which import the roles of paper directly from Japanese manufacturers and sell it to users in the United States.

The major problem in selecting fax paper is in matching the coating of the paper with the print head on the fax. With a less-than-perfect match (i.e., paper without a perfect balance for the heat of the print head), the copy will appear to be of poor quality. In short, performance quality of fax paper is far from standardized, and you need to follow the recommendations of the equipment manufacturer rather than arbitrarily select any fax paper for economy or some other reason.

Facsimile Services

You don't have to buy a facsimile machine to send fax messages. Services are available that will transmit a document for you. If you are a high-volume user, the service may provide you with a machine; otherwise, you would have to take your document to the nearest service offering facsimile transmission (no doubt the organization will offer a variety of services, fax transmission being only one). Your local Yellow Pages will list services in your area, or you could purchase a directory such as the *FAX/NET Public Access Facsimile Station Directory*, which lists more than nine-hundred independent fax stations across the United States.

Large communication services such as IIT World Communications that offer service on a subscription basis to a wide network of users provide not only fax service but telex and other data transmission. Since rates vary from one service organization to another, you need to request a variety of information and make comparisons. Check the range of services (e.g., electronic mail, fax, telex), rates for each, transmission speed, network served, whether individual transmissions are accepted or whether you must subscribe to a full service, and so on.

Most services are general; that is, you can send any type of message (e.g., text and graphics) by any appropriate means of your choice (e.g., fax) to almost any place of your choice (e.g., worldwide). Some, however, are more specialized, such as the U.S. Postal Service's INTELPOST (see chapter 8). INTELPOST, for example, uses fax machines as well as other transmission methods (e.g., Express Mail) to reach specified locations where the document can be picked up or delivered by regular mail. Some private delivery services are beginning to offer a combination of services—physical transport of a document, fax service, and other forms of data transmission.

Message transmission is continually evolving, and some facets of it are changing daily. Although it is difficult to keep up with the new technologies, it is easier to find competitive and economical services. Watch for sales material, journal articles, and other information, and update your product- and service-literature files regularly.

TELEX TRANSMISSION

One popular form of message transmission uses a keyboard machine commonly known as a teleprinter or teletypewriter. Telex and related forms of transmission are a keyboard-to-keyboard type of messaging. Unlike facsimile, this process involves a typewriterlike keyboard on which the message is prepared; thus the material transmitted is limited to text, whereas facsimile sends exact copies of graphics as well as text.

Some persons believe that since messages are prepared

at the keyboard with telex, errors are more likely to be transmitted. Facsimile, on the other hand, can send only already completed and, presumably, corrected documents, perhaps prepared earlier by a typewriter or word processor. However, there is still no guarantee that the copy prepared earlier for facsimile is error-free, so the assumption that telex messages are more likely to have errors may be an exaggeration. To others, in fact, the ability to keyboard a message and send it all at once— without moving from a typewriter, for example, to a fax machine—is an advantage.

Telex I and II

Telex was established by Western Union and has been used for many years. It is a much older technology than computer-based electronic mail (see chapter 8). Since Telex I and II have been used for a long time in business, standardization of teleprinters has occurred, and the cost is less than some of the newer technologies and services. Telex I is the original telex; Telex II was formerly called TWX for "Teletypewriter Exchange."

Equipment and operations. Telex I machines use a different code than Telex II machines. Telex I uses a five-bit Baudot code (named after the developer of the first major code) and transmits about sixty-seven words a minute. Telex II uses ASCII (American Standard Code for Information Interchange), which is a standard computer code, and transmits about one hundred words a minute. Telex II, the faster form of transmission, is billed by the minute, whereas Telex I is billed on a pulse rate (one pulse = one character).

Telex I and II are standard worldwide. Therefore, you can send messages anywhere without worrying about which subscriber service to use or which brand of teletype machine the receiver has. Each terminal—at the origin and the destination—has a machine that looks a little like a large typewriter mounted on a console or like a stand-alone word processor. You type the message on the keyboard and dial in to send it over the telephone lines.

At the destination the same type of terminal prints out a hard copy (paper) of your message. In other words, the same machine will send or receive a message.

Telex transmission is considered slow compared to some of the other forms of electronic messaging (see Teletex), and messages can be sent only in all capital letters. The quality of the printout of incoming messages is inferior too.

The machines code the message on a punched paper tape. This tape is then fed into a reader device, and the message is transmitted when you are ready to dial in and make the connection. Previously, the tape was punched as you typed, but that meant you couldn't correct an error before sending the message. Operators used to type several *E*'s or other letters after an error and then retype the word. Now, using word processors you can type and correct the copy on diskettes or other magnetic media and punch the tape from the corrected message. Thus the tape that is coded to transmit the message can be error free.

Since all telex terminals—sending and receiving—are compatible, everyone uses the same protocol (i.e., the same format). But you need to follow the instructions supplied by Western Union or one of the international carriers to use the equipment properly and to type and format your message correctly. Although the keyboard may remind you of a typewriter keyboard, the answerback mechanism is something not found on an electric or electronic typewriter. Messages begin, for example, by both parties identifying each other by way of this answerback. In fact, when you activate the terminal by pressing the "Call" button and then dialing the number designated by the telex service you are using, the first thing that will probably occur is that the service will in turn activate your terminal's answerback mechanism.

Subscriber services. Traditionally, volume messaging has been handled through subscription to a telex service. It doesn't matter which service you use, since all are interconnected. Usually, you can dial in to a network from terminals directly connected to your service, as a leased-line subscriber, from any communications carrier, and from other data terminals that communicate over the telephone lines. Since the industry has been deregulated, Western Union can connect you with overseas numbers and the international carriers can connect you with domestic numbers.

When you subscribe to a service, you will be given a dial number and a set of instructions for sending messages on your own communicating teleprinter or the service-supplied teleprinter. After you press the "Call" button to activate service and receive the answerback (identification) exchange, the system will prompt you, usually line by line, what to type, for example: your correspondent's name, company name, street address, city, state or province, country, and zip or postal code. Then you will type your own name, country, and telex number. After that, you will be told something such as "commence text," that is, to begin the body of your message. Specific step-by-step instructions will vary from one service to another, so you must study the written material you will receive and then follow the actual prompts you receive through the system after pushing the "Call" button.

In addition to Western Union, other services are FTC Communications, Graphnet, ITT World Communications, RCA Global Communications, TRT Telecommunications, and Western Union International (a subsidiary of MCI International). If you are just investigating the field, request a brochure of services and a current rate chart from each carrier (rates and services change frequently, so request new information on a regular basis). The combined subscribers of all the carriers mentioned above are listed in the annual *U.S. Directory for Telecommunications Subscribers* (free to telex subscribers). The information in this directory includes, for each subscriber, company name, address, carrier, telex number, and telex answerback.

Telex users must become familiar with a number of codes and abbreviations that are used in telex communications. The instructions you receive from the subscriber service you choose will explain the necessary short forms to use in telex communications, as well as give you important instructions (e.g., you cannot type certain letters in telex communications). The following are some of the abbreviations you may find in telex communications:

ABS	Absent subscriber, office closed
BK	I cut off
CFM	Confirm
COL	Collation
DER	Out of order
DF	You have reached the called number; proceed
EEE	Error
GA	Go ahead
MOM	One moment please
MNS	Minutes
MUT	Mutilated
NA	Messages to this subscriber not admitted
NC	No circuits
NCS	Subscriber's name changed
NP	No printer
OCC	Occupied; printer is busy
OK	Do you agree?
RAP	I will call back
RPE	Internal procedure error
RPT	Repeat
THRU	You are connected with
TPR	Teleprinter
W or WD	Word
WRU	Who is there?

You don't have to have a teleprinter to send and receive telex messages. Various interfaces have been developed to turn your word processor or computer into a complete telex center. Generally, you connect a modem to your computer and your telephone and then simply dial into the carrier of your choice. Thus you can have all of the editing capabilities of any computer or word processor and, at the same terminal, transmit your message through a telex network.

With immediate delivery and store-and-forward service, messages can be prepared and then delivered at a designated later time. Incoming messages can be stored in the carrier's central computer until you are ready to retrieve them, or they can be forwarded to your own electronic "mailbox" for later pickup. It also doesn't matter whether you choose to subscribe to Telex I or II. Even though both use different codes, service organizations use a switching process so that a Telex I subscriber, for example, can be connected to a Telex II subscriber.

Other Services

The types of available service and the equipment options keep changing. Many of these changes involve benefits such as an expanded network, easier ways to communicate by telex messages, and faster transmission speeds. Some involve the introduction of new services such as Teletex (not to be confused with a broadcast videotex called teletext).

Teletex. Western Union introduced Teletex service in 1983 in selected cities in the United States and between those cities and West Germany. The service was first developed and introduced in West Germany in 1981 and is designed for high-volume users. Teletex users can also transmit messages to telex subscribers.

Transmission by Teletex occurs at twenty-four hundred bits per second, or one in seven seconds, which is about forty-five times the speed of standard telex. Format and typography of a Teletex message resembles that of a traditional business letter rather than the uppercase letters and inferior print quality of telex. Teletex has other features, too, such as accents and diacritical marks, which are common in many foreign languages. The much greater speed of Teletex over standard telex means greater savings as well. (Contact Western Union for current page rates and monthly subscription fees.)

Teletex functions by using word processors or computers that are equipped to send and receive messages automatically. Therefore, it has the editing capability of a word processor or computer used with the telephone lines for high-speed transmission. At present, only some of the word processing manufacturers are offering telex compatibility and have plans to include Teletex. For Teletex to spread worldwide, manufacturers of the equipment used will have to meet the standards (e.g., compatibility) required by the Consultative Committee for International Telegraph and Telephone.

Leased-channel service. For very high-volume users— beyond the practical scope of standard telex or telephone— some services will lease an exclusive communications line between an organization and its overseas office. This line may be used to transmit teleprinter, voice, facsimile, electronic-mail, and other messages. A line may be leased for a monthly charge regardless of the time or volume usage, or there may be an additional message-unit charge.

Private-line switching. High-volume users may require a private line that links many of their offices. By employing various switching mechanisms, service companies can interconnect the user's private lines and also connect the private lines with other networks such as telex. This type of system can usually accept and switch messages from any location in the subscriber's communications network to any combination of other locations.

Packet-switching service. A packet-switching service interconnects computers or other data terminals and connects data terminals with computing facilities. Through such a switching service incompatible systems can communicate with one another, and one can use a wide variety of databases and other services.

INMARSAT service. This is a marine version of IN-TELSAT satellite communications. Through INMARSAT a properly equipped ship or offshore rig can contact any telex subscriber worldwide. It is an automatic, switched telecommunications service that functions much like any telex service with features such as unattended message reception (unlike radio marine service). Satellites are used for telephone, radio, and television transmission as well as data transmission. The largest satellite communications system today is INTELSAT.

Tie-line service. Tie lines, leased from a common carrier, are direct wire links between two points. They may, for instance, connect two or more private branch exchanges or provide a link between a firm and Western Union.

TELEGRAMS AND CABLES

Although businesses that send a lot of messages use electronic-mail systems, the telex network, facsimile transmissions, and so on, others still contact Western Union to send a traditional domestic telegram or an international cablegram. If the receiver doesn't have a receiving Telex or facsimile machine or an electronic "mailbox," you have to find other means of transmission, and telegrams and cables are one means of sending urgent messages (see also the information on Express Mail and overnight private delivery services in chapter 8).

Domestic Telegrams

Domestic telegrams can be sent over your telex machine or through Western Union. You can also type a telegram by typewriter, computer, or word processor and send a duplicate of it by facsimile. If you use a teleprinter, computer, word processor, or facsimile, you must follow the manufacturer's instructions for operating the equipment and the network's instructions if you are a subscriber to a telex or other service. You can also "dictate" your message to Western Union by telephone or type a copy and hand deliver it. Delivery is often in a matter of hours from the time it is phoned in or delivered.

Domestic service includes telegrams sent to any place in the continental United States, Canada, Mexico, and

Saint Pierre and Miquelon Islands. The three classes of service are the fast telegram, the night letter, and the mailgram (sent in conjunction with the Postal Service). Since rates and regulations change frequently, you should periodically request current information from Western Union.

Generally, the following items are charged (see *Fast telegram, Night letter,* and *Mailgram* for variations in determining charges): addresses other than one free address, street address of the sender, department name in signatures, and the message itself. Abbreviations of five or fewer letters count as one word (*NYC*). Initials in a name count as one word if there are no spaces (*JB Shore*). Figures (*$, #, and so on*) of five or fewer characters count as one word if there are no spaces between them. However, in messages to Canada and Saint Pierre and Miquelon Islands, each figure counts as one word. True compounds (*father-in-law*) count as one word. A word such as *STOP* used in place of a period counts as one word.

Fast telegrams. All messages are sent as fast telegrams unless you specify night letter or mailgram. Either plain language or code may be used, and the charge is based on a flat rate for a minimum of fifteen words plus an extra charge for each additional word. The following items are not charged: one complete address, attention line, name, city and state of sender, company name in signature, and punctuation marks. Otherwise, follow the guidelines above for counting charges.

Since telegrams are expensive, you should write your message as briefly as possible. Don't worry about complete sentences so long as the message is clear. For example, instead of saying "We would like to receive . . . ," simply say "Please send . . ." or "Send . . ." Also check the time difference before you decide upon the more expensive fast telegram (refer to the Global Time Chart in chapter 10). Would the more economical mailgram or night letter be adequate? A telegram sent from California at 4 P.M. would not likely reach a recipient in New York until the next day anyway.

Night letter. The night letter, slightly less expensive than the fast telegram, is usually delivered the next business day by 2 P.M. It can be sent any time until 2 A.M. Either plain language or code may be used, and the charge is based on a minimum of one hundred words with an additional charge for each additional group of five words. Refer to the general guidelines above in determining what words are charged. However, since there is a flat charge for a minimum of one hundred words, it is usually of little value to try to condense your message to fewer words.

Mailgram. Unlike fast telegrams and night letters, mailgrams are first sent to the recipient's local post office and then delivered the next day with the rest of the person's daily mail. Like the night letter, the mailgram charge is based on a minimum of one hundred words with an extra charge for additional words. Unlike the traditional telegram, the mailgram includes the name, address, and signature of the sender in counting words to be charged. But since the minimum charge for a mailgram also covers one hundred words, there again is usually little value in trying to condense the message.

Preparations. Ask Western Union to send you a supply of blank telegram forms. You can then simply fill in the blanks and have the full information ready even if you plan to telephone the message to Western Union. The typed version can be sent later as a confirming copy or used as your file copy.

Money orders. You can send money orders through Western Union by taking cash, check, or money order to your local Western Union office or telephoning Western Union and using Visa or Mastercard. Call to determine the current policy and the amount that can be paid by check.

Ships in port. To send a telegram to someone on a ship in port, include the full name of the passenger, the steamship line, name of the ship, stateroom number (if known), name of the port and pier, and the departure time.

Cablegrams

Like domestic telegrams, cablegrams (international telegrams) can be sent by telex or through Western Union or one of the international carriers offering cablegram service. You can also send a duplicate copy of a typed cablegram by facsimile. Again, like domestic telegrams, cablegrams are charged according to the number of words. Since each word in the recipient's address and signature are counted except for the country and routing symbols, many senders use registered code addresses and signatures (you can register through some of the major carriers). Code words and abbreviations (without spaces) count as one word for each five letters. Unlike domestic telegrams, cablegrams should not use symbols such as $, &, %, and # (spell out the symbol). Punctuation marks in numbers (*1,000*) count as one character within the word, otherwise as one word when used alone. A plain word is usually counted as fifteen characters per word. However, international carriers each have their own rates and procedures for counting charges. Therefore you should request current rates and instructions from each carrier that you plan to use.

International service includes full-rate messages (FR), letter telegrams (LT), and radiograms.

Full-rate messages. This is a fast service for cablegrams, usually with same-day delivery. These messages may be sent as plain language or in code, with a minimum charge for seven words. Since this service is faster, it is also more expensive. Users should check a global time chart (see chapter 10) to see whether, considering time differentials, the more economical letter telegram would also arrive in sufficient time.

Letter telegram. This is the international version of an overnight letter to certain countries. Letter telegrams may not be written in code, although a registered code address may be used. However, the minimum charge is for twenty-two words, rather than seven as with a full-rate telegram, and the rates are less even without an abbreviated or coded body. Delivery usually occurs the day after filing. Be certain to type "LT" after the address, or the message will automatically go as a full-rate cable.

Radiograms. You can send a full-rate cablegram to ships at sea in plain language or five-letter code words. Type the passenger's name, the name of the ship, its location (e.g., South Pacific), and the marine radio station (write as one word, such as *SANFRANCISCO-RADIO*). Type *INTL* (international) on the line above the addressee's name. Through some international carriers such as RCA Global Communications you can send photographs, drawings, and other documents by radio photo service.

Special services. You can add *RP* for "reply prepaid" to pay for your recipient's cost of replying. *PC*, for "paid confirmation," means that you are paying to be notified when (date and time) the message arrives. As mentioned earlier, registered code addresses may also be used on international cablegrams, and coded language may be used in full-rate messages. If an addressee has moved, you can type *FS* before the person's name to request forwarding. *NUIT* typed before the name means that you want the message delivered even after business hours.

CHAPTER TEN

Using Telecommunications Services

One item is a particularly important link in office operations—the telephone. Not only do office workers communicate directly with one another by telephone, they also use the telephone lines for sending telex and facsimile messages (chapter 9) and electronic-mail messages (chapter 8) and for other purposes such as accessing databases by computer. Since almost everyone uses the telephone for some purpose, office workers must know something about contemporary technology and basic procedures in using the equipment.

SERVICES AND EQUIPMENT

Like other modern technologies, telephone technology is still evolving, and the types of equipment and capabilities keep changing. Available services have been changing, too, particularly since the establishment of various operating companies to offer local telephone service and the expansion of other carriers, in competition with AT&T, that offer long-distance service.

The seven regional Bell operating companies (BOCs) that provide local service throughout the United States are U.S. West, Pacific Telesis, Southwestern Bell, Bell South, Bell Atlantic, Nynex, and Ameritech. They offer local calls and short-distance toll calls for designated geographic areas as well as inbound 800 service and outbound WATS (wide-area telephone service).

In addition to AT&T, the other companies that provide long-distance service by subscription are called "other common carriers" (OCC) or "specialized common carriers" (SCC), for example, MCI, Sprint, and Allnet. Usually, either you must select the carrier you want or one will be assigned to you. *Equal access* means that all carriers have the same access, and regardless of which carrier you use, you can dial 1 plus long distance without adding other numbers representing access codes. (*Dial* is commonly used in the industry to refer to both rotary dialing and pushbutton dialing.)

Rates and service vary among the common carriers, and you should compare costs and capabilities before making a choice or switching from one to another (some advertise savings of up to 40 percent). Some of these companies offer other services, such as private lines and voice data. Billing aids are also available in certain cases. For example, by dialing a code that you assign to a particular customer, you can easily keep track of all telephone costs that apply to that customer's account.

Pushbutton Systems

The pushbutton, or "key," desk telephone system is common in many offices. Telephones in one office may be interconnected to telephones in another office and, with the other telephones, also be connected to outside lines. Various configurations are possible with this technology. You may have one telephone in a small office that one person answers. In a slightly larger firm, a number of pushbutton telephones with buzzer buttons may be interconnected so that the person answering can signal others to pick up and take incoming calls. In other cases there are intercom buttons that you push before dialing certain digits to contact the person you want to reach.

Regardless of the particular procedure, all pushbutton systems have *hold buttons* used to retain a connection while the caller waits for some reason, and many have other features such as programming for *automatic* and *speed dialing*. A system that retains certain numbers in its memory enables you to call those numbers quickly merely by pushing a button or dialing an abbreviated code rather than redialing the full number each time. With a *routing* feature calls can be transferred automatically from a remote location to another telephone.

In larger systems where all incoming calls are received by a receptionist or other operator, a *message* feature such as a light on the telephone signals people that the operator has a message for them. Lightweight headsets are available for operators who want to have their hands free while talking on the telephone. Some *dial safeguards* are available with pushbutton systems; usually, this is in the form of a small device that prevents unauthorized persons from making outside calls. *Call sequencers* vary in function from a mechanism that merely causes a button to flash, indicating the next call in line, to more sophisticated devices that process unanswered calls after a certain number of rings and monitor incoming traffic to alert management if more operators are needed. *Speakerphones* are devices that enable users to speak without using the receiver. Several persons then can gather around the telephone and talk to the caller. *Picturephones* carry the technology a step further and enable you to see the person you're speaking with on a televisionlike screen.

Since telephone equipment is now sold independently by outside suppliers, you can check your local Yellow Pages for addresses and telephone numbers of sales outlets. Ask for the free product literature and compare prices, features, and service options. Ask about the cost and possibilities for upgrading. (For information about additional features and configurations, see Other Systems and Equipment.)

Exchanges

Telephone exchanges within an organization are switching devices that interconnect telephones in the various offices and, usually, also provide access to the outside public telephone network. As the technology has advanced, the equipment used to make the calls from office to office and to the outside has changed from manual to electromechanical, to crossbar equipment with common control, to computer-based systems, to digital equipment that integrates voices and data.

Digital telephones. Although the older equipment is disappearing, not all modern in-house telephone exchanges are digital; less expensive, sometimes refurbished, analog equipment is still common.

As in computer technology, the digital process transmits signals in varying discrete steps based on bits (binary digits), whereas the analog signal varies in a continuous manner. The most obvious external difference to a layperson is the digital display monitor (like that of a digital watch or clock) that shows various data such as information about the party calling and the cost of the call. Since digital systems are software driven, they can be upgraded without replacing the equipment. For the office seeking integration of various equipment and functions, the digital telephone system is easily linked to other computer activity (e.g., electronic mail).

PBX systems. Letters are used to describe the types of in-house telephone exchanges. *PBX (private branch exchange)* refers to the basic switching facility within an organization. In the contemporary working world, it is often thought of as an outgrowth of the early plug-in switchboards. If the exchange is manually operated, it is called *PMBX (private manual branch exchange)*. If the switching is accomplished automatically with the equipment, it is known as a *PABX (private automatic branch exchange)*. The computerized exchange is known as a *CBX (computerized branch exchange)*. All of these systems—and others—are variations of the familiar office switchboard. Depending on the system you have, you often must dial "9" or some other code first before placing a call to an outside location.

An exchange differs from an interconnected group of pushbutton, or "key," telephones in that the switching occurs in a central mechanism that is activated by dialing codes (e.g., the number "9" to make an outside call) instead of by pushing a button. Usually, an exchange can accommodate many more telephones than a pushbutton system. An operator typically handles the central exchange, or switchboard, unless the system will allow some direct dialing without operator intervention.

Equipment features. Telephones connected with an exchange system have the same features as a pushbutton system and often more. The hold button is standard, and features such as call sequencing, call rerouting, and so on are common. Codes are sometimes used before dialing a number to prevent others from placing long-distance calls without authorization. *Recorders* keep track of calls: to whom made, by whom, time spent, and the cost. With computerized switching, computers can be connected to the telephone lines to permit other forms of nonvoice transmission such as electronic mail (chapter 8).

Least-cost routing (LCR) equipment automatically dials calls by the most economical means, such as a WATS line (see Other Systems and Equipment), rather than by direct distance dialing (DDD). With a WATS extender connected to the exchange you can call company numbers from outside on the firm's WATS line. *Direct inward dialing (DID)*, whereby one can dial an in-house number from outside without going through the central exchange, can be arranged in different ways. It can be part of the PBX (or pushbutton) system or attached to it, or it may be arranged through the telephone company (Centrex system). Some new systems are especially designed for *voice-data* functions; such an exchange might be used for voice telephone traffic as usual and in addition handle data transmission between offices.

Other Systems and Equipment

Telephone technology is both complex and varied, and the options and uses will become more numerous as organizations move closer to the truly integrated office in which machines and functions are all interconnected. It is already difficult, and sometimes misleading, to discuss word processing, telex messaging, electronic-mail transmission, telecommunications, and other modern communications processes as independent technologies. Even now they are much more interrelated than commentators suggest in books, magazines, and conference presentations, where topics are intentionally segregated to facilitate an orderly discussion. However, these technologies are still relatively segregated in small and some medium-size firms.

To companies of all sizes, the number and variety of features is staggering. Some options, such as intercoms and answering machines, although widely familiar, vary greatly in capabilities and costs within their own category.

Intercom. In its simplest form, an intercom system provides two-way communication between persons in different offices, each of which is equipped with a loudspeaker and microphone and is connected to the other by a cable. Today you can have your choice of a separate intercom system or one operated through the in-house pushbutton or exchange telephone system. When the telephones are used, you usually push an in-house button or dial an in-house code to be connected to another office. An executive, for example, might press a button that buzzes in the secretary's office, and the secretary can then also press the desk telephone's intercom button and speak to the executive as if it were a regular telephone call from the outside.

Intercome systems have many of the special features that are associated with modern telephone equipment. *Camp-on busy*, for example, means that if your line is busy the call will go through as soon as you hang up. *Paging* mechanisms alert you by flashing light or sound (e.g., a beep) that an important call is waiting. Other features are background music while on hold, call transfer, and privacy from having others break in on a line in use.

Answering machines. These devices, usually compact desk models, which record messages from callers when you are away, are so popular that they are used in homes as well as in businesses. With a remote feature you can call your number from another location and activate the machine to play back your messages for you. Some machines have numerous other features such as message light indicator, fast forward or backward, message date-time indicator, telephone recording capability, remote announcement change, and quick erase.

An *answering service* is a staffed organization that ties in to your telephone line so that operators can pick up and answer your telepone if it rings a certain number of times indicating that you are away. Whereas an answering machine is usually purchased by the user, an answering service serves numerous customers and charges a monthly or other fee.

Paging. Various devices are available that, within a designated range, are activated when you have a telephone call. Sometimes called beepers because of the sound they emit, these small devices have to be kept with you at all times when you are away from the telephone and are ineffective as soon as you travel out of the signal area.

Remote call forwarding. Through the use of a special code your calls can be forwarded automatically to ring at another telephone. This arrangement would work if you wanted customers to be able to call a number in their local area while you were actually answering the forwarded call in a different location. Some businesses use remote call forwarding to service an area without having an office or representative physically located there. But forwarding requires that someone be at the remote location to take the call.

Voice mail. Unlike answering machines, voice-mail equipment enables users to leave voice messages and also respond with their own voice messages. Nonsubscribers can call and leave messages even though they cannot receive or respond to messages through the system. If desired, the same message can be sent to a number of persons. Since a message can be left at any time of the day or night, it doesn't matter whether or not the receiver is at the office when you send it. (See also Electronic-Mail Systems in chapter 8.) One can purchase the necessary hardware to use voice mail (e.g., a PABX with a voice-mail and telephone-answering capabilities) or subscribe to a telecommunications service bureau that has a network covering the desired geographic area.

Cellular radio. The new technology in mobile telephones is cellular radio communication. Wireless mobile equipment has been available in moving vehicles (cars, planes, trains, and ships) for some time, but this conventional precellular transmission has been hampered by overloaded channels causing long waits and by limited available mobile telephone numbers. The more recent cellular radio technology accommodates more network subscribers, since small geographic calls representing transmission centers divide into even more small cells as additional calls come in.

The mobile telephone itself functions in conjunction with a small radio-computer mounted on the vehicle. But the telephone must be operated within the coverage area of a cellular mobile phone company. Although this is presently a limitation, as the technology spreads so will the areas covered. Also, since one can access the public telephone network with a mobile telephone, calls can be made worldwide from a mobile unit. Mobile telephone numbers are listed in the regular telephone directory.

Leased lines. Private lines can be leased from AT&T or one of the other common carriers for exclusive use by a company that has enough volume to a designated area. Whereas WATS lines are used to cut costs of calls covering a wide area, leased lines are used to lower telephone expenses for calls to a concentrated geographic area.

Tie lines connect exchanges of a firm in two locations, thereby eliminating toll calls between offices of a company in different locations. A *foreign-exchange line (FX)* enables you to place or receive calls as if you were in another location. A firm thus might appear to have a sales office in a particular city when it really has a leased line to that city for handling calls without toll charges. To use a leased line from an office telephone, you might first have to dial a code such as "6" or "8" and then dial the number you want to reach.

Private lines can be leased for international communications too. Often you can reach the overseas destination simply by dialing an extension number. INTELSAT is a private-line service that transmit voice, data, and video signals by satellite. (The marine version of transmission to ships at sea is INMARSAT.) Most leased lines are available for a flat monthly rate and, sometimes, an additional charge for message units.

WATS. Wide-area telephone service, better known as WATS, is available through two types of lines—inbound and outbound. These lines are installed in your offices and are billed at rates that differ from regular telephone rates and are more economical in some cases. To dial a number from your office on the WATS line you may, depending on your system, first have to dial a code such as "7" and then dial the desired number.

An *outbound WATS line* is usually more cost effective when a large number of calls are made to a designated area. When the reverse is true—that a large number of calls are coming in from a wide area—an *inbound WATS line* may be needed. Customers and others, then, who would otherwise call collect, would be told by your company's operator to please call your inbound WATS number. This will be a number with an 800 prefix assigned to you when you establish inbound service. These 800 numbers are listed in a special WATS directory, and callers are then able to dial that number long distance at no charge to them. WATS lines are common in telemarketing and other sales activity where customer contact is encouraged.

Teleconferencing. Audioconferencing is a means of communicating with a number of people at the same time without the travel, hotel, and other person-to-person meeting costs. You can arrange teleconferences in two ways: dial the long-distance operator and explain the simultaneous connections you want (each connection is billed as a separate person-to-person call), or install dedicated equipment for audioconferences. Some computerized dial-in equipment can connect twenty or more persons at the same time. *Three-way calling* is a feature of some telephone systems that enables you to make conference calls without a reduction in voice quality.

A meeting-by-telephone is most successful for short conferences, when it is especially useful to save one, two, or more days of travel time for a meeting that may last only an hour or two. Nevertheless, the arranger must be prepared to conduct the telephone conference with the same control and organization that one would exercise over attendees at a traditional on-site meeting (see chapter 3). The participants should also be notified in advance to insure that they are available and prepared for the discussion. A hard copy (paper) of the meeting can be sent later by regular mail, facsimile, or some other means.

Videoconferencing. Since the cameras and transmission equipment and the special facilities required for video transmission are expensive, many firms who want to use this form of communication rent outside facilities equipped for this purpose. Videoconferences, where you can see the other participants on a televisionlike screen, are often used for special occasions: introducing a new product or discussing essential matters with sales field personnel.

Proceedings of a videoconference can be transmitted in one of two ways, by satellite or terrestrial means. The conference might involve large groups of participants gathered in conference rooms equipped with wide-screen monitors and one or more cameras. But in less ambitious situations two offices may each have a picturephone, so that persons in each office can see the others as they talk by telephone. Like the audioconference, a formal video meeting must be planned and conducted properly, and participants need advance notice to insure that they are present on time and prepared for the discussion. With videoconferences, a hard copy of the meeting or a videotape can be sent later to the attendees.

TELECOMMUNICATIONS PROCEDURES

It rarely takes long to learn how to use the telephone equipment in your office (e.g., your desk phone) or to understand the general capabilities of your company's overall telephone system. It usually takes more skill to handle the practical aspect of incoming and outgoing calls. Suddenly, you have to be careful not to cut off a caller who wants to be transferred to another number, or tactfully but firmly, you have to discourage a persistent caller who wants to talk to you or your boss. In addition, you may be required to maintain a desk file of important personal (e.g., physician) and business (e.g., travel agent) telephone numbers and keep a log of long-distance calls, as well as take telephone messages for others who are away from their desks. Although the practical aspect of telecommunications is usually the most difficult, it is also the most enjoyable to those who like to talk with others.

Telephone Etiquette

Visitors whom you meet at work form an impression of you and your organization from your physical appearance and from what you say and how you say it. Telephone callers also form an impression of you and your organization from what you say and how you say it. Whereas a smile or a frown would trigger an opinion if they met you in person, the sound of your voice will be their guide when you speak over the telephone. Tone and inflection are easy clues to boredom, annoyance, indifference, insensitivity, impatience, inattention, and other negative images.

Other qualities are important too. Avoid talking so fast that callers have trouble following you. Use a low-pitched voice, and avoid shrill or loud noises. If you tend to speak in a monotone, practice normal inflections that add personality to a voice. Check your enunciation and develop the habit of speaking clearly and carefully. Never talk with gum or a cigarette in your mouth or while chewing on something such as a pencil. Think while you are speaking to avoid blurting out the first thing that comes to mind—it may be the wrong thing. Experts believe that if you answer the telephone with a smile, it will be reflected in your voice.

Never leave your telephone unattended; have someone else pick up calls when you leave your desk. If you can be reached somewhere else, leave the address and telephone number. Develop a policy of answering calls promptly and always identify yourself ("Good morning, ABC Company, Ms. Rogers." Or "Good morning, Mr. Shaw's office, Wendy Rogers speaking").

If you must put callers on hold, ask them politely if they would please hold while you get the information you need for them. If you do not put them on hold, be careful not to bang the receiver on the desk. (But do not leave callers with an open line to overhear other office conversations.) Thank them for waiting when you return. During the conversation be considerate and patient. Listen carefully so that they do not have to repeat anything needlessly. At the conclusion, say good-bye, let the caller hang up first, and replace the receiver gently.

If you need to cut short a long-winded caller, do so tactfully. Say something such as "I want to thank you for calling, Mr. Jones. Let us know if we can be of help in any other way." Or: "That's good to know, Mr. Jones. I appreciate your filling me in, although I know how busy you are, so I won't keep you any longer. But thanks very much for calling."

Using the Telephone

Screening calls. Receptionists, secretaries, and others are often required to screen calls before putting them through to someone else. Some callers make it easy by stating their name and reason for calling ("Hello, this is Marla Beale. Is Mr. Smith in? I have the budget figures he wanted"). If they don't give their names and the office policy is to find out the names of all callers, you might say: "May I ask who's calling?" If the office policy also is to find out the purpose of the call, you might say: "May I tell Mr. Smith what this is in reference to?"

Usually, the preliminary exchange develops normally, but sometimes callers will not give their names or reasons for calling. Your strategy then depends on office policy. If you know that your employer definitely will not speak with someone under these circumstances, you might say: "I'm very sorry, but I'm not authorized to put through calls without the name and business of a caller. But if you could send Mr. Smith a confidential letter, I know he'll be happy to read it right away." Most offices, however, would rather put through an occasional nuisance call than risk offending an important contact who has some reason for maintaining secrecy.

If your boss is away from his or her desk, and it is still office policy to secure names and reasons for calling, take down all of the necessary information. Sometimes another person in the firm can help the caller just as well or better than your boss. Or perhaps you can take care of the matter yourself. But if you need to leave a message for your boss, you may use a blank slip of paper or one of the printed message forms sold in office-supply stores. The telephone message you take might include:

1. Caller's name
2. Caller's address
3. Caller's telephone number
4. Instructions: please call, returned your call, will call back, and so on
5. Caller's message (what call is in reference to)
6. Initials of person taking message
7. Date and time message was taken

Your employer may need information for the files or other data before discussing something by telephone. In that case, find the necessary facts and put the material on his or her desk right away before the person calls again or before your boss returns the call. If your boss is away when the call comes in, the caller also may want information. Avoid revealing too much. Company or personal business should never be explained to outsiders. For example, don't say, "Mr. Smith is out of the office this

week seeing a client in Tampa about some real estate."
Say, "Mr. Smith is away this week. Could I be of help?
Or perhaps you'd like to speak with someone else."

Transferring calls. Sometimes another person in the
organization can help a caller, and you want to transfer
the call so that the caller won't have to phone again.
However, first be certain that you cannot handle the
matter yourself and that you are transferring the call to
the appropriate person. People do not like being transferred from office to office. Once you are certain that the
transfer is necessary, tell the caller whom he or she
should speak with and ask if the caller would like to be
transferred ("Ms. Anderson in the Accounting Department could help you with that. I'll be happy to transfer
your call"). If the caller cannot wait to have the call
transferred, offer to give his or her name and number to
the appropriate person and ask that person to return the
call.

If the person wants to have you make the transfer, you
may want to tell the caller what to do if he or she should
accidentally be cut off. To make the transfer, follow the
procedure required with the telephone systems you have.
For instance, with an exchange monitored by an operator, you may have to depress the receiver button slowly
to cause a light to flash that the operator will see. But if
you depress the button completely, you will break the
connection, and the caller will have to call again. If an
operator responds to your signal, you might say, "Please
transfer this call to extension 2321." If callers cut you off,
hang up and wait for them to call back. If you call a
company and someone cuts you off during a transfer, hang
up and call again. If you are cut off during a person-to-
person call, dial the operator and explain that you were
disconnected.

Placing calls. The precise steps you would take in
making telephone calls depend upon your telephone system (e.g., dialing a code to get an outside line from your
office telephone), your telephone equipment (e.g., pushing a button for automatic dialing), and the telephone

services your company subscribes to (e.g., WATS). But certain procedures are common in many situations involving outgoing calls. Rates, however, are not the same everywhere. Local and long-distance charges vary from one telephone company or common carrier to another.

Station-to-station calls with all telephone companies and common carriers refer to those calls that you dial yourself (direct distance dialing, or DDD) or that an operator dials for you (operator-assisted calls) to a particular number, no matter who answers. *Person-to-person calls* are placed through an operator to a particular person, and you speak only with that person. Usually, you dial "0" followed by the number you are calling. An operator then asks whom you want to speak with. The person-to-person call is more expensive than the station-to-station call, but sometimes it is the best alternative. Perhaps the person you must speak with is rarely available, and you might have to make numerous station-to-station calls before making contact. First check, however, whether there is a free 800 number you could call.

A *credit-card call* is a call charged to your telephone calling card and later billed to you by the telephone company. Follow the instructions you receive with your calling card, which is often issued free upon request. If you are calling from a pay telephone, read the instructions on the front of the telephone. The following is a common sequence of steps to follow in using touch-tone telephones:

1. Press "0".
2. Dial the number you wish to reach.
3. Listen for a dial tone.
4. Enter your calling-card number (possibly including another code such as a private security number).
5. To make more than one call, do not hang up; press the "#" (or other) button and simply enter the next number you want to reach without reentering your calling-card number. With rotary phones you usually dial "0" and an operator will come on the line and ask for your calling-card and security number.

To receive information, follow the instructions in your telephone directory, which may be to dial 1 (in some areas), the area code, and 555-1212. An operator will come on the line and ask what city you want to reach. You then give the name and address of the person for whom you need a telephone number.

Time differentials must be considered when you place calls to locations in other U.S. or foreign time zones. Telephone directories often have a map of area codes in the front or back, and these maps also show U.S. time zones. Thus if you are in New York and you promised to call someone in Los Angeles at 10 A.M., remember to check the time difference so that you do not run up a phone bill calling at the wrong time. Time differentials are important also in determining when to make overseas calls. (Refer to the Global Time Chart on pp. 207-10.) Ask for the company providing long-distance service for you to send you a chart of international dialing codes and instructions for direct dialing through their network. Person-to-person overseas calls must be made through the overseas operator.

Collect calls are made by dialing "0" and giving the operator the telephone number and name of the person to whom the call will be charged. The operator will ask the called person if he or she will accept the charges. Companies that receive a lot of collect calls from outsiders often have an inbound WATS line installed (see Other Systems and Equipment, *WATS*).

Conference calls are arranged by dialing "0" and asking for the conference operator. This type of connection is described in Other Systems and Equipment, *Teleconferencing*; see also *Videoconferencing*. Like conference calls, *appointment calls* are prearranged. To call someone at a certain time, ask the operator in advance to make a person-to-person call at the designated time. When the outside connection is made, the operator will connect you as well. You can, in fact, give the operator a list of person-to-person calls you want placed at designated times (*sequence calls*). Conference, appointment, and sequence calls are all billed at higher rates than direct-dialed station-to-station calls.

Mobile calls to cars and trucks can be dialed the same as a regular telephone number. Numbers are listed in the regular telephone directory. To place a call to a ship at sea, call the long-distance operator and ask for the marine operator. Give full information: name of ship, name of person, stateroom number, and telephone number (if any). For additional information on placing calls, refer to Pushbutton Systems, Exchanges, and Other Systems and Equipment.

When you place a call for your boss, be certain that he or she is ready to come to the line immediately so that the called person will not be kept waiting. Many executives make a point of already being on the line when a prominent person or senior executive is being called. Otherwise, you might say, "Mrs. Brown? Mr. Smith of Cortland Industries is calling. Would you hold the line a moment, please?" Then immediately buzz your boss on the intercom and connect the two persons.

Cost Control

Unnecessary telecommunications expenses arise from abuse and poor judgment. Abuse is not always intentional. Employees have always used the office telephone for personal calls and often assume it is something they are entitled to do. Some employers control the use of WATS and regular long-distance lines through access codes known only to authorized personnel. In other words, without dialing the access code, one cannot make the long-distance connection. Employers also color-code pushbutton telephones (e.g., green = WATS) to help employees avoid dialing on the wrong line and running up a charge in error.

Excessive use of office telephones for personal business can sometimes be reduced by installing pay telephones in the company and removing regular telephones from areas that encourage personal use. A certain amount of abuse can be controlled simply by keeping employees better informed of what they may and may not do. This can be accomplished by telling them in person, by writing instruction memos, by passing out policy announcements, by posting visible signs next to telephones, by using stickers and color codes on telephones as guides and reminders to users, and so on.

Often, signs that costs are out of control come from certain patterns or changes in patterns. Employees may relax their record keeping of toll calls, or some employees may make more calls than others who have the same job. Perhaps the number of collect or third-party calls is increasing. Sometimes, however, the fault is clearly with management. A service may be subscribed to that does not provide a printout of calls, or the wrong service may be chosen, causing an increase rather than a decrease in telecommunications costs.

Poor judgment is the culprit in many cases. Rather than wait for a leased line to open up, employees may become impatient and use the regular long-distance lines. Less-expensive facsimile transmission (see chapter 9) may be just as appropriate or more so than a long-distance telephone call in some cases. Your WATS billings might be less with another carrier. Or your customers might be willing to pay for a long-distance call, in which case it might be pointless to have an inward WATS line. It also might be less expensive to buy rather than rent some of your telephone equipment. Perhaps you are using maintenance service outside of normal business hours when it is much more expensive. You may not be involving employees in cost-cutting measures; some of them may have good ideas and might be more willing to watch expenses if they were part of the decision-making process.

Calling-card and other telecommunications fraud leads to another expense. It sometimes goes undetected for a long period before someone uncovers it; much depends upon the amount of fraudulent use. Some forms of fraud are especially familiar. Slugs in pay telephones (and vendor machines) are common. Other fraud involves using unauthorized access codes to gain use of long-distance lines for personal business. To prevent calling-card fraud, whereby someone makes calls and charges them on another person's calling card, some telephone companies are adding security codes to the card numbers. But this won't help if wallets or purses that contain the cards and the security codes are stolen or if a criminal overhears someone using a public telephone read the number and code to an operator. At present, the only effective safeguards against fraud are greater controls and much tighter security systems.

Global Time Chart

To determine the time in listed countries, add the number of hours shown under your time zone (or subtract, if preceded by a minus sign) to your local time. Time differences are based on standard time, which is observed in the U.S. (in most states) from the last Sunday in October until the last Sunday in April. This may vary in other countries.

Time Difference to—	U.S. Time Zones			
	EST	CST	MST	PST
American Samoa	–6	–5	–4	–3
Andorra	6	7	8	9
Argentina	2	3	4	5
Australia (Sydney)*	16	17	18	19
Austria	6	7	8	9
Bahrain	8	9	10	11
Belgium	6	7	8	9
Belize	–1	0	1	2
Bolivia	1	2	3	4
Brazil (Rio de Janeiro)*	2	3	4	5
Chile	2	3	4	5
Colombia	0	1	2	3
Costa Rica	–1	0	1	2
Cyprus	7	8	9	10
Denmark	6	7	8	9
Ecuador	0	1	2	3
El Salvador	–1	0	1	2

Time Difference to—	U.S. Time Zones			
	EST	CST	MST	PST
Fiji	17	18	19	20
Finland	7	8	9	10
France	6	7	8	9
French Antilles	1	2	3	4
French Polynesia	−5	−4	−3	−2
German Dem. Rep.	6	7	8	9
Germany, Fed. Rep. of	6	7	8	9
Greece	7	8	9	10
Guam	15	16	17	18
Guatemala	−1	0	1	2
Guyana	2	3	4	5
Haiti	0	1	2	3
Honduras	−1	0	1	2
Hong Kong	13	14	15	16
Iceland	5	6	7	8
Indonesia (Jakarta)*	12	13	14	15
Iran	8½	9½	10½	11½
Iraq	8	9	10	11
Ireland	5	6	7	8
Israel	7	8	9	10
Italy	6	7	8	9
Ivory Coast	5	6	7	8
Japan	14	15	16	17
Kenya	8	9	10	11
Korea, Rep. of	14	15	16	17
Kuwait	8	9	10	11
Liberia	5	6	7	8
Libya	7	8	9	10

Time Difference to—	U.S. Time Zones			
	EST	**CST**	**MST**	**PST**
Liechtenstein	6	7	8	9
Luxembourg	6	7	8	9
Malaysia (Kuala Lumpur)*	12½	13½	14½	15½
Mexico (Mexico City)*	−1	0	1	2
Monaco	6	7	8	9
Netherlands	6	7	8	9
Netherlands Antilles	1	2	3	4
New Caledonia	16	17	18	19
New Zealand	18	19	20	21
Nicaragua	−1	0	1	2
Nigeria	6	7	8	9
Norway	6	7	8	9
Panama	0	1	2	3
Papua New Guinea	15	16	17	18
Paraguay	2	3	4	5
Peru	0	1	2	3
Philippines	13	14	15	16
Portugal	5	6	7	8
Qatar	8	9	10	11
Romania	7	8	9	10
San Marino	6	7	8	9
Saudi Arabia	8	9	10	11
Senegal	5	6	7	8
Singapore	12½	13½	14½	15½
South Africa	7	8	9	10
Spain	6	7	8	9
Sri Lanka	10½	11½	12½	13½
Suriname	1½	2½	3½	4½

Time Difference to—	U.S. Time Zones			
	EST	CST	MST	PST
Sweden	6	7	8	9
Switzerland	6	7	8	9
Taiwan	13	14	15	16
Thailand	12	13	14	15
Tunisia	6	7	8	9
Turkey	7	8	9	10
United Arab Emirates	9	10	11	12
United Kingdom	5	6	7	8
Uruguay	2	3	4	5
U.S.S.R. (Moscow)*	8	9	10	11
Vatican City	6	7	8	9
Venezuela	1	2	3	4
Yugoslavia	6	7	8	9

*Has more than one time zone.
Source: *Personal Directory for International Dialing*, Bell System, May 1982.

BUSINESS
WRITING

CHAPTER ELEVEN

Using the Right Style

Office workers who prepare letters, memos, and other messages, as well as reports, proposals, and publicity and other business material, must know the basics of correct contemporary style. Billions of dollars are generated through the written word each year, and errors are not only costly but an embarrassment; they readily reveal one's lack of knowledge and professionalism.

But often style is not a question of right or wrong. It is also a matter of a contemporary versus an old-fashioned image. Trends in punctuation, capitalization, spelling, and word division keep changing, and if you want to give others the impression that you are well informed and forward thinking, you may have to change your style to fit the times. Even persons who are certain that their writing is grammatically correct may need to review style guidelines periodically to insure that their writing style is consistent with all facets of effective, modern communications.

PUNCTUATION

Too much, too little, or incorrect punctuation will make your message more difficult to read and will increase the chances for misunderstanding. Proper punctuation is essential to insure that you don't take your reader on an unnecessarily difficult journey. To depict a certain writing style, as well as to achieve clarity, you will likely have to make some arbitrary decisions in punctuating your material. For example, you may prefer the modern *open style*, using punctuation only where it is absolutely essential to avoid misreading, or you may want to use the traditional *close style*, punctuating everywhere that it is technically, or grammatically, correct to do so. With both styles, however, certain punctuation is always required, such as a period at the end of a sentence or an apostrophe to show possession.

Apostrophe (')

The apostrophe is necessary when you want to show possession, omission, and certain plural forms.

Possession. Add an apostrophe and *s* to a singular word that does not end with an *s* sound (*manager's*) or that does end with an *s* sound and also forms another syllable in the possessive (*boss's*). But omit the *s* with a plural word that already ends in *s* (*weeks'*). Add an apostrophe and *s* to a singular name (*Hill's*) and an apostrophe alone to a name made plural by adding *es* (*Williamses'*). Add an apostrophe to distinguish between joint and separate possession.

> man's hat   witness's oath   thirty days' notice
> Louise Ryan's appointment   John Burns's speech
> the Adamses' car   Donna and Carl's project (joint)
> Donna's and Carl's projects (separate)

Exceptions to the rule for adding an apostrophe and *s* are the names *Jesus* (Jesus' message) and *Moses* (Moses' life). The *s* is also omitted in names ending with an *-eez* sound (Fortees' patent). In the case of common nouns, the *s* is omitted when pronunciation would be awkward if it were included (for *appearance'* sake, for *righteousness'* cause.)

Omission. Add an apostrophe where letters and numbers are omitted.

> they'll (they will)   rc'd (received)   '80s (1980s)

Plural. Add an apostrophe and *s* to form a plural word only if it might be confusing to omit it.

p's and q's   Ph.D.'s   1980s   CODs

Brackets []

Put brackets around comments and corrections that are not part of material being quoted and use them to enclose parenthetical remarks within parentheses. Do not space between the brackets and the material enclosed.

"No," she said, "we haven't set a date for next year's [1988] convention." The company is expanding its product line this year (after a slowdown last year [1986]).

Colon (:)

The colon has a variety of possible (but not always essential) uses: to introduce a list, quotation, or example (in place of a dash or period); to show a pause between two closely related sentences that are not linked by a conjunction (in place of a dash); between dates and pages and between cities and publishers in note references; to show ratios (in place of a hyphen) and clock time; and following letters salutations. Put two spaces after a colon, but omit the space when the colon links two numbers as in a ratio or clock time.

the following items: stationery, copy paper, and pens
The salesman was encouraged by one thing: the customer urgently needed new equipment.
Journal 2 (1986):   New York: New American Library, 1979   10:1 ratio   10:25 A.M.   Dear Ms. Edwards:

Comma(,)

Use the comma to separate three or more words or phrases in a series (*series comma*), to separate clauses of a compound sentence, and to show words omitted in a series. Use commas to set off *nonrestrictive* (not essential) clauses, introductory and transitional words and phrases, words in apposition, parenthetical expressions, and quoted material. Put one space after a comma.

electronic typewriters, word processors, and computers
Bill is our staff supervisor, and Harold is our market-
ing manager.
Four new employees were hired in the spring; three,
last fall.
The report, which has one hundred pages, is ready to
be typed.
When he's free, ask him to stop by my office.
Therefore, we will continue.
The president, Ms. Watson, is out of town.
Let's renegotiate, if you can call it that, while we still
have the opportunity.
"It's late," she said, "but we can still meet the
deadline."

Dash (—)

The dash is annoying to readers when it is overused.
But with judicious use it can effectively show sudden
interruption or emphasize clauses of explanation. Do not
use it with other punctuation marks in succession (*not*:
Today,—according to plan—the relocation begins). There
should be no space before or after a dash.

Graphs, charts, tables—these items are all useful
illustrations.
His car—the company car, that is—needs servicing.
Courage—that's what it really takes.

Ellipsis Points (. . .)

Use periods (less commonly, asterisks) in succession to
show the omission of words: Three dots show words
omitted at the beginning or in the middle of a sentence;
four dots represent words, sentences, and paragraphs
omitted at the end of a sentence (never more than four,
even though the end of one sentence and the beginning
of another is missing). Put one space between the dots
but no space between the end of a sentence and the dot
that represents a period.

"Production this year . . . is higher than last year. . . .

to date there is no evidence of greater efficiency . . . , although a report is due soon. . . . The committee will conclude work at the end of the month. . . ."

Exclamation Point (!)

Although the exclamation point loses its impact when it is overused, it can properly be used (sparingly) to show exceptional surprise, irony, or strong feeling. Put two spaces after it at the end of a sentence.

No! You can't be serious! Hurry! Bargain Sale!

Hyphen (-)

The hyphen has a number of uses: to divide words at the end of a line, to link compound words, to show fractions, to convert prefixes to a proper name, and to separate parts of numbers such as digits in telephone numbers. Note that not all compound terms are hyphenated. Some are written closed (*nonessential*) in contemporary writing, and some are hyphenated before a noun (*well-defined* path) but not after it (path is *well defined*). Do not space before or after a hyphen except a suspended hyphen (*two-* to three-week cruise).

self-made man   three- by five-inch cards   secretary-treasurer
vice-president   quasi-public corporation   one-fourth
    pro-American   1-800-556-1232

Parentheses ()

Use parentheses to enclose incidental comments and figures or letters in lists that are run into the text. Do not space between parentheses and the material enclosed.

The law is specific about that (see section 14a-b).
The open house is Saturday, June 19(?).
The company is hiring (1) word processor operators, (2) file clerks, and (3) PBX operators.

Period (.)

Periods are used at the end of a sentence, after certain abbreviations, and as decimals after numbers and letters in a list. *See also* Ellipsis Points. Put two spaces after a sentence but no space around decimals or periods within numbers and letters.

We're closed today. non seq. 11.671
a. Accounting, b. Sales, c. Research

Question Mark (?)

Use the question mark after a direct question and to show doubt (often enclosed in parentheses after the word in question). Put two spaces after the question mark ending a sentence but no space when it is enclosed in parentheses.

Have the visitors arrived?
Shall we meet on Monday? Tuesday? Wednesday?
Adam will direct the cleanup (?), and his junior staff
will assist him.

Quotation Marks (' ")

Use single and double quotation marks around precise quotations. The single marks show quotations within a quotation. Periods and commas go *inside* and semicolons and colons go *outside* the quotation marks. Also, use quotation marks for nicknames and titles of articles, essays, unpublished material, short poems, short musical works, and television shows. Do not enclose indented quotations (extracts), slang, general use of the word *yes* and *no*, or words following *so-called*. Do not space between the word quoted and the quotation marks.

"Remember," he said, "there are two key points in the chapter 'Selling Techniques.' "
John "Junior" Stedman "Business Trends" (article)
"A New Age" (essay) "Winterland" (short poem)

"Lavender Strings" (short musical work)
"Newhart" (television show)
My answer is yes.
He means the so-called new technology.

Semicolon (;)

Use the semicolon to separate clauses that do not have a connecting conjunction and to separate lists of items in a series that already have commas. Do not space between the semicolon and the preceding word.

Proper servicing of the equipment is important; in fact, it's essential.
The targeted cities are Boston, Massachusetts; Los Angeles, California; and Kansas City, Missouri.

Virgule (/)

The virgule is also called the slash, diagonal, and solidus. Use it in abbreviations, to mean *per*, in dates (instead of a hyphen) to show a span of periods or calendar years, in numbers, and between lines of poetry that are run into the text. Do not space before or after a slash, except put an equal space on either side between lines of poetry.

B/L   mi./sec.   fiscal year 1986/87   ¼ 3476/AM-117
A. H. Clough said: "Because we can't do all we would,/ Does it follow, to do nothing's good?"

CAPITALIZATION

Although authorities differ in matters of capitalization and punctuation of names and terms, they agree that one should follow a preferred style consistently. For example, it would confuse a reader to see *Industrial Revolution* in one paragraph and *industrial revolution* in the next paragraph when you're referring to the same event in each case. Contemporary style favors lowercase (small letters) over uppercase (capital letters) when there is a choice.

Thus you would write "John Smith, the *president* (not *President*) of ABC Company." The guidelines presented here generally reflect contemporary style, but you should follow the style used in your profession or office unless your employer encourages you to make your own determination.

Days and Time

Capitalize official names of holidays, festivals, seasons, days, and time, but lowercase general descriptive terms.

Religious and calendar days and time. Capitalize the names of religious seasons and holidays, secular holidays, calendar months and days, and time-zone abbreviations.

Easter Day   Good Friday   Yom Kippur   New Year's Day   D day   Labor Day   election day   January–December   Monday–Friday   summer/winter solstice   EDT (eastern daylight time), PST (Pacific standard time)

Education

Capitalize important words in official names and titles, but use lowercase for general descriptive terms.

Schools and colleges. Capitalize the official names of schools and colleges and the official names of departments and divisions. Lowercase general terms for a school or division.

University of Dayton   the university   School of Engineering   engineering school   the school   Department of English   English department   the department   Department of Physics   physics department   the department

Classes and programs. Capitalize the names of classes and the official titles of programs and courses. Lowercase general terms for a member of a class, a program, or a course.

Freshman Class   the class   a freshman   Asian Studies Program   the program   Geology 221   a geology course   the course

Degrees and honors. Capitalize initials that stand for academic degrees and the honors that are part of a formal name or title. Lowercase a general reference to a degree or fellowship.

Ph.D.   a doctorate   the doctor of philosophy degree
H. Q. Winthrop Fellowship   the Winthrop fellowship
the fellowship   Erik Anderson, Sc.D.   Dr. Erik Anderson

Geography

Capitalize most major geographical and political divisions and other official names, but use lowercase for general descriptive terms.

Major regions and divisions. Capitalize most major political divisions and parts of the world and important divisions or regions of continents and countries.

the Arctic   arctic winter
Far East   the East (world)   Eastern civilization
West Coast (U.S.)   the West (U.S.)   western U.S.
Middle Atlantic states   the states of the Middle Atlantic region   the States (United States)
the North (U.S. region)   northern (direction, locality)
the Occident   occidental culture
North American continent   the continent
West Africa   western Africa
western/eastern Europe (region)   Western/Eastern Europe (political division after World War II)
central Europe (region)   Central Europe (political division of World War I)
Roman Empire   the empire
New York State   the state of New York

Topographical names. Capitalize official topographical names. Lowercase general descriptive terms such as *river*, but do not use a descriptive word such as *river* with a foreign term that already includes the equivalent of that word (*Rio* Grande, not *Rio* Grande *River; rio* already means "river").

Atlantic Ocean   the ocean
Arkansas River   the river   the Arkansas and Mississippi rivers
Lake Mead   the lake   Lakes Mead and Powell
Sierra Nevada   the Sierras   the mountains
Rocky Mountains   the Rockies   the mountains

Popular and legendary names. Capitalize most popular and legendary names. Lowercase words derived from proper names such as *plaster of paris*.

Bay Area (San Francisco)   Foggy Bottom (Washington, D.C.)   Deep South (U.S.)   Old South   antebellum South   New World   Old World   the States (U.S.)   the states of the Middle Atlantic region   Roman culture   roman numerals   roman typeface

Public places. Capitalize the names of public monuments, buildings, streets, and so on. Lowercase a general reference to a room, street, fountain, and the like.

the U.S. Capitol   the capitol (building) in Texas   a capital city   Thirty-fourth Avenue   the avenue   the Walnut Room   room 16C   the room   Interstate 17   the interstate highway   rue de Paix   le rue

Government and Politics

Capitalize important words in official names and titles, but use lowercase for general and descriptive terms.

Acts and laws. Capitalize the official titles of acts, bills, plans, treaties, laws, amendments, and constitutions. Lowercase general references (*the constitution*) but capitalize *The Constitution* when it refers to the U.S. Constitution.

Kramer Act   the act   Marshall Plan   the plan   Fourteenth Amendment (U.S. Constitution)   the amendment   the Constitution (U.S.)   New Jersey Constitution   the constitution of New Jersey   the constitution (New Jersey)

Political parties and governmental bodies. Capitalize the official names of political parties (but not the word *party*) and the official titles of governmental, administrative, and deliberative bodies. Lowercase general references to a department, an assembly, and the like, and lowercase political terms ending in *-ism* such as *facism*.

Communist party   the party   Communists   communism   the Right   right wing   rightist   Labor movement   the movement   the General Assembly (U.N.)   the assembly   Indianapolis Board of Education   the board of education   the board   U.S. Department of Commerce   Commerce Department   the department   Parliament (British)   parliamentary

Political units. Capitalize political divisions and other designations that follow a name or are officially part of it. Lowercase general references to a city, a county, and so on.

Ottoman Empire   the empire   Florida State   the state of Florida   Marion County   the county of Marion   Sixth Ward   Ward 6   the ward   the Union (U.S.)   the Confederacy (U.S.)   U.S. government   the federal government   the government   Ministry of Justice   the ministry

History

Capitalize the important words in special historical and cultural events, but lowercase numerical designations, recent ages, and most periods. (Note that there are a number of exceptions to the general rule.)

Events and movements. Capitalize the official names of most important events and of movements that are derived from proper nouns. Lowercase most other general movements (but note various exceptions).

World War I the Great War the war Boston Tea Party Prohibition Great Depression the Depression (1930) the depression (all others) gold rush westward movement the movement civil rights movement the movement cold war baroque style cubism Gothic style neoclassic Neoplatonism Romanesque Stoic surrealism

Documents. Capitalize official titles of acts, treaties, and other formal documents. Lowercase general references to a doctrine, plan, and the like.

Mayflower Compact the compact Monroe doctrine the doctrine Marshall Plan the plan Medicare or medicare Medicaid or medicaid H. M. Rice Immigration Act the immigration act the act the Constitution (U.S.) California Constitution constitution of California the constitution (California)

Periods. Capitalize the formal names of certain historical and cultural periods and early times. Lowercase numerical designations, recent periods, and most other periods (but note various exceptions).

Middle Ages late Middle Ages Restoration Renaissance High Renaissance Stone Age Old Stone Age space age nuclear age colonial period antiquity ancient Rome romantic period Victorian era Christian Era Progressive Era Neolithic period Paleolithic period

Judiciary

Capitalize the important words in official names and titles, but lowercase general descriptive terms.

Courts, titles, and cases. Capitalize the official titles of courts, judicial titles when they precede a proper name, and all important words in legal cases. Lowercase general references such as *the case* and incomplete lower court names.

> U.S. Supreme Court   The Court (U.S. Supreme) Alabama Supreme Court   the supreme court (Alabama)   the court   Municipal Court of Milwaukee   the municipal court   the court   American Bar Association the bar   Justice White   the justice   *Stutgartt* v. *State of Montana*   the *Stutgartt* case

Lists

Capitalize the first word and proper nouns, but lowercase all other words.

Lists and outlines. Capitalize the first word of each item in a list or outline and any proper noun.

> I. Office procedure
>   A. Etiquette
>   1. Coworkers and in-house personnel
>   2. Clients and outside contacts

Military

Capitalize important words in names and titles, but lowercase general descriptive designations.

Titles and awards. Capitalize military titles that precede a proper name and official names of awards and citations. Lowercase general references such as *the captain; Admiral of the Fleet* and *General of the Army* are always capitalized before or after a name to avoid ambiguity.

> Joseph Blume, major   Maj. (or Major) Joseph Blume the major   James Dill, Admiral of the Fleet   the Admiral of the Fleet   Medal of Honor   the medal

Battles, groups, and craft. Capitalize the formal names of wars and battles, military groups, and military crafts and vessels. Lowercase general references to war, ships, planes, and so on.

> Vietnam War   the war   World War II   the Second World War   the war   Allied forces   Allied armies the Allies   National Guard   the guard   U.S. Coast Guard   the Coast Guard   Royal Air Force   British air force   U.S. Navy   the navy   Pacific Fleet   the fleet   SS *Valiant*   the ship   ICBM   missiles

Proper Nouns

Capitalize proper nouns, but lowercase general references and descriptions.

Persons, places, and things. Capitalize the names of particular persons, places, and things, including epithets, fictitious names, trade names, and words that are personified. Capitalize peoples, races, and tribes except when the description is based only on color, race, or local custom or is a noun, adjective, or verb derived from the capitalized description. Lowercase common and descriptive terms such as *tissue.*

> Prince Edward   Walter Reed   Atlantic Ocean   Europe Orientals   oriental culture   Negro   black   Don Quixote   quixotic   The Sun King   Uncle Sam   Mother Nature   the Grim Reaper   the Capitol (U.S. building) Romans   roman numerals   Ping-Pong   table tennis Kleenex   tissue

Religion

Capitalize the important words in religious names and titles, but lowercase general descriptive terms.

Names and titles. Capitalize the formal names for the Bible and books and divisions of the Bible as well as other sacred religious works. Capitalize references to the Deity and appellations of revered persons; special rites and services; and official names of specific churches.

Bible biblical Psalms Fourteenth Psalm a psalm
the Scriptures the Gospels the gospel truth Talmud
talmudic God the Trinity the Father Allah Greek
gods Resurrection Original Sin the Mass (the eu-
charistic sacrament) high mass (an individual cele-
bration) bar mitzvah First Methodist Church of Sante
Fe the Methodist church the church

Science

Rules and guidelines for capitalization of scientific terms
are extensive and vary among scientific organizations.
For detailed instructions consult stylebooks such as the
Council of Biology Editors Style Manual and the American Institute of Physics' *Style Manual.*

Proper names, terms, and symbols. One accepted style
is to capitalize the names of plants and animals above the
species level, geological eras, planets and satellites and
chemical symbols. Lowercase general descriptive terms
and meteorological phenomenon.

Homo (genus) *Homo sapien* (genus + species) Cac-
taceae succulents Pliocene epoch the later Pliocene
Mars the planet Big Dipper a constellation aurora
borealis Saturn's rings the Galaxy a galaxy H_2O
°C (degree Celsius)

Titles of Persons

Capitalize official titles preceding a name, but lowercase most titles in other instances.

Formal titles. Capitalize civil, military, religious, and
professional titles and titles of nobility when they precede a person's name. Lowercase most titles that follow a
name or stand alone, and always lowercase titles that are
merely job descriptions such as *programmer.*

President Reagan Ronald Reagan, president of the
United States the Reverend Wiley the rector Pope
John Paul the pope the papacy salesman Roy

Miller   the salesman   the Queen Mother   the queen of England   Her Majesty   Dexter Stonehurt, first earl of Triolette   the earl of Triolette   the physician Mildred Markham   Dr. Mildred Markham   the doctor

Titles of Works

Capitalize all important words in titles of works, but lowercase general references to a work.

Written work, broadcasts, music, and art. Capitalize the titles, including verbs, of written works; musical compositions, paintings, drawings, sculptures, and other artwork; television and radio programs and motion pictures; and mottoes and notices. Lowercase general descriptive terms such as *motto*.

Home and Office Encyclopedia (book)   *Fortune* (magazine)   "The Effect of Color on Productivity" (dissertation)   "Dallas" (television program)   *An Officer and a Gentleman* (movie)   the *Emperor* Concerto   Piano Concerto no. 5   *The Thinker* (sculpture)   *Black Dawn* (painting)   *The Divine Comedy* (long poem)   No Smoking (sign)   One for All and All for One (motto)

SPELLING

You can save time in composing messages and other written material by learning a few basic rules of spelling. Time spent initially in learning these rules will be time saved later when you apply them at work. But if you forget any of them, do not guess—consult this chapter again or use your dictionary.

Forming Plurals

With some words you can simply add *s* or *es* to form the plural, but in other cases the spelling of the rest of the word changes too.

Singular nouns. Add *s* in most cases and *es* in some cases.

    book/books   pen/pens   computer/computers
    box/boxes   class/classes   business/businesses

Irregular nouns. Change the spelling of irregular nouns or keep the same form.

    child/children   foot/feet   woman/women   mouse/mice
    corps/corps   economics/economics

Compound nouns. Usually, make the most important word plural. When both words are equally important, make both words plural. When no word alone is of importance, make the last word plural. When a compound ending in *-ful* is written as one word, add *s* to the end of it. When a compound has both a noun and preposition, make the noun plural.

    ambassadors at large   attorneys general   brigadier
    generals   bills of lading   courthouses   bookshelves
    mothers-in-law   accounts receivable   chiefs of staff
    cupfuls   notaries public   coats of arms   passersby
    pick-me-ups   tie-ins

Nouns ending in o. When the *o* is preceded by a vowel, add *s*. When it is preceded by a consonant, add *es* or, in a few cases, *s* (some have both forms).

    folio/folios   memo/memos   hero/heroes
    potato/potatoes   cargo/cargoes   zero/zeros/zeroes

Nouns ending in y. Usually, when the *y* is preceded by a vowel, add *s*. When it is preceded by a consonant, change the *y* to *i* and add *es*.

    attorney/attorneys   day/days
    country/countries   category/categories

Nouns ending in f, ff, or fe. No clear-cut rule exists to show when you add *s* or change the *f* to *v* and add *es*.

safe/safes   proof/proofs   chief/chiefs
leaf/leaves   shelf/shelves   life/lives

Nouns ending in s, ss, sh, ch, x, *or* z. Usually, when a singular noun ends in *s*, *ss*, *sh*, *ch*, *x*, or *z*, add *es*. When the singular word ends with a silent *s*, keep the same form in the plural. A few singular nouns keep the same form in the plural and some have more than one acceptable plural form.

lens/lenses   loss/losses   fish/fishes
church/churches   box/boxes   quartz/quartzes
corps/corps   hertz/hertz   cactus/cactus/cactuses/cacti

Abbreviations, numbers, and words. Usually, add *s*, although a few abbreviations repeat the initial letter. Add *'s* if *s* alone would be confusing. Some abbreviations keep the same form in the plural. Add *s* or *es* to numbers written as words.

dept./depts.   no./nos.   1980/1980s   p./pp.   r/r's
6/6's   Ph.D/Ph.D.'s   mi./mi.   twenty/twenties   twenty-two/twenty-twos   do and don't/do's and don'ts

Writing Prefixes

You need to consider style as well as accuracy in writing prefixes. Many offices have a standard style that all employees must follow; in other cases, it is up to you.

Style. Contemporary writers omit the hyphen and write all prefixes closed, unless the prefix precedes a capitalized proper noun, is meant to convey a different meaning as in *re-form* (to form again), or would make reading difficult without the hyphen.

nonessential   antinuclear   anti-intelligence
anti-American   redesigned   semiconscious
predetermined   pre-World War I   overworked
biannual   interdependent   subhuman
underdeveloped   socioeconomic   multifaceted

Spelling. When a word begins with *s*, keep the double *ss* formed by adding *mis-* or *dis-*.

spell/misspell   simulate/dissimulate   step/misstep
agree/disagree   regard/disregard   print/misprint

Writing Suffixes and Verb Endings

The spelling rules pertaining to word endings are useful guides for daily business writing. But since numerous exceptions apply in many cases, consult a dictionary whenever you are uncertain about the treatment for a particular suffix or verb ending.

One-syllable words. When the word ends with one vowel followed by one consonant, *double* the final consonant in most cases before adding a suffix or verb ending that starts with a *vowel* (but: *tax/taxed, bus/buses, row/rowed*).

ship/shipping   stop/stopped   run/runny
bet/betting   sad/sadden   win/winning

When the word ends with one vowel followed by one consonant, *do not double* the final consonant before adding an *-ly* ending.

sad/sadly   glad/gladly   bad/badly

Multisyllable words. When the word ends with one vowel followed by one consonant and the accent falls on the *last* syllable, *double* the final consonant in most cases before adding a suffix or verb ending that starts with a *vowel* (but: *prefer/preferable, refer/reference, transfer/transferable*).

regret/regrettable   begin/beginning   occur/occurred
control/controlling   deter/deterring   prefer/preferred

When the word ends with one vowel followed by one consonant and the accent does *not* fall on the *last* syllable, *do not double* the final consonant in most cases before adding a suffix or verb ending that starts with a *vowel* (but: *program/programming, cancel/cancellation*).

credit/credited   travel/traveling   counsel/counseling
cancel/canceling   total/totaled   profit/profited

When the word ends with more than one vowel followed by one consonant, *do not double* the final consonant in most cases before adding *any* suffix or verb ending (but: *equip/equipped, cordial/cordially*).

appeal/appealing   conceit/conceited   despair/despairing
repair/repaired   despoil/despoiling   repeal/repealed

When the word ends with more than one consonant, *do not double* the final consonant before adding *any* suffix or verb ending.

forewarn/forewarned   forlorn/forlornly
transcend/transcending   desert/deserted
backward/backwardness   abolish/abolishment

Words ending in silent **e.** *Drop* the *e* in most cases before adding a suffix or verb ending that starts with a *vowel* (but: *use/useable* or *usable, agree/agreeing, mile/mileage*).

beguile/beguiling   arrive/arrival   glare/glaring
sale/salable   gesture/gesturing   desire/desirous

Keep the *e* in most cases before adding a suffix that starts with a *consonant*. But *drop* it when another *vowel* proceeds the final *e*.

like/likely   awe/awesome   sincere/sincerely
trouble/troublesome   argue/argument   due/duly

Words ending in **ce** *or* **ge.** *Keep* the *e* in most cases before adding a suffix or verb ending that starts with the vowels *a*, or *o*.

manage/manageable   advantage/advantageous

enforce/enforceable   charge/chargeable
notice/noticeable   service/serivceable

Keep the final *e* before adding the suffixes -*able* and -*ous* but *drop* it before adding *ible*.

outrage/outrageous   knowledge/knowledgeable
courage/courageous   deduce/deducible
force/forcible   convince/convincible

Words with ie. In most cases follow the rule "*i* before *e* except after *c* or when sounded like *a* as in *neighbor* and *weigh*" (but: *neither, leisure, financier, conscience*).

retrieve (*i* before *e*)   deceive (except after *c*)
freight (or when sounded like *a*)
tie/tying   lie/lying   die/dying

Words ending in y. When the word is preceded by a consonant, change the *y* to *i* in most cases before adding *any* suffix or verb ending *except* one already beginning with *i*.

modify/modification   worry/worried   likely/likelihood
heavy/heaviest   try/trying   modify/modifying

Adjectives of one syllable (a) have two forms in the comparative and superlative and (b) usually keep *y* before -*ly* and -*ness*. Words with -*ship* and -*like* and in derivatives of *lady* and *baby* keep the *y*, and words ending in *y* preceded by a *vowel* usually keep the *y* before *any* verb ending (but: *day/daily, pay/paid*).

dry: drier/driest or dryer/dryest   dry/dryly/dryness
secretaryship   ladylike   buy/buying   employ/employment

Words ending in -ation. Change the suffix to -*able* instead of -*ible*. But since no rule exists to indicate the use of -*able* or -*ible* with other words, consult a dictionary when you are in doubt.

application/applicable communication/communicable
reparation/reparable education/educable
estimation/estimable registration/registrable

Words ending in -ize, -ise, and -yze. No rule exists in American usage to indicate the use of *-ize, -ise*, and *-yze*, although most of the words end in *-ize* and only a few in *-yze* (British usage favors *-ise* over *-ize*).

authorize summarize criticize
compromise advertise exercise
analyze catalyze paralyze

Words ending in -ance/-ancy/-ant or -ence/ency/ent. When a word has a *c* that sounds like *k* or a *g* that has a hard sound, in most cases use *-ance, -ancy,* or *-ant*. When the word has a *c* that sounds like *s* or a *g* that sounds like *j*, use *-ence, -ency,* or *-ent*.

extravagance/extravagancy/extravagant
significance/significantly/significant
transcendence/transcendency/transcendent
belligerence/belligerency/belligerent

Words ending in -sede, -ceed, and -cede. Only one English word ends in *-sede*; only three English words end in *-ceed*; and the rest in this classification end in *-cede*.

supersede proceed exceed succeed
precede concede recede intercede

WORD DIVISION

One of the principal reasons for dividing words at the end of a line is to avoid an unattractive, uneven right-hand margin in typed or typeset material. But since too many end-of-line hyphens also look unattractive, you should avoid (1) having more than two successive lines ending with a hyphen and (2) dividing the last word in a paragraph and the last word on a page (except in legal documents where writers divide the last word to show continuity).

Syllabication

Divide words after a *syllable*—one or more letters in a word that form a unit. For example, *Webster's Ninth New Collegiate Dictionary* shows three units in the word *syl-la-ble*. You could properly divide (hyphenate) the word at the end of a line after *syl-* or *la-*. American dictionaries syllabicate according to pronunciation, and spelling dictionaries, also known as "word books" and "word finders," often show pronunciation as well as syllables. In certain cases, pronunciation is an essential key to accurate word division.

prog-ress (a noun meaning "advancement")
pro-gress (a verb meaning "to proceed")
pres-ent (a noun meaning "a gift")
pre-sent (a verb meaning "to give or introduce")

One-syllable words. Do not divide them.

stayed (*not* stay-ed)   house (*not* hou-se)
through (*not* th-rough)   three (*not* th-ree)

Short words. Do not divide words of five or fewer letters.

woman (*not* wo-man)   boxes (*not* box-es)
only (*not* on-ly)   into (*not* in-to)

One-letter syllables. Do not separate one letter at the beginning or end of a word from the rest of the word. Divide a word with a one-letter syllable *within* the word only *after* the letter (but see Prefixes and Suffixes and Hyphenated Compounds).

abate-ment (*not* a-batement)
cafe-teria or cafete-ria (*not* cafeteri-a or caf-eteria)
appli-cation or applica-tion (*not* applic-ation)

Although in many words *-able* and *-ible* are suffixes that should *not* be divided, in other words they are not suffixes and the word *should* be divided after the *a* or *i* (consult a dictionary when you are uncertain how to divide words with *-able* and *-ible*).

Nonsuffix: ca-pable or capa-ble (*not* cap-able)
eli-gible or eligi-ble (*not* elig-ible)
pos-sible or possi-ble (*not* poss-ible)

Suffix: ser-viceable or service-able (*not* servicea-ble)
man-ageable or manage-able (*not* managea-ble)
de-ductible or deduct-ible (*not* deducti-ble)

Two-letter syllables. Avoid separating a two-letter syllable from the beginning or end of a word *unless* you leave three characters (including punctuation) on the top line or carry three characters to the next line.

be- / ginning (*better*: begin-ning)
at- / tention (*better*: atten-tion)
start- / up, (up, = 3 characters)

Double consonants. Divide a word *between* the consonants that are doubled when adding a suffix or that appear *within* a word, but *do not divide* a word between the double consonants that fall at the *end* of a root word.

control-ling (*-ing* added)
regret-table (*-able* added)
foun-tain (*n-t* within the word)
gram-mar (*m-m* within the word)
call-ing (*ll* at the end of the root word)
bless-ing (*ss* at end of the root ward)

Prefixes and Suffixes

A *prefix* such as *non-* is added to the front of a base word (*nonessential*) and a *suffix* such as *-ment* is added to the end of a base word (*management*), thereby creating a word that conveys a different meaning.

Dividing prefixes. Divide a word *after* the prefix rather than *within* it.

anti-democratic over-estimate non-support
under-developed de-emphasize socio-economic
pre-eminent post-war inter-agency sub-compact

Dividing suffixes. Divide a word *before* a suffix rather than *within* it. Note that in some cases the portion separated includes the suffix plus one or more letters from the base word (consult a dictionary when you are uncertain about the correct syllabication in words with a suffix).

depend-able (suffix *-able*) manage-ment (suffix *-ment*)
standard-ize (suffix *-ize*) irresist-ible (suffixe *-ible*)
trust-worthy (suffix *-worthy*) convales-cent (*c* + suffix *-ent*) coura-geous (*ge* + suffix *-ous*)
signifi-cant (*c* + suffix *-ant*) adver-tise (*t* + suffix *-ise*)

Hyphenated Compounds

Some compound words are written closed (*statewide*), but others have hyphens (*president-elect*). Divide a compound word with a hyphen *only* at the point of the hyphen.

father-in-law (*not* fa-ther-in-law) all-inclusive (*not* all-inclu-sive) self-evident (*not* self-evi-dent) quasi-public (*not* quasi-pub-lic) vice-president (*not* vice-presi-dent) owner-operator (*not* owner-opera-tor)

Abbreviations, Acronyms, and Contractions

Do not divide abbreviations, acronyms, and contractions.

RAM (*not* R-AM) SALT (*not* SA-LT) Sc.D. (*not* Sc.-D.)
ibid. (*not* ib-id.) COD (*not* C-OD) wasn't (*not* was-n't)

Numbers and Dates

Avoid dividing numbers but, if essential, divide *only* at the comma and keep the comma on the top line. Avoid separating number-word groups. Divide numbers in lists *only* before the number. Divide dates *only* between the day and the year.

> $2,791,-043 (*not* $2,79-1,043)   page 71 (*not* page /
> 71)   104 First / Street (*not* 104 / First Street)
> (1) rules, / (2) regulations, and (3) procedures (*not*
> [1] rules, [2] regulations, and [3] procedures)

Names

Divide only between the first (plus middle) name and the last name. When a title follows the name, if possible divide between the name and the title or between parts of the title.

> John M. / Harris   John M. Harris / vice-president
> John M. Harris, vice- / president

Punctuation

Divide *after* punctuation marks such as a dash or hyphen.

> My report— / "Sales Power"—is still in progress (*not*
> My report / —"Sales Power"—is still in progress).
> The senator- / elect will speak tonight (*not* The
> senator / -elect will speak tonight).

CHAPTER TWELVE

Writing Letters and Memos

Composing letters and memos is a daily activity in most offices. The messages range from one- or two-sentence notes to lengthy discussions filling numerous pages. Many of them are individually prepared on a typewriter or by computer or word processor. Others—letters with identical messages—may be reproduced by one of the duplicating processes such as offset printing; by automatic typewriter such as magnetic-tape machine; or by computer or word processor. Form letters may contain blank spaces where someone can later type in the date, inside address, and salutation. Form letters prepared by automatic typewriter, computer, word processor, or another automatic or electronic process may automatically merge a mailing list of inside addresses and other items of information with the otherwise standard letter message. This gives each form letter the appearance of an individually prepared letter.

Although the means of preparation or reproduction may vary, as may the need for individuality (the personal touch), all messages reflect the competence and professionalism of the sender. Accuracy, neatness, tone, format—all of these facets of letter writing reveal a great deal about you, your company, and its product or service. Whatever your goal may be—to sell something, to motivate someone, to deal with a problem, to create goodwill—you have a lot to gain by developing your letter-writing abilities to the fullest.

FORMAT GUIDELINES

Parts of Letters

Many offices have an established letter and memo format that all employees are expected to follow. The principal letter styles shown in this chapter are the full block, block, modified block, simplified, and official formats. The correct position of the various structural parts of letters are shown in the formats illustrated in this chapter.

Dateline. Type it two or more lines below the letter-head, flush left or right depending on the format used.

Reference line. Type it two lines below the dateline, flush left or right depending on the format used; place your reference first and the addressee's reference line (if any) two lines beneath yours.

Personal or confidential notation. Type it flush left beneath the reference line, two to four lines above the inside address (or above the salutation in the official style).

Mail notation. Type it flush left only on carbon copies two lines above the personal notation.

Inside address. Type it flush left several lines below the dateline, reference line, and so on, depending on the letter size (see also the example of an official-style letter where the inside address appears below the signature line). Omit the job title in an inside address if it causes the address to run over four lines. See Style Guidelines, Forms of Address, in this chapter.

Attention line. Type it flush left two lines below the inside address. An attention line on a letter otherwise addressed only to a firm insures that the letter will be opened and read; an attention line on a letter addressed to another person insures that it will be read even though the addressee may be absent.

Salutation. Type it flush left two lines below the attention line. Use the styles recommended in Style Guidelines, Salutations, in this chapter.

Subject line. Type it two lines below the salutation (or three lines below the inside address in the simplified format), with or without an indentation depending on the letter format used.

Body. Type it single spaced with or without a paragraph indentation depending on the letter format used.

Complimentary close. Type it two lines below the body, flush left or slightly right of center page depending on the letter format used. See Style Guidelines, Complimentary Closes, in this chapter.

Signature line. Type it four lines below the complimentary close (five lines below the body in the simplified format), aligned with the close (flush left or right of page center). See Style Guidelines, Signature Lines, in this chapter.

Identification initials. Type them flush left two lines below the signature. Some firms omit the initials on the original. The signer's initials are first, followed by the dictator's, followed by the typist's (BK:JR:tm).

Enclosure notation. Type it flush left two lines below the identification initials. Examples are *Enc.*; *Encs. 3*; *Enclosure*; *Enclosures: Brochure, Filmstrip; Under separate cover: Report.*

Carbon-copy notation. Type it flush left two lines below the enclosure notation. A blind-copy notation is typed in the upper left corner of a letter *only* of the copy going to the person designated to receive a blind copy. Some of the various abbreviations that are used are *cc* (carbon copy), *bc* (blind copy), *rc* (reprographic copy), and *pc* or *Copy* (photocopy).

Postscript. Type it flush left or indented depending on the format used, two lines below the last notation of the letter. Use the postscript only for unrelated remarks, not something you merely forgot to say in the body. Type the signer's initials after the last word.

Continuation page. Type a stacked heading on any additional pages such as

John Jones
January 6, 1987
page two

or type the information across the page:

John Jones　　　　January 6, 1987　　　　page two

Letter Formats

Full-block letter. In this style all principal parts are typed flush with the left margin, including paragraph openings. The order in which the various parts appear (dateline before reference line, salutation before subject line, and so on) is illustrated in this sample full-block letter:

December 12, 1987

Our file Project X

PERSONAL

Mrs. Edward Lynley
Technical Consultants, Inc.
1804 Newsome Street
Prescott, AZ 86302

Dear Barbara:

Subject: Center for Advanced Research Project X

The Board of Trustees of the Center for Advanced
Research cordially invites you to attend a private
organizational meeting to mark the implementation of
Project X. Since you have devoted so many hours of
your time to developing the concept for this exciting
research project, we sincerely hope you can join us on
this important occasion.

Laboratory C will be open from four o'clock until five
o'clock in the afternoon for organizing members to
tour the impressive new facilities that will house
Project X. Cocktails will be served in the adjoining
lounge from five until seven o'clock for you and the
members of the Project X founding team as well as a
few special friends of the center.

We're looking forward to seeing you again, Barbara.
Please do let me know if you can join us for
cocktails at the conclusion of the tour of Laboratory C.

Cordially,

Forest B. Winthrop III
Chairman of the Board

jt

Enc.

cc: Members of the Board of Trustees

P.S. Mark Rogers sends his best regards and is looking
forward to visiting with you at the meeting. FBW

December 12, 1987

Our file Project X

PERSONAL

Mrs. Edward Lynley
Technical Consultants, Inc.
1804 Newsome Street
Prescott, AZ 86301

Dear Barbara:

Subject: Center for Advanced Research Project X

The Board of Trustees of the Center for Advanced
Research cordially invites you to attend a private
organizational meeting to mark the implementation of
Project X. Since you have devoted so many hours of
your time to developing the concept for this exciting
research project, we sincerely hope you can join us
on this important occasion.

Laboratory C. will be open from four o'clock until five
o'clock in the afternoon for organizing members to
tour the impressive new facilities that will house
Project X. Cocktails will be served in the adjoining
lounge from five until seven o'clock for you and the
members of the Project X founding team as well as a
few special friends of the center.

We're looking forward to seeing you again, Barbara.
Please do let me know if you can join us for cocktails
at the conclusion of the tour of Laboratory C.

Cordially,

Forest B. Winthrop III
Chairman of the Board

jt

Enc.

cc: Members of the Board of Trustees

P.S. Mark Rogers sends his best regards and is looking
forward to visiting with you at the meeting. FBW

Block letter. (See page 244.) In this style paragraphs are typed flush left as they are in the full-block format, but the dateline and reference line are positioned at the right margin, and the closing and signature lines are positioned slightly right of the page center.

Modified-block letter. In this style the dateline and reference line are against the right margin, paragraphs and subject line are indented, and the closing and signature are slightly right of the page center.

December 12, 1987

Our file Project X

PERSONAL

Mrs. Edward Lynley
Technical Consultants, Inc.
1804 Newsome Street
Prescott, AZ 86302

Dear Barbara:

Subject: Center for Advanced Research Project X

The Board of Trustees of the Center for Advanced Research cordially invites you to attend a private organizational meeting to mark the implementation of Project X. Since you have devoted so many hours of your time to developing the concept for this exciting research project, we sincerely hope you can join us on this important occasion.

Laboratory C will be open from four o'clock until five o'clock in the afternoon for organizing members to tour the impressive new facilities that will house Project X. Cocktails will be served in the adjoining lounge from five until seven o'clock for you and the members of the Project X founding team as well as a few special friends of the center.

We're looking forward to seeing you again, Barbara.
Please do let me know if you can join us for
cocktails at the conclusion of the tour of Laboratory C.

Cordially,

Forest B. Winthrop III
Chairman of the Board

jt

Enc.

cc: Members of the Board of Trustees

P.S. Mark Rogers sends his best regards and is
looking forward to visiting with you at the meeting.
FBW

Simplified letter. In this style everything is flush left,
but the salutation and complimentary close are omitted.
Notice, in the following example, the extra line of space
above and below the subject line (the word *subject* is
omitted) and between the last paragraph and the signature.

December 12, 1987

Our file Project X

PERSONAL

Mrs. Edward Lynley
Technical Consultants, Inc.
1804 Newsome Street
Prescott, AZ 86302

CENTER FOR ADVANCED RESEARCH PROJECT X

Barbara, the Board of Trustees of the Center
for Advanced Research cordially invites you to attend

a private organizational meeting to mark the implementation of Project X. Since you have devoted so many hours of your time to developing the concept for this exciting research project, we sincerely hope you can join us on this important occasion.

Laboratory C will be open from four o'clock until five o'clock in the afternoon for organizing members to tour the impressive new facilities that will house Project X. Cocktails will be served in the adjoining lounge from five until seven o'clock for you and the members of the Project X founding teams as well as a few special friends of the center.

We're looking forward to seeing you again, Barbara. Please do let me know if you can join us for cocktails at the conclusion of the tour of Laboratory C.

FOREST B. WINTHROP III—CHAIRMAN OF THE BOARD

jt

Enc.

cc: Members of the Board of Trustees

P.S. Mark Rogers sends his best regards and is looking forward to visiting with you at the meeting. FBW

Official letter. In this style, similar to the modified-block letter in its paragraph indentation, the inside address is at the bottom of the letter, two lines below the signature. This style is best reserved for formal or official correspondence, although some people use it on executive-size stationery (for example, the seven- by ten-inch Monarch letter). When used as a more formal letter than the other styles, certain elements (such as a postscript) should be omitted.

December 12, 1987

Dear Barbara:

The Board of Trustees of the Center for Advanced Research cordially invites you to attend a private organizational meeting to mark the implementation of Project X. Since you have devoted so many hours of your time to developing the concept for this exciting research project, we sincerely hope you can join us on this important occasion.

Laboratory C will be open from four o'clock until five o'clock in the afternoon for organizing members to tour the impressive new facilities that will house Project X. Cocktails will be served in the adjoining lounge from five until seven o'clock for you and the members of the Project X founding team as well as a few special friends of the center.

We're looking forward to seeing you again, Barbara. Please do let me know if you can join us for cocktails at the conclusion of the tour of Laboratory C.

Cordially,

Forest B. Winthrop III
Chairman of the Board

Mrs. Edward Lynley
Technical Consultants, Inc.
1804 Newsome Street
Prescott, AZ 86302

Parts of Memos

Memo formats vary widely from letter-size printed stationery to simple note pads. The correct position of the various structural parts of a memo are shown in the following example of a common memo format. The principal parts of a memo include the heading, the body, and miscellaneous notations.

Heading. The heading is usually printed at the top of memo stationery and includes guide words such as *Date, To, From*, and *Subject*. Major words in the subject line should be capitalized.

Body. Type it two to four lines below the last line of guidewords, flush left or indented, as preferred.

Miscellaneous notations. Type them in the same position as a traditional letter. Although a memo has no complimentary close or signature line, some writers place their initials two lines below the body, often typed slightly to the right of the page center.

Memo Format

The following is a common memo format used on standard business letterhead.

TO: <u>Department Heads</u>   From: <u>William Rossetti</u>

Subject: <u>June 7 Meeting</u>   Date: <u>May 4, 1987</u>

This will confirm that the next staff meeting will be held Friday, June 7, at 10:30 a.m., in the Conference Room. A revised agenda is attached.

Please let me know right away (extension 713) if you will be unable to attend. Thanks very much.

WR

kf

pc: David L. Durston, General Manager

Envelopes

The correct position of the address and various notations on an envelope are illustrated in the sample envelope. The style shown is that recommended by the U.S. Postal Service for processing by optical-character reader. Leave a bottom margin of at least five-eighths inch and a left margin of at least one inch.

[RETURN ADDRESS]

SPECIAL DELIVERY

ROZ: 7163-21-41C
NEW MANUFACTURING CO
ATTN MR. KT SMITH
33 N 64 ST RM 210
PRINCETON NJ 08540

STYLE GUIDELINES

The letter and memo formats illustrated in this chapter show you the correct position of the various structural parts. In particular, writers often have trouble selecting the right style for salutations, forms of address, complimentary closes, and signature lines. The following guidelines cover the areas of particular concern.

Salutations

Capitalize the first word and the person's name and title, and use formal greetings such as *My dear Mrs. Lewis* only in formal or official letters. Abbreviate *Mr.*, *Mrs.*, *Messrs.*, and *Dr.*, but spell out religious, military, and professional titles (e.g., *Professor*). Use the title a woman prefers if you know it; otherwise use *Ms.* When you don't know the gender, use the person's full name; when you don't know the name, use a title such as *Director* or *Sir or Madam*. Use *Ladies and Gentlemen* on a letter to a firm composed of both men and women. When the salutation mentions two or more persons, name the person with the highest position first. The following are examples of acceptable forms:

Dear Ms. Winthrop
Dear Captain Hurst
Dear Mss. Kent and Ortega

Dear Ms. Kent and Mrs. Ortega
Dear Ms. Lange and Mr. Burns
Dear Mssrs. Parker and Jeffreys (two men)
Ladies (women only in firm)
Gentlemen (men only in firm)
Ladies and Gentlemen (both men and women in firm)
Dear Sir or Madam (name and gender unknown)
Dear M. R. Power (gender unknown)
Dear Employees (letter to group)

Forms of Address

Always precede a name with a title (*Dr., Mr., Ms.,*
and so on) unless *Esq.* or *M.D.* follows the name. Avoid
academic degrees after a name in an inside address, but
if a person prefers that you use them, omit the titles *Dr.,
Mr., Ms., Miss,* or *Mrs.* before the name. You may use
a title such as *Professor* or *Dean* as long as it does not
mean the same thing as the degree that follows the name
(do not, for example, write *Dr.* Evan Starr, *Ph.D.*).
When there are several degrees, put the one pertaining
to the person's occupation first. Use *The Honorable* when
a person has held an official title, but do not use political
titles such as *Senator* and *President* after retirement (*Judge*
is an exception). Address a letter by job title when the
person's name is unknown (*Dear Editor*).

Use *Ms.* for women in business unless they prefer *Miss*
or *Mrs.* or have a professional title such as *Dr.* Follow
the woman's preference for use of maiden, married, or
combined maiden-married last names in business. For
formal social occasions, always use *Miss* and *Mrs.* for a
married woman, use her husband's full name. Socially,
divorcees may use *Mrs.* with a maiden-married name
combination and no first name, or *Miss* and the first
name and maiden name, or *Mrs.* with the first name and
married last name. The following examples show how the
name and title would appear on the envelope and in the
inside address (follow the person's preference in placing
or omitting the comma before *Jr.* and *Sr.*):

Mr. Louis Caruthers, Sr./Dear Mr. Caruthers
Dr. Kenneth Murray III/Dear Dr. Murray

Kenneth Murray III, M.D./Dear Dr. Murray

Eloise Jacobs, Esq./Dear Ms. (or Dr. if applicable) Jacobs

Dr. Eloise Jacobs/Dear Dr. Jacobs

Dr. Mary Hartwell and Mr. Frank Hartwell/Dear Dr. and Mr. Hartwell

Drs. Mary and Frank Hartwell/Dear Drs. Hartwell

Director of Marketing (name unknown)/Dear Sir or Madam

The Honorable Jeanne Barker/Dear Madam or Dear Ms. Barker

Ms. Carla Bennett/Dear Ms. Bennett (business)

Mrs. Joseph Russell/Dear Mrs. Russell (formal social—married or widowed woman)

Ms. (or Mrs.) Lola Wana/Dear Ms. (or Mrs.) Wana (business—divorced woman, former married name)

Ms. (or Miss) Lola Ortega/Dear Ms. (or Miss) Ortega (business—divorced woman, maiden name)

Ms. (or Miss, Mrs.) Lola Ortega-Wana/Dear Ms. (or Miss, Mrs.) Ortega-Wana (business—divorced woman, combined last names)

Mrs. Ortega-Wana/Dear Mrs. Ortega-Wana (formal social—divorced woman, combined last names only)

Miss Lola Ortega/Dear Miss Ortega (formal social—divorced woman, maiden name)

Johnson Industries/Ladies and Gentlemen

Ms. Cecelia York and Mrs. Dorothy Bledsoe/Dear Ms. York and Mrs. Beldsoe

Complimentary Closes

The trend is toward informal closes in business correspondence:

Sincerely
Sincerely yours
Cordially
Cordially yours
Regards
Best regards
Warmest regards
Best wishes

The following closes should be reserved for formal and official correspondence:

Respectfully
Respectfully yours
Yours truly
Yours very truly
Very sincerely yours
Very cordially yours

Signature Lines

Type a person's name exactly as he or she signs it. Place only *Mrs.* or *Miss* in parentheses before the name. *Ms.* and *Mr.* may precede the name in parentheses only if the signer's gender would otherwise be unclear.

For women in business, type their first names and maiden or married last name in the signature line. In formal social correspondence, type her husband's full name preceded by *Mrs.*—all in parentheses; however, the written signature should contain her *first* name and married last name. Socially, if a divorcee uses a maiden-married combination, type Mrs. and the two names in parentheses—no first name; the signature, however, would include the first name.

A secretary signing a letter for her employer should type *Secretary to Mr./Ms. Last Name* (no first name unless someone else in the firm has the same last name). Follow these examples in business letters:

Firm

Sincerely yours,
ACCOUNTING SPECIALISTS

John Davis

John Davis
Manager

Woman, any marital status
Cordially,

Ellen Purdue

Ellen Purdue
Marketing Manager

Title to indicate female gender (any marital status)
Sincerely,

T. L. Johnson

(Ms.) T. L. Johnson
Personnel Director

Title to indicate man
Sincerely,

Leslie Parsons

(Mr.) Leslie Parsons

Secretary's signature
Sincerely yours,

Nora Donaldson

Nora Donaldson
Secretary to Mrs. Channing

Secretary signing for employer
Sincerely yours,

Leonard Jarvis
km

Leonard Jarvis
Customer Relations Manager

Follow these examples in formal social correspondence:

Man with honorary title Esq.
Yours very truly,

Donald Franklin

Donald Franklin, Esq.

Married or widowed woman
Yours very truly,

Janet Cramer

(Mrs. Dean S. Cramer)

Single woman
Yours very truly,

Mary Proxmire

(Miss) Mary Proxmire

Divorced woman, maiden-married name
Yours very truly,

Helen Vinson-Whiteside

(Mrs. Vinson-Whiteside)

Divorced woman, maiden name
Yours very truly,

Helen Vinson

(Miss) Helen Vinson

LANGUAGE GUIDELINES

Modern letter writing has come a long way since the days of verbose and stilted messages. Today, letter writers carefully observe these guidelines:

Tone

Use a friendly, conversational tone, mentioning the person's name in the opening and closing whenever possible. ("Thanks so much for your advice, Tom; I really appreciate it.")

Opening

Make your opening clear and to the point; briefly state the purpose of your message in the first sentence or paragraph. ("It's time to start thinking about a theme for our next conference, Dave.") If your purpose is to sell or motivate, make the opening especially enticing.

Ending

Make your ending paragraph as short as possible and leave the reader with the impression you want. ("I'll be eager to learn your decision, Bill. Please let me know by Monday, December 5.") But include all necessary instructions—time, date, any other necessary facts. Never leave a reader wondering how to respond. Also, try to avoid merely repeating in summary what you said earlier.

Concrete Terms

Choose clear, specific words and judiciously avoid vague, weak terms such as *centers on* and *revolves around*.

Pompous Language

Avoid stuffy, pretentious language such as *commence* for *begin*, *terminate* for *end*, and *endeavor* for *try*. Be natural and unpretentious.

Short Words and Sentences

Generally, pick simple, short words and simple, short sentences over longer, more cumbersome alternatives.

Nondiscriminatory Language

Keep your language completely free of bias: avoid references to color (refer to heritages such as Asian-American, if necessary). Refer to men and women equally (*men* and *women*, not *men* and *girls*; *guests* and *spouses*, not *guests* and *wives; Mr.* Harris and *Ms.* Wallace, not *Mr.* Harris and Cindy).

Do not emphasize a woman's physical appearance when her professional capabilities should be stressed (say a *capable* supervisor, not a *pretty* supervisor). Do not emphasize a person's handicap unless it is pertinent and then make it incidental (say "Edna Stillwell, an employee who is hearing impaired, will teach the class," not "the deaf employee Edna Stillwell will teach the class").

Trite Expressions

Avoid trite expressions such as "I beg to inform you" or "I remain, faithfully yours."

Word Choice

Watch for errors in word choice, such as *due to* when you mean *because of; scarcely* when you mean *hardly.*

Wordiness

Be ruthlessly economical in your writing (*it is often the case that* is a rambling, wordy way of saying simply *often; month of July* is a wordy way of saying simply *July*).

Active Voice

Use the active voice whenever possible (*we think*, not *it is thought that*).

Editing

Carefully edit your correspondence for accuracy of information; adequate detail; appropriate tone for the recipient; courtesy; neatness; style of punctuation and capitalization; appropriate letter or memo format; consistency in writing style and language; and absence of cliches, irrelevancies, pretentious language, vague words, jargon, gobbledygook, euphemisms, trite expressions, and bias.

MODEL LETTERS AND MEMOS

Nearly three dozen model letters and memos are shown here, each one about a different topic. They are meant to be used as guides in composing your own messages. In some cases you may be able to substitute a few facts and use the rest of the letter or memo intact; in other cases you may have to change the tone and other aspects to suit your own situation and intended reader.

Traditionally, the memo format was reserved for internal correspondence; today, busy office personnel use the easily prepared memo format for informal contacts with clients, customers, business associates, and others outside the firm. For instance, why would one take time to prepare a formal letter when all one needs to say is "Here's the brochure you requested, George. Let me know if you have any questions."

Many of the model letters shown here could also be sent in a memo format (for example, Acknowledgment, Appreciation, Inquiry, Orders, and Reminder), and some of the memos could be sent as letters (for example, Announcement, Commendation, and Criticism). Often the choice depends on how well you know the recipient, how formal you want to be, and how important the time-saving features of a memo are to you.

Acknowledgment

Reply promptly and use a simple, straightforward approach.

Dear Jim:

Thanks for sending the revised program data. You're right—it looks much more impressive now that most of the time slots are filled.

I really appreciate your efforts in getting this
material to me in time to meet our deadline, Jim.
The printer expects to have the first proofs for you to
check by May 5.

Best regards,

Adjustment

An adjustment in response to a legitimate complaint
requires fairness and understanding—as well as an apology—to protect your company's image and your own and
to retain the goodwill of the customer or associate.

Dear Ms. Von Braun:

We were indeed sorry to learn that several of the
multistrike ZR19 printer ribbons you received were
defective. Thank you for returning the carton of forty-
eight ribbons so promptly.

Another carton of multistrike film ribbons is being
sent to you today by United Parcel Service. It was
carefully inspected before packing to insure that all
ribbons are in perfect condition.

We appreciate your continuing interest in our
products, Ms. Von Braun, and sincerely regret any
inconvenience this has caused you but hope that you
will be pleased with the new ribbons.

Thank you for your patience.

Sincerely,

Announcement

Some announcements are printed and posted on bulletin boards, some are reproduced on cards for mailing,
some are distributed as brochures or press releases, and
some are sent as letters or memos. Many announcements
are brief messages that consist of a clear, accurate statement of the essential facts.

TO: Departmental Managers

SUBJECT: International Mail Service

The company mailroom has installed equipment that enables us to dial into the INTELPOST system twenty-four hours a day, seven days a week.

INTELPOST is a Postal Service program for the electronic transmission of copies of original documents to twenty-eight foreign countries (see attached list). The transmitted copy is often available at the foreign destination within an hour. The cost is $5 a page (less for volume use). Any document may be sent—text or graphics—except glossy photographs (although a pho-tocopy of a glossy is acceptable). The size should be between 8½ by 14 and 5 by 5 inches.

Departmental personnel who want to use the INTELPOST service can request further information from Henry Schoenberg, mailroom supervisor, extension 3112.

Apology

A sincere apology for an error, oversight, or other problem does more than anything else to soothe someone's ruffled feathers. Add a solution or suggest some action whenever appropriate.

TO: James Rowe

SUBJECT: Production Manager

I'm sorry to let you know, Jim, that the No. 11 cables you requested from the parts department on April 7 are still out of stock. However, the manufacturer has them on back order and has guaranteed shipment by June 2.

Please accept my apology for the delay. I know you have a schedule to keep, so I promise to keep more of the cables on hand in the future. In the meantime, if there's any way I can be of help, please let me know.

Appointment

Accurate details (time, place, date, and so on) are important in letters concerning appointments and should be stated clearly in any request and restated in any letter of confirmation.

Dear Mr. Hendricks:

Thanks for letting me know that you will be in Milwaukee the week of January 9 and would like to discuss our retooling problems. Would you be able to meet me in my office at ten o'clock, Monday morning, January 9?

Please let me know whether this time will be convenient for you. I'll look forward to seeing you soon.

Sincerely,

Appreciation

Appreciation is a natural response to almost any thoughtful or commendable act, and the expression should be warm and sincere—but not gushy.

Dear Pam:

It was very thoughtful of you to help us complete the grant forms for our proposed renovation project. Your experience in working with grants certainly took the bite out of an otherwise formidable task.

Thanks ever so much, Pam. We truly appreciate your time and effort in our behalf.

Best wishes,

Collection

Collections are commonly undertaken by specialists such as collection agencies and attorneys. However, some offices handle collections internally or at least precede outside action with one or a series of letters, beginning with a casual reminder and ending with a prelude to legal action.

Dear Mrs. Steinberg:

This is just a friendly reminder that your payment of $211.98 will be very much appreciated. If your check is already in the mail, Mrs. Steinberg, please disregard this notice and accept our thanks. But if you haven't yet mailed it, won't you take a moment to send us your payment today?

Sincerely,

Commendation

Concentrate on the subject's achievements and omit anything else that would detract from the focus of the letter or memo—praise for the subject.

TO: Loni Morris

SUBJECT: Mailing-List Conversion

You did a marvelous job, Loni, in converting our antiquated card list into a modern, computer-based list. With the merge capabilities of our new software, we can finally send volume personalized client letters— a feature already proven to be productive by our competitors, as you correctly pointed out at our last meeting.

I have a meeting with Ted Corosin, our general manager, on Tuesday, and I intend to let him know what an outstanding job you did. The head office is always eager to learn about important contributions such as yours, and I know they'll add their thanks to mine for your initiative and foresight.

Congratulations, Loni, on another successful project!

Complaint

The most effective letters of complaint are those that are written not in irrational anger but with a calm hand, stating facts clearly and accurately and presenting a fair and reasonable request for adjustment.

Dear Mr. Walker:

Our March 27 order for thirty word-processing guides and supplementary exercise manuals has arrived incomplete. We received the thirty guides but none of the exercise manuals.

If the manuals are being shipped to us separately, please disregard this notice. But if they were unintentionally omitted or are unavailable now, I'd appreciate knowing the expected delivery date right away. Our workshop begins on Monday, July 14, and it is essential that we receives the rest of our order on or before Friday, July 11. Unfortunately, the guides alone, without the exercise manuals, are of no use to us in a workshop setting.

Please phone me immediately at 777-1111 so that I can complete arrangements for our summer program. Thank you very much for your help, Mr. Walker.

Sincerely,

Confirmation

The best way to avoid misunderstandings or confusion is to confirm everything in writing, restating any essential facts such as time, place, and date.

TO: Jeanne Shield

SUBJECT: Conference Planning Committee

Thanks again, Jeanne, for asking me to serve on the Conference Planning Committee. As I indicated at lunch today, my schedule is flexible for the coming months, and I'd be happy to serve on the committee.

I'll look forward to receiving your preliminary notes and will be at the May 6 meeting at 10:30 A.M. in your office.

Congratulations

Acts and occasions both large and small warrant recognition, and one should not hesitate to congratulate someone on developing a new idea, setting a sales record, beating a deadline, celebrating an anniversary, or achieving anything else that is more than routine. Always offer praise and recognition sincerely and enthusiastically without any hint of envy.

Dear Mr. Michaels:

I'm delighted to send you my very best wishes on your twenty-fifth anniversary with P & Q Engineering Specialists. Our firm is very fortunate to have benefited from your substantial contribution to its growth and progress during these exciting—sometimes difficult—years.

It's no secret that you have always given more than a hundred percent of your loyalty, your expertise, and your goodwill to coworker and client alike. Small wonder that your career has steadily advanced and that the firm has the pleasure of honoring you at an anniversary dinner next week for having reached this important milestone.

We warmly salute you, Mr. Michaels, and are truly grateful for the impressive example and inspiration you offer to all of us. Heartiest congratulations!

Cordially,

Credit

Letters involving credit require honesty, accuracy, confidentiality, and—in the case of refusals—consideration for the feelings of the recipient.

Dear Ms. Bronstein:

We're happy to send you, in confidence, the credit information you requested on Davison Graphics.

We have supplied type to this firm for about five years, and their purchases have ranged from $500 to $1,500 a month. Our records show that they have paid our invoices regularly within thirty days, and we consider their performance very satisfactory.

Let me know if there is anything else I can do to help, Ms. Bronstein.

Sincerely,

Cricitism

Tactless criticism can wound an employee and hinder future communications, productivity, and job satisfaction. Hence one must avoid a blunt or condescending tone.

TO. Marc Lewis

SUBJECT: Classroom Procedure

I enjoyed sitting in on your data-processing class yesterday and am impressed with the enthusiasm you've generated among the attendees. That's always good to see.

Everything moved smoothly after the daily lesson plans were distributed, and its clear that you know how to motivate your students. It's a shame that we have to lose ten to twelve minutes of time from each class in distributing the daily lesson plans and waiting for everyone to settle down. Let's try something different—let each attendee pick up the next day's plan on his or her way out *after* each class session. I know there will be times when this may be less convenient, but gaining at least ten minutes a day for twenty-five class days means an extra four hours of time available for instruction during the life of each program. That's significant when our goal is to train each attendee to the maximum in the short time available.

Let me know if you have any further thoughts or questions about this, Marc. I really appreciate all your efforts to make our training classes such a big success.

Employee Motivation

To motivate someone to respond in a particular way, you must be very persuasive, which means selecting facts to present that will appeal to the recipient. But the temptation to color the facts or stretch the truth should be shunned.

Dear Hal:

I was pleased to learn that you have been asked to head a new committee to form a liaison among company departments. The Board of Directors certainly picked the right candidate for the job, and I hope your answer will be yes.

I can't think of anyone who is better qualified than you to set the standards for departmental cooperation. Your congeniality coupled with your methodical approach to organizational matters practically insures the success of this idea. It's no secret that departmental rivalry has seriously hampered productivity on more than one occasion, and a liaison committee to foster closer ties and cooperation among departments is long overdue. I can promise you that your efforts toward this goal won't go unnoticed and will earn the admiration and gratitude of everyone on the Board of Directors, as well as the many employees who are eagerly waiting for any sign of improved departmental relations.

If you decide to move ahead with this, Hal—and I sincerely hope you will—don't hesitate to call on me or any other member of the board to discuss ideas, policy, procedures, problems, or anything else that comes to mind. In the meantime, all the best to you.

Regards,

Evaluation

Memos that analyze and report on the merits of something (or someone) may vary in length depending on policy and office requirements. In any case, write in a concise, straightforward style.

TO: Milli Hoxmier

SUBJECT: New Word Software

I've completed the study you requested on updating our word-processing software. New Word has all of the features that were described as essential in our preliminary study report:

1. Computer-assisted instructions (training disk)
2. On-screen preview of documents (before printing)
3. Editing via keyboard or mouse
4. Format files for standardizing documents
5. Merge capability
6. Expandable spell-checker
7. Glossary-storage capability

Since it is an extremely powerful program, with more features than most, it has no disadvantages that should influence a decision to purchase it. However, we should consider the following factors:

1. Members of the secretarial pool are trained to use a significantly different word-processing program.
2. Converting to New Word will require time-consuming modifications in existing documents and extensive retraining of all support personnel.

3. Our field offices are geared exclusively to the use of the old program, and future document exchange will be affected.

4. Approximately a year after conversion, the capabilities of New Word will foster cost advantages that ultimately will outweigh conversion costs.

As you can see, conversion would create problems and expenses in the short run (up to a year) and efficiencies and cost savings thereafter. Before making a decision at our next meeting, I would suggest (a) that we discuss this with our field offices and (b) that we ask New Word Corporation for its suggestions in minimizing conversion difficulties.

Let me know if you have any questions, Milli.

Follow-up

Unanswered communication must be followed up at appropriate intervals, either repeating essential facts or enclosing a copy of the original unanswered message. But do not suggest that the recipient is thoughtless or forgetful.

Ladies and Gentlemen:

Last month we requested specifications and prices on your heavy-duty surge-protection devices. The information has not yet arrived, and we must have it in time to place an order by April 1.

Could you send us the information and prices this week? Thank you.

Sincerely,

Goodwill

Friendly letters that build goodwill and create a favorable impression of a person or a firm can be sent on numerous occasions—holidays, anniversaries, awards, promotions, outstanding service, and so on.

Dear Joan:

I just read your article "Debt-Reduction Guidelines for Middle-Class America." It's wonderful!

Your ideas are superb, Joan, and offer a truly sensible solution for the millions who need help in money management. I can't tell you how gratifying it is to know that someone has a completely fresh approach to an old problem. Congratulations on a very impressive piece!

Best wishes,

Inquiry

Most inquiries are short and sweet, containing only the facts necessary for the recipient to respond.

Ladies and Gentlemen:

Please send me the name and address of the J-C Copier sales and service dealer handling the region including Penn City, Tennessee. Thank you.

Sincerely,

Instructions

To avoid misunderstandings, instructions must be stated clearly and with adequate detail for readers to know what to do. When a problem necessitates the instructions, the tone must bear an element of firmness as well.

TO: All Employees

SUBJECT: Copier Log Entries

Since we installed a copier in the supply room for use by all offices, there has been increasing negligence in recording copier usage in the log-entry notebook. This record is essential for accounting purposes, and our bookkeeper must allocate the cost of all copies made to the appropriate category of use—advertising, marketing, and so on. Without entries there is no way to know to which accounts to charge the cost of copies made.

Hereafter, to insure that log entries are recorded for all copies made, we are implementing the following procedures to be followed by all personnel using the general copier:

1. Before entering the supply room, pick up a copier record slip from the clerk monitoring the supply desk by door.
2. After you have finished, record the number of copies made, your name, and your department on the slip.
3. Upon leaving the supply room, give the completed slip to the clerk monitoring the supply desk by the door, and he or she will file the record slip for later use in bookkeeping.

We hope this simple procedure will rectify the problem so that we can continue to provide a general copier for use by all personnel. To help us make this possible, we ask that you carefully follow the above procedure and respect any related requests made by the supply clerk, who has been instructed to insist upon a completed record slip from everyone leaving the supply room.

Thank you very much. We appreciate your patience and cooperation.

Introduction

A letter of introduction may be mailed in advance to the recipient or given to the subject who will hand carry it to the recipient. Sending the letter in advance thoughtfully gives the recipient time to decline a meeting with the subject.

Dear Ms. Cavanagh:

I'm happy to introduce David Willis to you as a possible candidate for a position in your company. I believe he will be contacting you next week to request an interview.

Dave is leaving Ewing Wholesalers to move to the West Coast, where he hopes to find a suitable supervisory position in refrigeration engineering. For the past seven years he has been project supervisor of a team of six refrigeration engineers at Ewing, where he has successsfully completed three major innovative projects in recent years. All of us at Ewing will miss his skill and dedication and believe he will be an asset to any firm with needs in his area of expertise.

I'd appreciate any consideration you can extend to Dave. Thanks very much, Ms. Cavanagh.

Cordially,

Invitation

For many occasions it is appropriate to send an invitation by letter. In any form of invitation the details (time, date, and place) should be clear. The tone in a letter depends upon whether the letter is sent to a casual friend (perhaps inviting someone to lunch) or a prominent person (perhaps asking the person to address a conference). Replies customarily follow the style and tone of the invitation.

Dear Dr. Edelston:

The Board of Directors of the Centerville Telecommunications Society read with great interest your excellent article in the June issue of New Telecommunications. Your discussion of breaking the new-technology language barrier deals with a topic that our members have been eager to understand better, and we would like to invite you to speak about this matter at the October meeting of our society.

The meeting will be held at 7:30 P.M. on Friday, October 14, in the Centerville High School Auditorium, one block off Highway 40 east, at the edge of town, where about sixty members will be present. We usually ask our speakers to arrange for a twenty-minute address followed by a ten- to fifteen-minute question and answer period. Since our membership includes many newcomers to the field, a significant amount of introductory information would be appropriate.

In hopes that you will be able to accept our invitation, I'm enclosing a data form and a questionnaire for you to complete and mail to us by September 30. As you will see on the data form, the society provides dinner, overnight accommodations, and an honorarium of $50 to visiting speakers.

We do hope you can join us on October 14, Dr. Edelston. I'd appreciate having your reply by September 14 so that we can finalize our program.

Sincerely,

Notice

The bylaws of some organizations require that meeting notices follow a prescribed form. In the case of an informal meeting notice, a brief memo is appropriate.

TO: Sales Staff

SUBJECT: October Meeting

The next sales meeting will be held on Thursday, October 7, from nine until eleven o'clock in the morning, in the conference room.

An agenda will be mailed on September 20. If you have any topics to be included, please send them to me by September 19.

I'd appreciate hearing from you right away if you're unable to attend. Thanks very much.

Orders

Although routine orders involve little more than a request for an item, with adequate description and reference to the form of payment, other matters such as cancellations, changes, and apologies for delays require more skill in composition.

Dear Mr. Kline:

We would like to change our February 6 order for typewriter maintenance service at Holt and Biscome Enterprises.

We had requested a contract for eleven electric machines and two electronic models. Our check for $980 for one year's service beginning March 1 was enclosed with our initial request. Since then we have purchased two more electronic machines and would like to include them in the blanket coverage. In a telephone conversation with you on March 13 you said that additional coverage, prorated for a partial year, would amount to no more than $125. Please arrange for this amendment to our coverage and send us an invoice for the additional amount.

I'm enclosing a copy of our present contract and will look forward to receiving a revised agreement. Thanks very much.

Sincerely,

Reference

A reference, or a letter of recommendation, may be typed individually and sent to a specific person who has requested the information, or a general letter may be composed and given to the subject who then makes duplicate copies and sends them to prospects at will.

To Whom It May Concern:

I'm pleased to have this opportunity to comment on the substantial contribution that Margo Jamison

has made to Pruett Nationwide Insurance Company.
For six years, as director of our publications office,
she was responsible for the production of our company
house organ, taking each issue from concept to
printed copy.

Ms. Jamison worked skillfully under pressure and
successfully rallied the ongoing support of a busy
staff of six writers, artists, and production personnel.
Her talent and published expertise gave our house
organ a degree of professionalism that others in the
magazine business would envy.

Margo Jamison would be an asset to any firm
seeking a responsible, experienced editor and
publisher. The appropriate organization would benefit
immensely from her exceptional capabilities.

                              Sincerely,

Rejection

A rejection can cause hurt feelings and discourage further
efforts unless it is presented tactfully and thoughtfully.

Dear Mr. Ott:

We have carefully considered your request for a
raise effective January 1, and I'm sorry to let you
know that the institute cannot grant the increase at
that time.

Although your two years of employment at the
Research Institute have been very satisfactory, and
we are especially pleased to learn that you wish to
expand your responsibility, the institute was unable
to meet its funding goals last year, which has imposed
additional budget restraints in a number of areas,
including the payroll division.

However, another salary review will be conducted
at the end of the year, following the midyear fund
drive, and you will be notified then if any budget
restraints will be lifted. In the meantime, please

accept our thanks for your continued dedication to our program. We genuinely appreciate your efforts and hope you continue to enjoy your work at the Research Institute.

Sincerely,

Reminder

It is often prudent to remind someone of a date or a deadline—just to be certain that they won't forget or that there is no misunderstanding. But to be useful, a reminder should arrive in time for the recipient to make plans or take other action.

Dear Lee:

I just wanted to let you know that the workshop committee is still planning to meet for lunch at the Jewel Inn at noon on Thursday, November 5. So that I can reserve a table for us, I'd appreciate it if you would telephone me at 213-3000 or drop me a note this week to confirm that you are still planning to attend.

Thanks very much, Lee. I'm looking forward to seeing you on the fifth.

Best regards,

Report

The memo format is suitable for many small, informal reports. See chapter 13 for a description of other report styles.

TO: Brad Levitt

SUBJECT: Remodeling and Progress Report

We have completed the following stages of the first- and second-floor remodeling project:

First Floor: Lobby repainted and recarpeted and new furniture installed; east-wing suites repainted; west-wing suites repainted and recarpeted; conference-room paneling repaired and air cleaner installed; east hallway recarpeted; west hallway recarpeted

Second Floor: Hallway recarpeted; computer-room security system installed

The following work has been approved and will be undertaken in January and February:

First Floor: East-wing suites to be recarpeted; conference room to be recarpeted; east hallway to be wallpapered; west hallway to be wallpapered

Second Floor: Hallway to be wallpapered; new furniture to be installed in executive rooms 201 and 204

The estimated completion date is February 15. Although there were some delays in installing the computer-room security system, overall we are on schedule and within budget.

The next progress report will be sent to you on January 1. In the meantime, Brad, if you have any questions, just let me know.

Request

The request, which may involve more detail than a routine inquiry, asks for something and states what action the recipient should take.

Dear Mrs. Hunt:

I'm seeking research material concerning voice-data communications to use in preparing an article I'm writing for the New Technology Journal. Does your company have reports, brochures, or other literature on this subject available to the public? Or do you have a price list for books or magazines that you may have for sale?

I'd very much appreciate receiving any information
you may have by August 17. Thanks so much for
your help.

Sincerely,

Reservations

Details (time, date, place, accommodations desired,
credit card number, and so on) are crucial in making
reservations and should be stated clearly both in requests
for reservations and in any confirmation or change in
plans.

Ladies and Gentlemen:

Please reserve a dinner table for fourteen at 7:30
P.M., on Sataurday, May 16, in the Orchid Room. We
would like optional cocktails and full-course coq au
vin dinners ($12.95) for everyone.

The check should be presented to Paul Arrette,
branch manager, Esmond Financial Consultants,
host for the evening.

Please confirm this reservation to me at 502-8686.
Thank you.

Sincerely,

Sales Promotion

Although most promotional letters are prepared by
specialists, some customer contacts serve the same purpose.

Dear Mr. Wallace:

To meet your growing needs, we're constantly
looking for ways to develop new and improved
utility paper. I'm happy to say we've created a new
eighteen-pound weight word-processing paper that

may meet most of your needs and still save you money
over the alternative twenty-pound professional paper.

Wendy Macauley, our field representative, will be in
Jackson on Monday, September 2, and will contact
you to see whether it would be convenient to stop at
your office to show you this exciting new paper and
explain the potential savings to you. I know you're
going to be impressed with this discovery, Mr.
Wallace, so I hope you'll have time in your busy
schedule to meet with Ms. Macauley. In the meantime,
do call if you have any questions.

Cordially,

Solicitation

Whenever you're asking for something—money, assistance, a favor—you need to be enticing. Provide incen-
tive when you can and explain clearly how the contributor
can respond easily.

TO: All Employees

SUBJECT: Wilshott Handicapped Children's Fund

Most of us are among the lucky ones in life who have
never had to manage in spite of a handicap. Most of
us have children who have been similarly blessed. One
of the things that makes us proud to work at
Wilshott Industries is that we never forgot those who
haven't always shared our good fortune. It's that
kind of sensitivity that led to the establishment of the
Wilshott Handicapped Children's Fund more than a
decade ago.

Every year Wilshott's Board of Directors agrees to
match the amount of employee donations collected
for handicapped children, and every year we try to
beat the previous year's record. Last year we collected
$9,843, so our total contribution was $19,686 with
Wilshott's matching donation. How about it—can we
set our sights high again and double that amount this

year? A lot of disabled youngsters are counting on
us to give them a chance for a reasonably normal life.

Throughout April, someone in every department w
call upon coworkers to ask for a generous donation—
as much as you can afford to give. Please don't hold
back. I'm going to double the amount I gave last
year. Will you do the same?

Thanks very much for your help—from all of us on
the fund committee and from handicapped children
everywhere.

Sympathy

Expressions of sympathy are a necessary part of business as well as social life, and they should be handled sensitively without becoming macabre.

Dear Mr. Adams:

Please accept my deepest sympathy on the death of
your wife. Everyone in the firm admired her tireless
work for numerous charities, and I know that she will
be greatly missed.

Do let me know if there's any way I can be of help
during this difficult time.

With sincerest sympathy,

Thank you

Any act of special kindness requires a message—usually brief—of sincere gratitude.

Dear Ms. Appleton:

It was such a pleasure to meet you in Atlanta and
tour your impressive assembly plant. Thank you for
taking time away from your regular schedule to help
me understand more about the important activity
that precedes packaging in my division.

I sincerely appreciated your thoughtful attention, Ms. Appleton, and hope that soon you will give me a chance to show you our packaging operations in Greensboro. Many thanks.

Best wishes,

Transmittal

A memo format is typical for brief messages intended only to identify an enclosure and the sender. However, more detail may be included when further explanation is in order.

TO: Cindy Anderson

SUBJECT: Annual Report

I thought you might like to see the enclosed proof (no need to return it) of our next annual report. It's being checked now for errors in the public relations department and is scheduled for printing on Friday, August 30.

FORM AND GUIDE LETTERS

Form Files

When certain types of letters or memos are used frequently, and you merely change names or other isolated facts, it is useful to have copies on file for reference. If you prepare your correspondence by typewriter, keep a forms-file folder or notebook with sample letters and memos—or even model paragraphs—that you can imitate or copy verbatim, rather than compose each succeeding message from scratch. Such guide letters will save you substantial time and effort.

Computer Forms

If you prepare your correspondence by magnetic-tape typewriter or by computer-word processor, you can copy letters and memos that would make good models onto a separate forms document file (for example, onto one or more floppy disks in the case of a computer or word processor). You will need to devise an index for this file, possibly by basic type of message (acknowledgment, apology, congratulations, sympathy, and so on).

You should follow the instructions with your particular software, but generally, when you need to send a letter or memo, you can then locate and call up a suitable model and examine it on your monitor. After that you can either edit the model there and print it out or you can copy the model onto another document disk and edit (and save) it there, leaving the original model as it is on your forms document file disk. If your model is formatted (margins set, spacing indicated, and so on), there will be little for you to do in preparing the new letter—simply key in the modifications (new date, new inside address, and so on) and print it out on your business letterhead.

If your word-processing software has a merge feature, you will be able to merge an entire address list with your selected model letter. Mailing lists are also commonly stored on tape and can be merged with the body of a letter by high-speed magnetic-tape typewriter. All of these methods are means of sending essentially the same message to many people but having each letter printed out to look as if it was individually prepared.

Printed Forms

Some offices use printed forms—partial messages that are duplicated on an offset printing press or by some other means of reproduction. The date, inside address, and possibly other data are then typed on the already printed body of the letter or memo. Depending on the quality of reproduction, such messages are often easy to recognize as mass-produced forms, rather than individually typed messages, especially if the typed-in address and other data don't match the ink density and style of the preprinted portion.

However, this procedure is adequate for many routine, repetitive mailings. Such forms can be printed with tiny pinhead dots at precisely the points where the date and inside address should be typed. This will help the typist align the typed-in copy (date, inside address, and so on) without spending a lot of time shifting and adjusting the paper in the typewriter.

Sources of Forms

Whatever method you use to send letters—printing press or quality mimeograph, magnetic-tape typewriter, word processor, computer, electric or electronic typewriter—you will benefit from developing a forms file of good models. To do this, save copies of similar, repetitive messages; copy models from letter books or handbooks such as this one; save well-written correspondence from others; and compose your own models when you can't find any other samples appropriate for your business.

Personalizing Forms

To make a form letter or memo appear more personal, use good-quality paper, sign the form in ink (do not use rubber stamps), and send it by first-class mail. Also, to help you decide whether to use a form and whether your present form letters and memos are adequate, consult the following checklist:

Form-Letter Effectiveness Checklist

	Yes	No
Is the form letter designed so that a typist can make typed fill-ins easily?	( )	( )
Has a test been made to see whether a file copy of the letter is actually needed or whether the prescribed number of copies can be reduced?	( )	( )
Is the letter easily understood on the first reading?	( )	( )

Is it free of old-fashioned letter language, such as "reference is made to," "you are advised that," and "examination of our records discloses"?( )　( )

Has a "usage" test been made to see whether it is practical to carry a printed stock?　( )　( )

Does the letter concern a routine business or informational matter?　( )　( )

Is there a mark to show the typist where to begin the address so that it will show in the window of an envelope?　( )　( )

Will the supply on hand be used up in a few months' time?　( )　( )

Is the letter identified in any way, for example, by a number printed in one of the corners?　( )　( )

If you were the person receiving the form letter, would you consider it effective and attractive? ( )　( )

Has a test been made of typed letters to see whether it is practical to replace any of them with form letters?　( )　( )

Has provision been made for reviewing all requests for form letters to make sure that unnecessary, poorly written, and poorly designed letters do not slip into print?　( )　( )

Do you have standards that you expect all form letters to meet?　( )　( )

Are form letters put into use by written instructions explaining when they are to be used, enclosures (if any) that should be made, and carbon-copy requirements?　( )　( )

Do you have a systematic way of numbering form letters?　( )　( )

When form letters become obsolete, are immediate instructions issued to discontinue their use and to remove old stock from supply cabinets and desks?　( )　( )

Source: National Archives and Record Service, Records Management Division, General Services Administration, Washington, D.C.

Note: A checkmark in the "No" column indicates the need for corrective action.

CHAPTER THIRTEEN

Preparing
Business Reports

Reports fill a variety of needs in the working world. The primary function is to inform. But reports may be written with different objectives in mind: to sell, to persuade, to debate, to explain, to solicit, and so on. Some reports follow a standard format and may even be submitted on a printed form; others are informal and may be prepared as a memo or letter; and some are formal, prepared according to a very specific format. All of them, however, involve—to some extent, at least—organization, research, writing, and final preparation. Since effective communication is vital to a successful career, you need to know the do's and don'ts of proper report writing.

TYPES OF REPORTS

Informal Reports

Very short reports may be prepared as a letter or memo on regular letterhead stationery. For details on writing style and letter format, review chapters 11 and 12, including the model memo reports in chapter 12. Letter or memo reports may be no more than a response to someone's request for information and may have a casual, conversational tone, but they should nevertheless provide all necessary facts in a logical sequence.

Some short reports, for example expense and time-study reports, must be submitted on standard forms. If your organization does not have its own forms, you can purchase standard forms at office-supply stores. Although a form requires abbreviated information, you must still use correct grammar and clear, concise statements.

When more is required than a letter or memo, but not as much as an extensive formal report, the short-style report is appropriate. This report is prepared on plain paper (not letterhead stationery) and resembles a formal report in its use of businesslike language and at least some of the parts found in a formal report. (See Formal Reports.) It will likely open with (1) a preliminary one- to two-paragraph summary of the report thesis, the findings, and your conclusions and recommendations; (2) a one- to three-paragraph introduction, including the history, objectives, and scope of the report; (3) the discussion and analysis in which you develop your theme and present your argument and associated documentation; (4) a brief statement of your conclusions and recommendations; and (5) possibly an appendix of supplementary material.

Formal Reports

Formal reports vary also and may omit some of the traditional parts, such as the report cover. Proposals for both public and private grants, for example, usually must be prepared according to the requirements of the funding agency. Often these requirements include a strict format that must be followed and perhaps even a printed form that must be used. But all formal reports must clearly and logically develop the theme with a forceful presentation, including good documentation (tests, statistics, and so on) and businesslike language and tone. Some or all of the following parts are appropriate in a formal report:

Cover. A wrapper that encloses the pages of the report; it gives information such as the report title, the date of the report, the name and job title of the preparer, and possibly the company name and location.

Flyleaf. A blank page inserted after the cover.

Title page. The first page of the report after the cover

Model Title Page

ARTIFICIAL-INTELLIGENCE APPLICATIONS

Prepared for
Harrison Ross, President
Ross Enterprises
1721 East Avenue
Pittsburgh, Pennsylvania 15213

Prepared by
Helen Jorgenson, Consultant
Computer Services, Inc.
22 Wilson Boulevard
Chicago, Illinois 60606

---

and flyleaf; it gives the report title, the date of the report, the name and job title of the preparer, possibly the preparer's company name and address, and the name, job title, and possibly the company name and address of the person to whom the report is submitted. Refer to the model on page 286.

Letter of transmittal. A cover letter typed on regular letterhead stationery; it may be part of the report, inserted immediately after the title page. The transmittal letter is always addressed to the person for whom the report is prepared. It identifies the report by title, explains the purpose of it, and briefly states important features, persons who contributed to it, and any other relevant facts, especially any information not given in the body of the report. It may conclude by offering to answer questions or provide further information. If the report includes a letter of authorization, it is placed immediately after the transmittal letter. If a foreword written by an outside advocate is included, it is placed immediately after the authorization letter.

Table of contents. An outline of the main sections (for example, the headings and subheadings) in the report and the associated page numbers; a long, formal report commonly follows the numbering style of books, with small roman numerals for the front-matter pages and arabic numerals for the rest of the report, beginning with the introduction.

Lists of illustrations and tables. A page(s) prepared in a format similar to that of the contents page; it lists the titles and captions of all tables and figures in the report, with associated page numbers. You may have one list for illustrations (photographs, charts, and diagrams) and another for tables (straight tabular matter).

Abstract. A summary or synopsis of the report, varying in length from a few paragraphs to a few hundred pages; it may be a condensed version of the information in the report, or it may discuss the objective of the report and what the report has accomplished. An abstract may be written in narrative form like a traditional book preface, or it may use subheads, with numbered lists or one or more paragraphs after each subhead.

Introduction. The statement of the problem that opens the report body; it should state briefly what the subject of the report is, the purpose of the report, and what conclusions the report will present.

Background. A section immediately after the introduction providing information needed to understand the main body; it may be called Methodology, Review of Research, Company Policy, Scope of the Study, History and Philosophy, or any other appropriate topic.

Data analysis. The main discussion of the problem; it develops the theme of the report in a logical, step-by-step manner. There may be numerous sections, with each one introduced by a descriptive subhead. Additional, supporting material should be referred to during the discussion and positioned in the appropriate places in the manuscript. (Refer to the descriptions of tables and illustrations in Manuscript Preparation.)

Conclusions and recommendations. A summary of the results of the study and suggestions for further action (if appropriate); it is often called Summary, Conclusions, Recommendations, or a combination such as Summary and Conclusions or Conclusions and Recommendations. These final sections are brief reminders of the purpose of the report, its key points, the logical conclusions reached, and what should be done (recommendations) based upon the results of the study. If appropriate, the language should be persuasive. It should be conclusive and original and should not merely repeat earlier sentences and paragraphs.

Appendix. Supporting material such as forms and tables; it consists of documentation that is not inserted in the body of the report. Usually, each appendix is numbered or lettered (for example, Appendix A: Sample Questionnaires).

Notes. A section where text and other footnotes are collected; it may consist of source and discussion notes or only source notes, with discussion notes typed at the bottoms of text pages. (See the discussion of references in Manuscript Preparation.)

Glossary. An alphabetical list of definitions of unfamiliar terms used in the report and other terms pertinent to the field of study; it is often a separate section but may be prepared as one of the appendixes (for example, Appendix E: Glossary).

Bibliography. Resources cited and those used in preparing the report; it may be called Selected Bibliography if it does not include all works cited in the report. Sometimes it is called Works Cited or Works Consulted.

Index. An alphabetical list of names, key subjects, and terms used in the report and the page numbers where they are found; it may be brief or detailed, with various levels of terms. Refer to the index at the end of this book for an example of style.

ORGANIZATION AND PLANNING

Planning Ahead

Report writing is not different from anything else in that you can work more efficiently and accurately if you know in advance what you need and what you must do. Haphazard, disorganized activity can lead to lost time, errors and omissions, and an inferior product.

Many people develop a block with any writing project, and for them the first step in report writing is the hardest. Planning ahead helps remove this block to getting started. The first step will be easier if you begin by making a list of things to do: Put the various steps to take in proper sequence and then follow them, one at a time—order books and other necessary material, set up interviews and make other appointments, go to the library, determine a format for the report, decide how to prepare it (by typewriter, computer, or other means), and so on.

Developing the Thesis

One of the first things to do is to develop a thesis: (1) decide what you want your message to accomplish, (2) determine to whom you want to direct the message, and (3) decide what and how much information to include. To clarify everything in your mind, put the three steps *in writing* and keep the list in front of you—along with your list of things to do—as you work.

Preparing an Outline

No one should ever begin researching a report without preparing an outline. First devise a topic outline. You may change the topics and their order later, but a preliminary outline gives you a guide to follow. For example:

A. Nondiscriminatory communication
   1. Racial and ethnic discrimination
   2. Discrimination against the handicapped
   3. Sexual discrimination

Your outline topics may serve as headings and subheadings when you start writing the text of the report.

When you are ready to start writing, convert your topic outline into a sentence outline. These sentences can be used as the opening under each topic in the final report. For example:

1. Racial and ethnic discrimination = The goal of every writer should be to eliminate racial and ethnic discrimination.
2. Discrimination against the handicapped = Focusing on a person's disability rather than capability is the worst form of discrimination against the handicapped.
3. Sexual discrimination = When you write with sex-

ual bias, you may be insulting 50 percent (or more) of the work force.

In most cases you will have to complete some or all of your research before you can convert your topic outline into a sentence outline. Once you reach the drafting stage, you can continue the conversion process: topics expanded into sentences, sentences expanded into paragraphs, paragraphs expanded into sections, and sections expanded into chapters.

RESEARCH

Sources of Information

Make a list of sources of information for your proposed topic: your own company files, library, and personnel; other companies; educational and research institutions; libraries and bookstores; professional and technical associations; local clubs; and so on. Depending on what you need and the source of the information, you may use various fact-finding methods and tools. For published material you may need paper, index cards, pen and pencil, and access to a copier; for interviews and on-site material, you may need a tape recorder and cassettes, a camera and film, a questionnaire form, and note-taking tools. Use your ingenuity in locating possible sources of information. Check the Yellow Pages of your telephone directory and ask others for suggestions.

Library Research

A substantial amount of information can be found in company, public, and specialized libraries. A library's card catalog will list published books, often by author, title, and subject. Various reference works (for example, *Reader's Guide to Periodical Literature*) index periodicals, and you can ask the reference librarian whether copies are available. Many libraries also keep clippings and pamphlets in *vertical files* (file cabinets). Ask your reference librarian for help in locating sources of information for the topic you are researching.

The following are the two principal library classification systems, although a particular library may deviate slightly from the basic pattern. The ten Dewey Decimal categories may be subdivided as needed (100, 110, 120, 120.1, 120.2, 120.3, and so on), and the twenty Library of Congress categories may be combined as needed (HG, MN, and so on). Additional numbers and letters indicate further subdivisions of categories.

Dewey Decimal System

000. General works
100. Philosophy
200. Religion
300. Sociology
400. Philology
500. Natural science
600. Useful arts
700. Fine arts
800. Literature
900. History

Library of Congress System

A. General works and polygraphy
B. Philosophy and religion
C. History and auxiliary sciences
D. History and topography outside the United States
E.,F. American history and topography
G. Geography and anthropology
H. Social sciences
J. Political sciences
K. Law
L. Education
M. Music
N. Fine arts
P. Language and literature
Q. Science
R. Medicine
S. Agriculture and plant and animal husbandry
T. Technology

U.   Military science
V.   Naval science
Z.   Library science and bibliography

The following are some of the reference works that you will find in a well-stocked library:

Encyclopedias and fact books. These references (for example, *McGraw-Hill Encyclopedia of Science and Technology*) provide a wide variety of descriptive information on almost any topic in any field.

Atlases. These references (for example, *Goode's World Atlas*) provide detailed maps of cities, states, provinces, countries, regions, and continents. Some of them offer information, such as climatic conditions, soil composition, topography, and various types of manufacturing and production.

Dictionaries. These references (for example, *Webster's Third New International Dictionary*) provide not only definitions but spellings, pronunciations, and other information about words and terms. Word books commonly omit the definitions and show spelling, word division, and often pronunciation.

Style books. These references (for example, *The Chicago Manual of Style*) describe proper capitalization, punctuation, citation, and other matters pertaining to the form of written material.

Directories. These references (for example, *Million Dollar Directory*) give names, addresses, and often other pertinent facts about people and organizations in different professions and areas of business activity.

Indexes. These references (for example, *Business Periodicals Index*) are guides to published material, providing author, titles, subjects, publication facts, and so on for material published in periodicals or as books.

Business and financial publications. These references (for example, *Federal Reserve Bulletin*) provide current business and financial facts.

Investment guides. These references (for example, Moody's manuals) provide facts about securities.

Computer Research

Databases. You can access electronic libraries known as *databases* from your own office if you have a telephone, the right computer equipment, and a modem. A *modem*, or modulator/demodulator, converts data into signals that travel over the telephone lines. Depending on the databases you access, you may receive a list of citations for the topic you want to research or both citations and abstracts (summaries) of the published works.

Database services are available by subscription and/or hourly-rate charges. Ask your local reference librarian for a source of current database names and addresses. Also, many computer magazines regularly report on new database services. Some services provide information about specific subjects only (for example, LEXIS—legal citations and abstracts). Other services have more subjects, and some services even provide access to numerous databases (for example, DIALOG).

Computer-search services. Some firms provide computer-search services (check your Yellow Pages), and libraries that have a computer sometimes offer such services too. Usually, you give the organization a list of key words pertaining to your research topic; these words are then coded and fed into the computer, which prints out a list of related reference sources. Computer-search services are especially useful when you need to locate numerous sources or hard-to-find sources.

The Interview

Before you conduct an interview you need to locate people who are likely to have the information you need and then persuade them to see you. If you are successful in arranging an interview, you need to be fully prepared *before* meeting your subject. Prepare a questionnaire and take with you pen, pencils, paper, and sufficient other note-taking material. Ask for permission to record the session, and be certain your recorder and cassettes are working properly. Also ask for permission to take any desired pictures and be certain your camera and film are ready. (See the sample Model Release, Photographic Release, and Interview Release.)

Learn as much as you can about your subject in advance and try to put the person at ease immediately. Ask concrete questions about specific actions or situations (*not* "Tell me something about XYZ"). Be persistent if you need more facts, but continue questioning courteously so that you do not antagonize the subject. Take backup notes even if you are using a recorder. If you plan to quote the subject verbatim, use an interview-release form. Follow up later with a phone call—or even another appointment—if some points are not clear or if you suspect inaccuracies.

WRITING

Preparing Drafts

After you have prepared a topic outline, conducted your research, and converted your topic outline into a sentence outline (see Organization and Planning), you are ready to start writing. Many people try to get an initial draft written as quickly as possible and deal with style, correct spelling, and other matters later when they are ready to polish and refine the rough draft. Other people like to write slowly and edit and polish as they write.

For matters of style (punctuation, capitalization, spelling, and word division), refer to chapter 11. In addition, follow these basic language guidelines:

1. Use short words and short sentences as much as possible.

Model Release

TO:_____

_____

_____

    I hereby give _____ the absolute right and permission to copyright and/or publish and/or resell photographic portraits or pictures of me, or in which I may be included in whole or in part, for art, advertising, trade, or any other lawful purpose whatsoever.

    I hereby waive any right that I may have to inspect and/or approve the finished product or the advertising copy that may be used in connection therewith or the use to which it may be applied.

    I hereby release, discharge, and agree to save _____ _____ from any liability by virtue of any blurring, distortion, alteration, optical illusion, or use in composite form, whether intentional or otherwise, that may occur or be produced in the making of said pictures or in any processing tending toward the completion of the finished product.

Date_____   Model_____

Guardian_____   Address_____

Witness_____   _____

Photographic Release

Dear_____.

May we please have permission to reproduce the photograph(s) indicated below for inclusion in _____
_____
and for any and all revisions, adaptations, and subsidiary and/or derivative rights, uses, or works of the Work for all commercial and trade purposes in perpetuity throughout the world.

In signing this permission, you warrant and agree to hold us harmless that you are the absolute owner of the photograph(s) and the use contemplated by this permission will not infringe upon the copyright or any other right of third parties.

Sincerely,

_____

MATERIAL TO BE REPRODUCED:_____
_____
_____
_____
_____

Permission is granted by: _____ Date: _____

Form of Copyright Acknowledgment:_____
_____
_____
_____

Interview Release

TO:

_____

_____

_____

I, _____, have examined _____

by _____ and affirm that I am quoted
accurately in the manuscript.

Date_____   Address_____

Signature_____   _____

2. Use active sentences ("We tested the machine," *not* "The machine was tested by us").

3. Use transition words (*therefore, however, moreover,* and so on) as needed to make one sentence (or paragraph) slide smoothly into another.

4. Use an effective lead, or topic, sentence for each paragraph.

5. Use brief descriptive headings for sections.

6. Use clear, concise words (avoid weak, vague terms such as *revolves around* and *centers on*).

7. Be specific (for example, say "savings of five hundred dollars" *not* "substantial savings").

8. Avoid pretentious language (such as *commence* for *begin* and *utilize* for *use*).

9. Avoid trite expressions (such as "permit me to say that" and "wish to state").

10. Use nondiscriminatory language (such as "Asian and black heritages" instead of "disadvantaged minorities").

11. Use italics sparingly (for words being defined; for unfamiliar foreign terms; for legal cases; for craft and vessels; for genera, subgenera, species, and subspecies; and for titles of publications, long poems, plays and motion pictures, paintings, operas, and long musical compositions); underscore the words that you want to be italicized in the final, printed version.

12. Do not use verbatim quotes merely to avoid the effort of composing your own statements.

13. Beware of libel—a false or malicious statement in writing that injures another person's reputation; examine your draft for unintentional slurs against race or religion. Check with an attorney if you have any doubts.

14. Consult the applicable statutes in regard to invasion of privacy when you intend to describe, photograph, quote, or otherwise portray someone in printed material and always obtain releases for use of photographs and other material (see the sample release forms in this chapter).

Use of Quoted Material

Prepare quotes running more than eight lines as *extracts*, that is, separate, indented blocks of copy. Use double quotation marks at the beginning and end of quotes *within* the text, but do not use opening and closing quotes for extracts. Any words of your own that you insert in a precise quotation must be enclosed in brackets, not parentheses. If a word in the original is misspelled, write [*sic*] after the word. If you want to emphasize something write [emphasis mine] after the passage to which you added your own underlining.

Use ellipsis points (dots, or periods) to show omitted material. For example:

> Do not indent the first line of an extract if it falls in the *middle* of the first paragraph quoted [emphasis mine]. Use three dots to show material . . . omitted in the middle of a sentence. Use four dots to show material omitted at the end of a sentence. . . . Also use four dots to show sentences missing between paragraphs. . . .
> . . . use three dots and indent the first line to show the omission of the first part of the paragraph. . . . According to the *XYZ Style Book*, "When four dots are used, their [*sic*] is no space before the first dot since it represents a sentence period." Use three dots at the end of a sentence when it is a sentence fragment such as . . .

Use quotation marks sparingly in general text. For example, do not put words following *so-called* in quotes; do not enclose general use of *yes* and *no* in quotes ("She said yes"); and do not put colloquial, slang, or inexact terms in quotes when the meaning is obvious ("Management was busy putting out fires").

Quotation marks are necessary, however, to enclose titles of articles, essays, unpublished material such as a dissertation, short poems, short musical works, and television shows. Put periods and commas *inside* quotation marks, but put semicolons and colons *outside* quotation marks.

Editing

There are two popular sayings about writing: "Amateurs write and professionals rewrite," and "Amateurs check things once and professionals check things twice." Editing and revision are clearly as important as the initial writing. This step is usually the one that transforms the basic information into logical, readable, consistent, and accurate prose.

Editing checklist. To edit your rough draft, thoroughly reread it several times, looking for different problems each time. First, you might check the consistency of style (punctuation, capitalization, and so on) and format (margins, subheads, and so on); next, you might double-check—one or a few things at a time—the position and sequence of front matter, text, and back matter; the numbering and position of illustrations (including captions) and tables; the numbering and position of footnotes and bibliography entries; the appropriateness of chapter titles and subheads; the effectiveness of the opening and closing; the smoothness of sentence and paragraph transitions; the accuracy of grammar and word choice; and anything else pertinent to your report.

Make up a checklist of things you want to review and check off each one when you're certain the report has no further need for improvement in each area. As you edit and polish your writing, keep a picture of your reader in mind. Is your language suitable for the audience? Have you written clearly and simply, avoiding the temptation to impress readers with your great intellect and knowledge of long, unfamiliar words and complex, confusing concepts? If you learn to be critical of your own writing, you will lessen the risk that your readers will be critical of it.

Editing by computer. Editing by computer saves the time otherwise spent retyping all or many pages of the draft. With a computer (and word processing software) or a word processor you can add, delete, reword, and reposition words, sections, block of copy, or full pages—observing your changes as you make them on the monitor (televisionlike screen)—without retyping an entire page. Instead, the computer records the specific changes on each page, adjusts all other copy (all pages) accordingly, renumbers all of the pages, and signals the printer to print out the revised draft. Many printers will print out several copies of a document. (See chapter 7 for more about word processing.)

Typemarking. When a report manuscript is sent to a printer (or compositor) for typesetting, someone must select typefaces, type sizes, and other features of the intended format. If this is not done in your organization or by someone you hire to do it (for example, a freelance designer or editor), the printer will make the choices for you.

To avoid an appearance you don't like, ask the printer for sample typefaces and sizes. Examine other printed material (this book, for example) to see how chapter titles, subheads, footnotes, and other elements can be set, including the use of bold, regular, and italic letters. Notice spacing around headings and between lines (leading). Discuss these matters with the printer and ask for assistance in marking the manuscript so that it will be set in the style you prefer.

MANUSCRIPT PREPARATION

Format

Most reports are prepared on white bond paper, 8½ by 11 inches, twenty-pound substance. Erasable paper should never be used for the finished copy, since it smudges so easily.

Pica is larger than elite type and hence easier to read. Similarly, letters in ten-pitch type are spaced farther apart than in twelve-pitch type and are easier to read. But if space must be conserved, you may prefer the smaller, tighter style of elite, twelve-pitch type.

Use left and right margins of about 1¼ inches and top and bottom margins of 1 to 1¼ inches. If the report is to be bound, be certain to increase the margin by the amount of the binding. For example, if you want left and right margins of 1½ inches and the binding on the left will use up ½ inch, set your left margin at 2 inches.

Add extra space above and below subheads. For example:

MAJOR SUBHEAD

Minor Subhead

Run-in subhead. This example has two line spaces above the major head and one line space above and below the flush-left minor subhead.

Indent paragraphs five to ten spaces and indent the complete left margin of extracts—verbatim quotes that run eight lines or more. (See Use of Quoted Material.) Use parallel subheads within a section, for example, (1) Researching a Report, (2) Writing a Report, and (3) Typing a Report, *not* (1) Researching a Report, (2) The Writing Process, and (3) How to Type a Report. Underscore a word to signify italics. But use underlining, quotation marks, and all capital letters sparingly, since too much of these forms of emphasis is annoying and distracting and often makes reading more difficult.

Computer specifications. Format specifications may all be set at one time with a computer (or word processor). You can type in the desired specifications (margin width, position of page numbers, space between lines and paragraphs, and so on) before you begin typing the report copy, and the computer will automatically arrange everything on each page accordingly.

Although this ability to format in advance is a timesaving feature, you still may have to print out and examine several pages, changing some of the specifications each time, before you are satisfied with the overall appearance. Once it suits you, the rest of the report can be prepared with little or no format adjustment. With certain software you can save the specifications and recall

them easily for future use, which means you won't have
to work out the design details the next time you have
another report to prepare.

Illustrations

Preparation guidelines. Photographs, charts, diagrams,
graphs, and other graphic material are all treated as
illustrations, as opposed to tabular items, which are treated
as tables. Reports that have halftones (photographs), and
complex artwork will likely be typeset and printed. But
whether you type (computer or typewriter) a report or
have it typeset and printed, several rules apply to both
situations.

1. Each figure must have a caption (title) and may
have a separate legend (brief description or commen-
tary). Some figures use combined caption-legend, for
example: "Figure 8.5. Population Trends, 1980–85. The
growth pattern established early in 1980 and 1981 accel-
erated during 1982 and continued through 1983."

2. When part or all of the figure is taken from another
source, permission must be secured from the copyright
owner, and the figure should have a source note crediting
the origin and positioned immediately beneath the illustrations. (The model table in this chapter has an example
of a source note that could also be used with a photograph or drawing.)

3. Each figure must be mentioned in the text (for
example, "See figure 7.3") to alert the reader that an
illustration accompanies the discussion.

4. Use consecutive numbering throughout the report
or use a double-enumeration system in each chapter, for
example: Chapter 1—Figure 1.1 (or 1-1), Figure 1.2, Figure 1.3; Chapter 2—Figure 2.1, Figure 2.2, Figure 2.3.

5. When the final version of a report is being prepared
by typewriter or computer, you may position illustrations
(a) within the text at appropriate places, (b) in groups at
the ends of appropriate chapters, or (c) all together in
one group after the last appendix. When a report is being
sent to a printer, original artwork and photographs should

be kept apart from the report manuscript, although photocopies may be placed within the report as described in (a), (b), and (c) merely to show position. (Type a separate list of captions and legends to accompany original photographs and artwork going to a printer.)

6. Eliminate all purely cosmetic illustrations—those that are unnecessary and do not significantly support the text discussion.

7. On the back of each original illustration going to a printer, or on a tissue or acetate overlay, note the page number where the piece is first mentioned in the text. You may also write other instructions to the printer on such an overlay, but do not press down on the face of the illustration while writing the instructions, because the crease may show up in reproduction.

Photographs. Submit photographs as 8- by 10-inch black-and-white glossies unless the report is going to be published in full color. If you want only a portion of a photograph to be used, put small lines (crop marks) in the white border of the photograph with a grease pencil to show the area you want the printer to use. Remember that photographs reduce proportionately. For instance, if you want an 8- by 10-inch-wide print to fit a space 2 inches wide, you will get an 80 percent reduction in *both* dimensions: (1) *width*: 10.0 inches minus 8.0 inches, or 80 percent, equals 2.0 inches; (2) *height*: 8.0 inches minus 6.4 inches, or 80 percent, equals 1.6 inches.

Line drawings. Charts, graphs, diagrams, and other line drawings do not have tonal values like a photograph. They may consist of pen-and-ink drawings prepared by an artist or computer-rendered drawings. Submit all such artwork to a printer in clear, sharp lines on a clean, white background. More complex line drawings may contain Benday (shaded) patterns or other variations (you often see such shadings in pie, bar, and column charts and in other graphic comparisons).

Tables

Numbers and titles. Unless a table is very brief and simple, it should have a number and a title. Type the number flush left, with the title on the same line or two line spaces below the number. Type subheads to a title, such as "In Millions," in parentheses flush left, two line spaces beneath the title. Place a single horizontal rule between the table title and the column headings.

Table 16.3

Sales Volume by Country
(In Millions of Dollars)

Number the tables with arabic numerals consecutively throughout the manuscript or use a double-enumeration system within each chapter: Table 1.1 (or 1-1), Table 1.2, Table 2.1, Table 2.2, and so on. Number appendix tables separately (A.1, A.2, B.1, B.2, and so on). Refer to each table by number (or letter) in the text (for example, "see Table 5.4") in proper numerical order.

Small unnumbered tables may be typed within the text discussion. Larger tables are best typed on separate sheets and positioned at the ends of appropriate chapters or all together after the last appendix (after the illustrations if they are also grouped together here).

Column heads. Each column in a table should have a heading, except for the left-hand list (*stub*), which may not need one. The stub heading should be singular, but other column heads may be singular or plural. Type subheads such as "Thousands" and "%" in parentheses at the end of the column heading or on the first line below all other words in the column heading. Separate the levels of a decked head with a horizontal rule (see Model Table). Capitalize all important words in column headings, and place a single horizontal rule beneath the headings to separate them from the table body.

Indent subheads under a stub item two or three spaces (see Model Table). Indent the word *Total* at the end of

Table 7.9

Sales of Keyboard Templates by Region, 1985–88
(In Thousands of Dollars)

| | Annual Sales | | | |
	1985	1986	1987	1988
East				
Coastal[a]	$ 50	$ 61	$ 64	$ 65
Inland[b]	43	40	50	50
West	76	80	80	91
North	41	39	44	47
South	27	29	30	36
Totals	$237	$257	$268	$289

Source: Computer Aids Society, CAS Bulletin 14 (1988): 3–4. Reprinted with permission.

Note: Figures for template sales are based on annual reports from members of the Computer Aids Society and do not include sales by nonmember companies.

a. "Coastal" refers to all states actually bordering on the Atlantic Ocean.

b. "Inland" refers to all states east of the Mississippi River excluding those bordering on the Atlantic Ocean.

the stub two or three spaces more than the word immediately above it. Except for proper nouns, capitalize only the first word in a stub item.

Table body. Double-space the table body and center short items in a column, but type long items flush left within each column. Align all figures at the decimal point and put commas in numbers of one thousand or more (*5,782*).

Type a % or $ symbol only after or before the top figure in a column, except a $ sign is usually repeated in the final row of "total" figures. Use either an extra line space or a ruled line above the final row of figures representing column totals. When no data are available for a particular item, center a dash (two hyphens) in the appropriate blank space. Use a footnote to explain deviations you have made or other discrepancies in figures (such as rounding off numbers). Type a final rule between the body of the table and the footnotes beneath it.

Notes. If the information is not original, type a table source note flush left (or with a paragraph indent), double-spaced, beneath the body of the table (see Model Table). Remember to request permission to use the table data from the copyright owner.

General table notes followed by other notes are also positioned flush left (or with a paragraph indent) immediately beneath the source note. Use a general note, not a numbered or lettered footnote, with remarks pertaining to the table title. The footnotes may have numbers, letters, or symbols (1, 2, 3; a, b, c; *, **, ***). But avoid using footnote letters such as *a, b,* and *c* in the body of a table already containing other small letters, and avoid using numbers when the table body already has numbers in it.

References

Citations and discussion notes can be handled in several ways: bottom-of-page notes, end-of-chapter note sections, a single end-of-report note section, a name-date reference list.

Notes. Number footnotes consecutively. The number in the text is typed as a raised (superior) figure. Always place this number *at the end* (never in the middle) of a sentence and *outside* the punctuation marks, for example: "Four million people voted between ten and eleven in the morning."[1] The number preceding the footnote itself is usually typed "on line" (aligned with the note text).

You may type discussion footnotes apart from the reference-source footnotes. Give discussion notes letters (*a, b, c*) or a sequence of symbols, (*, **, ***) and place them at the bottom of appropriate text pages. (If the discussion notes are very long, however, they should be typed in a notes section, not at the foot of text pages.) Number and collect the reference notes in a notes section at the end of each chapter or at the end of the report (end notes) after the last appendix or other supporting material (illustrations and tables).

To avoid numerous repetitive notes consisting only of different page numbers or ibid., give a numberd note the first time cited and add a statement to that note such as: "Page numbers for further reference to this work will be cited in the text."

The following are sample numbered notes, including succeeding references to the same work (see Model Table for an example of table footnotes):

1. David Marsh et al., *Office Practices*, 3 vols. (New York: Watts Publishers, 1982), 1:211.

2. Ibid., 210.

3. Neil Costa, "Word Processing," *Computers Today* 3, no. 16 (June 1986): 16–17; idem, "Effects of the Computer Revolution in One-Person Offices" (M.A. thesis, Doyle University, 1986), 62–63.

4. Marsh et al., *Office Practices*, 1:5.

5. Editorial, *Washington Post*, 7 July 1985.

6. Henry Farraday, "The Modern Office" (Paper presented at the annual meeting of the Office Worker's Association, Milwaukee, Wisconsin, March 16, 1983); Henry Farraday and Edna Johnson, eds., *Control Rooms*, 16 mm., 30 min. (Distributed by Business Films, Inc., Phoenix, 1984.)

Unnumbered notes. General notes are used to acknowledge someone's contribution or to refer to the source of an entire chapter or other division in the report. This type of note should be typed as an unnumbered footnote at the bottom of the first page of the chapter or division, or it may immediately precede note 1 on the list of numbered chapter notes or end notes. Credit notes with a copyright notice are usually typed at the bottom of the opening page of the chapter or division. The copyright owner from whom you request permission to use the outside material often specifies the wording you must use. (See Model Table for an example of a table source note.) Otherwise, the following examples show possible wording for credit lines:

Adapted from J. O. Harris, *Office Lighting* (Boston: Systems Publications, 1982), 4–21, by permission of the author and publisher. Copyright 1982 by J. O. Harris.

Portions of this chapter were first published in "Business Theories," *New Business Digest* 7, no. 5 (1981): 14. Reprinted with permission.

I gratefully acknowledge the assistance of Marcia Simpson in the preparation of this section.

This study was supported by Grant I-4A70-62, Business Technology Foundation, Washington, D.C.

Ask your employer or publisher to specify the maximum number of words that you may quote from another source without securing permission from the copyright owner (for example, less than one hundred words from an article or less than three hundred words from a book). Even when permission is not needed, a text footnote or table or figure source note is nevertheless required for any material taken from another source.

Reference lists. Instead of using numbered notes sections or bottom-of-page footnotes you may use an author-date system of citation. With this style you cite sources in the text in parentheses by name and year of publication, for example: (Jones 1982, 2:17). The 2:17 refers to volume 2, page 17. If there had been two 1982 Jones citations, you would arrange them alphabetically by title and label the first one 1982a and the second 1982b. Use a long dash, as shown below, for the name in additional entries (books authored are arranged alphabetically first, followed by books edited in alphabetical order).

A name-date text-citation system requires alphabetical lists of sources cited at the ends of the chapters or one list after the appendixes. Since this is strictly a source list, discussion notes will have to be typed at the bottoms of text pages or in a separate notes section.

You may call a name-date reference list References, Bibliography, Works Cited, or any other appropriate title. A list titled Select (or Selected) Bibliography would not be appropriate since it implies that not all works cited in the text are included in the list. You may also have one alphabetical name-date list titled References or Works Cited and another alphabetical list titled Bibliography or Select(ed) Bibliography.

The following are typical entries in an alphabetical reference list:

Costa, Neil. 1986a. "Effects of the Computer Revolution in One-Person Offices." M.A. thesis, Doyle University.
———. 1986b. "Word Processing." *Computers Today* 3, no. 16 (June): 16–17.
Editorial. 1985. *Washington Post,* 7 July.
Farraday, Henry. 1983. "The Modern Office." Paper presented at the annual meeting of the Office Worker's Association, Milwaukee, Wisconsin, March 16.
Farraday, Henry, and Edna Johnson, eds. 1984. *Control Rooms.* 16mm, 30 min. Distributed by Business Films, Inc., Phoenix.
Marsh, David, et al. 1982. *Office Practices,* 3 vols. New York: Watts Publishers.

Bibliography. If you include an alphabetical list of sources in addition to any name-date reference list, be certain that full data is given for each entry here and in any text footnote citation corresponding to the bibliography entry (the data in footnotes and bibliography must be consistent). Several entries by the same author may be arranged alphabetically or chronologically, with books authored first and those edited last. Use a long dash for the name with entries of additional titles by the same author, as shown below.

Use the title Select(ed) Bibliography when the list does not include all sources cited in the text and footnotes. In other cases, you may call the list Bibliography, Works Cited, or Works Consulted. Follow this style:

Costa, Neil. "Effects of the Computer Revolution in One-Person Offices." M.A. thesis, Doyle University, 1986.
———. "Word Processing." *Computers Today* 3, no. 16 (June 1986): 16–17.
Editorial. *Washington Post,* 7 July 1985.
Farraday, Henry. "The Modern Office." Paper presented at

the annual meeting of the Office Workers' Association, Milwaukee, Wisconsin, March 16, 1983.

Farraday, Henry, and Edna Johnson, eds. *Control Rooms*. 16 mm, 30 min. Distributed by Business Films, Inc., Phoenix, 1984.

Marsh, David, et al. *Office Practices*. 3 vols. New York: Watts Publishers, 1982.

Index

To prepare an index you need a copy of the finished version of the report: a copy of the final typed version or, if the report has been typeset, a copy of the page proofs. The typed or typeset material must show the final arrangement of text and illustrations with final page numbers.

Selecting index terms. Underline all key words on the typeset page proofs (or on a photocopy of a typed report). You may notice the same term appearing on several pages. Continue underlining the term on *each* succeeding page. In the margins make a note of general subjects that you want to include. Later you can decide which words should be main headings and which should be subentries. Or you can make some of these decisions while you are underlining. You might, for example, put one check mark by terms that should be main entries and two marks by terms that should be subentries.

Transferring terms to cards. Transfer each underlined term and each subject you wrote in the margins to small index cards. Write each term on a *separate* card and note on the card the page number where you underlined the term. Double-check each page number before you set one card aside to go on to the next. If you already marked the proofs to distinguish between main entries and subentries, transfer the same marking to each card along with the term and page number.

Alphabetizing the cards. Put all cards in alphabetical order. You will likely discover several cards that have the same term but different page numbers, for example, *Management* 5, *Management* 31, *Management* 27. Combine them into one card: *Management* 5, 27, 31.

Separate the cards into main entries and subentries. If you marked the proofs to show this and transferred the check marks to the cards, you can easily distinguish single check marks (main entries) from double check marks (subentries). If you did not make this distinction on the proofs, make a decision now and alphabetize the cards you select as subentries behind appropriate main-entry cards. You may, for example, take the card that states *Management* 5, 27, 31, and collect behind it four other cards:

Management 5, 27, 31
    Management policies 7, 9–10
    Management theories 14, 26–27, 31
    Management training, 5, 11
    Supervision 3, 13, 24, 30

Editing the cards. After all of your entries are arranged alphabetically with subentries grouped alphabetically behind appropriate main-entry cards, edit the cards before you type the index. Check spelling, wording, capitalization, and so on, and change entries to subentries or vice versa as needed. You may, for instance, want to make "Supervision" a separate main entry rather than a subentry under "Management." After editing, the final wording of the above example might look like this:

Management. *See also* Supervision.
    policies, 7, 9–10
    theories, 14, 26–27, 31
    training, 5, 11

Typing the index. If the index is to become part of a typed rather than typeset report, type it on the same type of paper as the rest of the report, probably twenty-pound white bond, 8½ by 11 inches. Type main entries flush left and indent subentries three to four spaces. Double-space the index (unless the report is single-spaced) and continue numbering it along with the rest of the report. See Format for additional details (margins, position of page numbers, and so on).

If you are submitting an index to a printer for typesetting, type it double-spaced and number it as a separate manuscript, beginning with 1. Proofread the typed index against the edited cards and make final adjustments and corrections *before* you submit the manuscript for typesetting.

TYPESETTING

After your manuscript has been edited and typemarked, it is ready for typesetting. If you do not have an in-house typesetting and print shop, request quotes from three outside typesetters or printers (ask to see other work they have done and names of other customers). You may decide to deal with separate typesetting and printing firms, although it is often more economical and convenient to have typesetting and printing handled at one location.

Cold Type

Copy prepared by typewriter, word processor, or computer is often referred to as cold type. It can be photographed directly and an offset printing plate prepared from the negatives. Also included in this category is photocomposition. Modern electronic machines have a typewriterlike keyboard, and images created are transmitted to paper or film. The final copy can be photographed for printing the same as in typewriter composition. Cold type such as typewriter composition may be less expensive and faster than hot type, but the quality is sometimes inferior, depending on the equipment used. Compare samples of both processes before making your selection.

Hot Type

Methods of composition that cast metal type such as Linotype and Monotype are referred to as hot type. Linotype machines produce solid lines of type cast in a molten type metal, forming a slug that is dropped into a galley (tray). Thus the entire line has to be reset to correct an error. The Monotype process, sometimes more expensive than Linotype, casts single letters and assembles them into lines in a galley.

PROOFREADING

Galley Proofs

After the report has been typeset the printer (or typesetter) will provide *galley proofs*, long sheets of typeset material without the illustrations, running heads, and final page breaks. These sheets are used by customers to proofread the typeset copy. They can also be cut apart and pasted onto page-size sheets to prepare a *dummy*, a page-by-page layout of the proposed publication.

To proofread the galleys, mark corrections in the margins using the symbols shown in the chart of proofreader marks below. Avoid rewriting at this stage, since changes are expensive once copy is set into type. But if you must add material, put a caret in the text and note in the margin what is to be inserted. Use a separate sheet for the new copy if it is too long to fit in the galley margins.

Proofreader Chart

In Margin	In Text	Meaning
ℰ	letters	Delete.
ℰ̃	letters	Delete and close up.
stet.	writing ~~reported~~	Let it stand.
no #	chapters (Examples show	No paragraph.
#	editingand	Add space.
out; sc	national of the	Something missing; see copy.

In Margin	*In Text*	*Meaning*
sp. out	Ⓢpeople	Spell out.
◠	info⌒rmation	Close up.
⊏	⊏ the division	Move left.
⊐	⊐he division	Move right.
tr	ind⤺ctive	Transpose.
‖	‖tell the	Line up, or align.
	client and	
¶	editing ⌐However	New paragraph.
?	͜1986	Question to author.
?	Is it true ∧	Insert question mark.
!	Great ∧	Insert exclamation mark.
/=/	non ═American	Insert hyphen.
ˇ/ˇ	as she said ∧Today ∧	Insert quotation marks.
↑	revision ∧however	Insert semicolon.
↑	the following copy ∧	Insert colon.
∧	blue ∧ red ∧ and	Insert comma.
	green	
⊙	this report ∧	Insert period.
∨	the readers ∨	Insert apostrophe.
	viewpoint	
b	✗ook	Change to b.
caps (or ═)	Summary	Set in capital letters.
lc	P̸REFACE	Set in lowercase letters.
bf (or ⁓)	Writing and Editing	Set in boldface type.
ital (or —)	Writing Handbook	Set in italic type.
s.c. (or ═)	a.m. or p.m.	Set in small capital letters.
c. + s.c.	Editing Guide	Set in caps and small caps.
∨∨∨	k ∨e∨y ∨topics	Correct spacing.
▭	▭Open the	Indent one em.
	discussion	
(rom.)	*Introduction*	Change to roman type.
③	footnote ∨3	Set as superior number.
①	B ∧R	Set as inferior number.
[/]	∧a + b∧	Insert brackets.
(/)	∧a + b∧	Insert parentheses.
⅟M	and chapters ⌢M these	one-em dash.

Source: From *The Practical Writer's Guide: An Easy Access Source Book*, by Mary A. De Vries. Copyright © 1986 by Mary A. De Vries. Reprinted by arrangement with New American Library, New York, New York.

Page Proofs

After the proofread galleys have been corrected, the printer will provide page proofs on which the copy is divided into final pages with running heads, page numbers, footnotes, and so on in the proper position. Usually, boxes are drawn or blank spaces are shown to indicate the place where illustrations will appear in the final product.

Page proofs, like galley proofs, should be corrected in the margins using proofreader marks. Check whether pages are of equal length; that no short line (widow) appears at the top of a page; that heads, page numbers, and figure captions are correct; and so on.

Final Proofs

Repros. The corrected page proofs are prepared as reproduction proofs (often called repros) on a coated white paper suitable for photographing. This is the last chance to make corrections before preparations for printing are made, although changes are costly at this stage.

Press proofs. Negative proofs or press proofs are the final stage before printing. These proofs are commonly prepared on a sensitized paper that may cause the images to be brown, blue, or some other color. Negative or press proofs show the actual illustrations as well as the copy and should be checked for completeness and position of material before approving the proof for printing.

PRINTING

After you have approved the final proof (a negative or press proof), your report is ready for printing. If you did get printing quotes in preparation for typesetting, request three quotes now from prospective printers. Look at samples of their work and ask for names of other customers. Also ask to see samples of text and cover paper as well as an ink chart if your project will be in color.

Inquire about the different binding methods too (spiral, glue, side or saddle stitching, and so on).

If you want to copyright your work, contact the Library of Congress in Washington, D.C., and ask for free copyright forms and instructions. For copyright to be effective, your work must contain the notice: © 19XX by XYZ Company. The work must be properly registered upon publication (before it is disseminated and falls into the public domain).

Offset

In offset lithography a photograph negative of the reproduction proof is used to prepare an offset plate. This plate is inked to make an impression on paper. Since the offset method uses plates made by photographing material, a great variety of needs can be accommodated. Ordinarily typed copy, for instance, can be photographed and printed on an offset press. Quality varies according to the original copy and the particular offset press.

Letterpress

The letterpress method uses a relief principle. Type and illustrations are prepared as raised surfaces (such as a wood or linoleum cut), which are inked and pressed against the paper to make an impression. Letterpress printing can be used for newspapers, magazines, books, and a variety of material.

Gravure

The gravure process is based on the intaglio principle. Instead of raised surfaces, depressions are cut into a plate. The ink, which is wiped from the surface of the plate, stays in the depressions and these images are pressed onto the paper. Gravure work is often used for color reproduction and specialty jobs such as label printing.

CHAPTER FOURTEEN

Handling
Publicity Material

Businesses regularly publicize their activities. A manufacturer might publicize the development of a new product or new form of technology. A service establishment might publicize the opening of another store or a change in its service. The opportunities to make the public aware of an organization are numerous. Job promotions and retirements can be announced, a business-social event can be reported, a contribution to a worthy cause or some form of community service can be publicized, and so on.

Organizations that need customer or client patronage and public support should take advantage of every possible opportunity to report favorable or informative activity to the outside world through articles, press releases, letters, brochures, print and broadcast advertisements and public service announcements, and any other form of message transmission.

Specialists are often retained to prepare material such as newspaper and magazine ads or broadcast spots. A large firm may have its own advertising and public relations departments or may retain an outside agency. Many agencies specialize in either advertising or public relations; others handle both at least in part since the line is often blurred between the two fields.

Usually, one associates *advertising* with a paid announcement, particularly with messages that ask the reader or listener to buy a product or service. One associates *public relations* with an introduction of something to the public, particularly with indirect sales efforts such as building a favorable public image or promoting a cause. One associates *publicity* with efforts to attract public attention by disseminating information or promotional material. But no matter how the means of reaching the public is classified, office personnel should be aware of the types of publicity that will help them gain the good-will, patronage, and support of customers, clients, and the general public.

PRESS RELEASES

Anyone can write a press release (also called news release). You don't even need special letterhead stationery, although it might help to catch the eye of a busy editor if you have stationery that boldly states *PRESS (or NEWS) RELEASE* at the top. However, you can also use your regular business letterhead; either way, the message must follow the standard release format.

Editors, who deal with vast amounts of incoming material while rushing to meet a deadline, do not have time to untangle garbled prose presented in an unfamiliar format. Since publications usually have much more newsworthy material than they can use, you need to do everything possible to encourage editors to select your release for publication. This includes presenting your news in a format they prefer and paying particular attention to the submission deadlines for each issue or edition.

Mailing Lists

Compiling the list. Compile a press-release address list of appropriate magazines, newspapers, wire services, newsletters, radio and television stations, and any other logical target for your information. Public relations writers commonly distinguish between the *trade press* (publications devoted to a specific industry or profession) and the *popular press* (publications and broadcast stations serving the general public).

Ask your local reference librarian for a copy of a trade directory such as *Ayer's Directory of Newspapers and Periodicals* or *Standard Rate and Data* for names and addresses of journals, newspapers, and other publications. For specialized coverage, look for a directory for the specific area involved. If you want to reach the Catholic press, for instance, check the *Catholic Press Directory*. For radio and television stations, consult a source such as the *Radio and TV Directory*. Your reference librarian can tell you which sources of addresses are available in your local library.

Addressing the envelopes. When you know the names of publication editors or station directors, use them. Otherwise, select a title in preparing an address. For instance, send releases for radio and television stations to the news director if there is one or otherwise the program director. Depending on the type of news item you are preparing, address releases for newspapers to the city or state editor, or if the newspaper has business, industrial, and other specialty editors, select the appropriate category. Do the same thing with periodicals—select an appropriate title for the type of news item you have. You wouldn't, for example, send an item of local interest to a state editor. Nor would you send an item about a new development in food preservation to a political editor.

Use the same care in selecting the publication itself for your list. If your release is about safety in the transportation industry, there is no point in sending the release to a gourmet-cooking magazine. If different releases that you send are appropriate for different publications, compile a full list and separate or code the addresses according to the type of message. For example, you might send news of a high-level executive appointment to more publications than news of a technical-engineering breakthrough. If your list is maintained by computer or magnetic-tape typewriter, you can easily code it so that addresses of certain targeted publications can be retrieved instantly.

Release Files

If you send numerous releases, keep both a chronological file of the releases and an index-card file arranged by subject (company promotion, new product/service, and so on). On each subject card, type the dates and a capsule of any other essential information pertaining to all releases about that subject. Editors may contact you later for more information about a product or an executive promotion. If you have a subject cross-file, you can quickly look up the appropriate card to find the release date and then locate a copy of the release by date in the chronological files.

Format

Type a press release double spaced on twenty-pound white bond paper, 8½ by 11 inches, with a margin of about 1¼ inches on each side. Use only one side to the page. Indent paragraphs five to ten spaces. Refer to the model press release below for the correct position of the various elements.

Source. Type the name of the person or organization sending the release in the upper-right corner, including the person's address and telephone number. You may type "For further information call" above the source data if this line is not already printed on the stationery. Leave three to four inches of space after the source before typing the release data. Editors use this space to write their headlines. You may write your own headline to give editors an indication of what the story is about, but otherwise a headline is unnecessary and, in fact, probably will not be used.

Release date. After the three to four inches of space following the source, center in capital letters the date and time that the editor may publish the material, for example: FOR RELEASE MONDAY, JUNE 5, 9 A.M. However, unless a specific release time is essential, simply state: FOR IMMEDIATE RELEASE

Model Press Release

For further information call:

> E J. Conley, Marketing Manager
> Windham Sporting Goods, Inc.
> 1414 Second Avenue
> Boston, MA 02106

FOR IMMEDIATE RELEASE

Boston (June 5). The introduction of an improved water-repellent fabric in Windham camp gear will be the focus of the Windham Sporting Goods exhibit at the Great Outdoors Fair on March 16 in Springfield, Missouri.

According to William Purlman, president of the company, tests have proved the new fabric, Repello-lite R, to be twice as effective in repelling moisture as the leading water-proof garment on the market today. The test results were released by the independent research firm of Dewer & McDavitt after comparing the industry's four leading repellent materials under simulated water-stress conditions.

-more-

Dateline. Type the dateline at least two lines beneath the release date. The dateline is in effect the first word(s) in the first paragraph. It shows the date and place where the story occurred. But you may omit the date if the story is for immediate release. The first paragraph (indented) of a release might begin:

Boston (June 5). James Harper, president of XYZ Industries, died today of an apparent heart attack.

Page ending. At the end of each page, center *-More* or *(More)*. Type the succeeding page number three times— for example, *2-2-2*—at the top of the next page and leave an inch or more space before continuing the text. At the end of the release center *-30-* or *###*.

If you are enclosing a photograph, type "Photograph enclosed" a couple of lines beneath the end-of-page symbol. Do not write on the back of the photograph except to add a short identifying number or label with felt-tip pen. Instead, type the caption on a separate strip of paper and paste it at the bottom of the photograph with the typing facing the same way as the face of the photograph.

Keep in mind that editors commonly edit from the bottom up, which means that if your release has six paragraphs and the publication has room for four, the editor will likely delete the last two paragraphs. Because of this type of pyramid editing, it is essential that you write facts in the order of importance, placing the least important last.

Writing style. The first requirement is that the story be newsworthy. Editors will discard something that does not qualify as a legitimate news item of interest to readers. Moreover, they will doubt your credibility as a reliable source of information. Most subjects should also be timely (no one wants to read about yesterday's news). Any one of the following would qualify as a newsworthy element: conflict, controversy, humor, public interest, money, tragedy, secrets, and irony.

Although the opening must catch the reader's attention, the prose should be lean and concise. Omit adjectives (*tremendous* loss), adverbs (performed *superbly*), and passive verbs (it *was decided* by the president). Stick to facts and present them in a logical order as briefly as possible. The lead must answer the questions *who, what, where, when*, and if possible *why*, for example:

The introduction of an improved water-repellent fabric (*what*) in Windham camp gear will be the focus of the Windham Sporting Goods (*who*) exhibits at the Great Outdoor Fair on March 16 (*when*) in Springfield, Missouri (*where*).

Clearly identify people and places. *Springfield* alone would leave readers wondering if it was a city in Illinois, Missouri, or elsewhere. Familiar names such as *Smith* must include the first name or two initials. If there might be several persons having the same first and last names, even further identification is necessary: *John Smith of East Meadows in Denver* or *John Smith, product manager, Right Industries*.

ARTICLES

Many press release ideas form the basis of a publishable article. Other ideas are not suitable for a release but require the greater detail that an article allows.

A professional writer may be retained to write a proposed article if your firm does not have in-house personnel with writing experience. The article also may be prepared by employees, provided that they follow the same requirements that a professional writer would observe.

The Market

Your local library probably will have one or more directories such as *Writer's Market* that describe length, topic, and submission requirements for articles in each periodical. Select appropriate publications for your topic. For example, if you want to direct your article to industry executives in a certain field, don't send it to a magazine that is published for consumers in general.

Format

Closely follow any specifications listed in the directory you consult. If a magazine typically uses articles of five hundred words with black-and-white glossy photographs, do not submit a fifteen-hundred-word article with color slides. In addition to studying the specifications listed in directories, purchase copies of prospective magazines and notice the style of previously published articles. Is the tone formal and businesslike or humorous and conversational? Are there many or few illustrations? Are there footnotes? Where are they positioned—at the ends of the articles or at the bottoms of pages—and are they called "Notes" or "References"? Are the article titles short, descriptive, and straightforward? Are there subheads in the text? How many levels of subheads are there? Are they centered, typed flush left, or run into the text, paragraph style? Do the articles have lists? Are they numbered, unnumbered, or preceded by a symbol such as a bullet? Make a list of everything you can see about the format and follow the same style when you prepare your article manuscript.

Type the manuscript on twenty-pound white bond paper, 8½ by 11 inches. Use margins all around of at least 1¼ inches, with a top margin of at least 3 inches on the first page. Double-space everything, including extracts and notes. Refer to chapter 13 for details concerning footnote style, page numbering, style of extracts, levels of subheads, and preparation of tables and illustrations. Essentially the same rules that apply to these matters in report writing apply in article writing.

Language

Although it is very important to follow the style and tone of previously published articles in a particular magazine, you can safely observe these rules in most cases:

1. Use short words and short sentences whenever possible, but vary the sentence length for added interest.
2. Delete jargon and colloquialisms and define unfamiliar technical terms.

3. Use the active voice (*I believe*, not *it is believed*) and choose nouns and verbs over adjectives and adverbs.

4. Be positive (*the tool will be ready February 1*, not *the tool won't be ready until February 1*).

5. Delete all needless words (*February*, not *the month of February*).

6. Don't summarize what you're going to talk about (not *next I'll discuss the product's potential*); simply start discussing it.

7. Develop a tantalizing lead sentence that makes the reader want to read on—perhaps a personal question (*How often have you been hit with increasing insurance rates because your firm didn't meet the listed safety standards?*) or a startling statement (*Last year more than 40,000 firms from coast to coast paid higher insurance rates because they failed to meet the listed safety standards*).

8. End the article with a snappy wrapup that answers any lingering questions in a reader's mind—without rambling on or beginning a new discussion when it's time to draw everything to a logical conclusion.

The Query Letter

Since each magazine has different requirements and there is no guarantee that your article will be published even if you follow those requirements, a query letter makes good sense. The objective is to write to the publication, describe your proposed article, and ask if the editor would be interested in having you develop it. If you write a tempting query letter, the editor may say yes, in which case you have the article sold or at least have an indication of interest before you go to the trouble of writing it. Or the editor may say no to what you propose but ask if you could prepare a different version of that topic. Or the editor may say no on all counts, in which case you at least didn't waste time writing the article for one magazine's requirements when something different will be required for the next one on your list.

Use the editor's name in the query letter's inside address, if available, but if necessary, address your letter to the appropriate editor (e.g., fashion editor). Give the essential facts in your query, including a summary of the topics, the proposed length, whether you plan to include illustrations, and when you would be prepared to submit the article. For example:

Dear Ms. Nordstrom:

One thing that individual bank customers can't easily assess is whether a bank's investment policy is sound. But there are surprisingly obvious clues for everyone to see—if you know where to look. Would you be interested in an article that alerts your readers to easy-to-spot signs of a sound or shaky bank-investment policy? Those signs are critical in judging not only whether a bank is serving its customers well but whether it is heading for failure.

I would be happy to prepare an article on this topic of about 1,200 words. The piece would have one table that rates bank policies from poor to good but would have no photographs or artwork.

As a financial planner, I regularly prepare evaluations of banking and other investment practices as they pertain to consumers in general and bank customers in particular. A brief personal biography is enclosed along with a brochure describing my firm's financial-planning services.

I would be glad to make any adjustments in the proposed article that you might require and look forward to hearing from you. Thanks very much.

Sincerely,

Be prepared for a rejection, but don't be discouraged. If all of the publications you contact say no, you may need to consider whether your idea is appropriate for those magazines, whether it duplicates something they have already published (or that someone else has already published), whether it fails to meet their format and size specifications, and so on. Perhaps you merely need to tailor the idea more to their needs. Or perhaps it is time to abandon that idea and develop a new one.

BROCHURES

The term *brochure* is used to describe a variety of printed literature containing descriptive or advertising material. Although the definition varies among professionals and users, smaller pieces of printed material (one to six pages or panels) are often referred to as fliers, circulars, or folders. Larger pieces (eight or more pages) are commonly called pamphlets or booklets. Regardless of size, complexity, or terminology, a wide variety of printed material is used as mailers and handouts in publicity efforts.

Format

Although a brochure may be any size, the weight, cost, and other factors may influence the size you choose. If the piece will be used as an envelope insert, it must be a size that will fold to fit your envelope. Weight is also an important consideration. Heavy paper is more durable (you probably want the customer to keep the brochure) and often looks more expensive than lighter paper. But it weighs more and thus can substantially increase your postage costs. Your budget may restrict you to a one-ounce package, so be certain to weigh a sample before you select the paper stock.

Because brochures vary so much, you should consider all elements to be used in the piece. Will it have photographs? What type of paper will enhance them the most? Do you want (or can you afford) to use full color, two colors, black ink only, or something else? Will the paper fold or perforate (if you need a tear-off) satisfactorily? How much space do you need for the copy without making the brochure look crowded? What other factors are pertinent to your particular mailer or handout?

Design

You may want to have a freelance artist or an advertising agency prepare a layout for you. This is a rough drawing of the proposed finished product, with areas blocked off where text and illustrations will appear. Often it is done in the color(s) you choose, or that the artist recommends, and may be sketched on a sample of the proposed stock (paper). Give the artist a good idea of the amount of text that you will have, number and type of illustrations, and anything else that will appear in the final brochure. Once you have approved a layout, take it to a printer—preferably three printers—and ask for a price quote in the quantity you desire.

Writing

If you write the copy yourself, determine in advance any size or other restrictions. Assume, for example, that postage costs and envelope size will limit you to six columns, or panels, each about three by nine inches (excluding the margins). Further assume that about three panels will be used up by (1) the cover, (2) a tearoff return card, and (3) two illustrations. That leaves about three panels for text.

Next, on a blank sheet of typing paper, make a three-inch row of x's, for example:

xxxxxxxxxxxxxxxxxxxxxxxxxxxxxxxxxxxxxxxxxxxxxxxx

Set your margins to fit this width and underneath the row begin typing your copy double-spaced. Aim for about six or seven lines of text for every inch of brochure space. After the brochure design is established and type size is selected, you may have to adjust your copy, deleting or adding a few lines. Even in the early stages, however, it helps to have a rough estimate of available space, and typing your drafts accordingly will make the later task of revising and editing much easier.

ADVERTISEMENTS

Part of your publicity campaign may consist of paid advertising in newspapers, magazines, and on radio or television. Although newspapers and magazines often can prepare ads for you based upon the information that you submit, this is such a specialized area, and a firm's advertising program is very important to it. For that reason, many executives believe that all but the simplest ads should be prepared by an advertising agency or a company's in-house advertising department. Advertising agencies usually receive a discount from the media but they may charge an additional fee for art and other services. Inquire about all possible costs and ask to see a portfolio of work done for other clients.

Requirements

The specialists you employ will know the print and broadcast requirements for the various media. Newspapers, for instance, charge by agate line, or $1/14$ inch deep by one column wide. Magazines commonly sell space in pages or fractions thereof. Broadcast time is usually sold as fifteen-, thirty-, or sixty-second spots or as program time. Ask the agency you retain for rate cards, which will indicate how much space or time you can purchase at a certain cost. Don't hesitate to express your budget limitations and to ask for full cost estimates when dealing with an agency. Discounts may be offered for repeated messages.

State your message and advertising goal as clearly as possible to the agency and carefully proofread and review any material they prepare for you. Be prepared to "educate" the people handling your account. You can do this with previously printed material, through discussion, and by introducing agency representatives to others in your organization. Be helpful in every possible way, although not to the extent that your constant interference is counterproductive to the creative process.

LETTERS

Advertisers rank the letter as the most important form of mailing. Direct-mail letters may be individually typed, printed, mimeographed, or prepared by computer, word processor, or automatic (e.g., magnetic-tape) typewriter. The section Form and Guide Letters in chapter 12 describes methods of preparation.

Guidelines

Consider the following suggestions and guidelines when you begin planning your direct-mail letter:

1. A successful mailing package often includes a form letter, brochure, reply card (self-mailer or with business-reply envelope), and outside envelope.

2. Indented paragraphs are more common than blocked (flush-left) paragraphs.

3. Personalized letters—for example, prepared individually by computer, word processor, or magnetic-tape typewriter—do better than printed or mimeographed letters.

4. Underscoring, testimonials, and other forms of emphasis help to enhance a message and increase response.

5. Two-page letters are usually more successful than one-page letters.

6. Two-color letterheads—often with a second color used in the text as well—attract more attention than one-color designs.

7. Specific deadlines for reply increase response.

8. Special offers such as a free gift increase response.

9. Special devices such as paste-on reply stamps increase response.

10. Liberal terms are more effective than no special terms or conservative terms.

11. Handwritten envelopes and postage stamps have a negative effect on response.

12. Follow-up mailings increase response.

Direct mail can be very expensive, and advertisers need to study their proposed package carefully. Does it clearly state all pertinent facts—price, delivery rate, requirements for ordering, and so on? Are incentives and attractive sales features emphasized? Are the letter and circular attractive and enticing? Is the reply card or order form easy to use? Advertising agencies and other direct-mail specialists can help you prepare an effective mailing and guide you to productive mailing lists. Since direct mail is a serious investment, it merits serious attention and should be carefully coordinated with your overall advertising and promotional program.

FACTS
AND FIGURES

Arabic and Roman Numerals

I	1	XL	40
II	2	L	50
III	3	LX	60
IV	4	LXX	70
V	5	LXXX	80
VI	6	XC	90
VII	7	C	100
VIII	8	CC	200
IX	9	CCC	300
X	10	CD	400
XI	11	D	500
XII	12	DC	600
XIII	13	DCC	700
XIV	14	DCC	800
XV	15	CM	900
XVI	16	M	1,000
XVII	17	MM	2,000
XVIII	18	MMM	3,000
XIX	19	$\overline{MV}$	4,000
XX	20	$\overline{V}$	5,000
XXX	30		

Note: Repeating a letter repeats its value: II = 2.
A letter placed after one of greater value adds to it: XI = 11.
A letter placed before one of greater value subtracts from it: IX = 9. A dash line over a numeral multiplies the value by 1,000: $\overline{X}$ = 10,000.

Diacritical Marks

´	Acute accent
`	Grave accent
˘	Breve
ˇ	Haček
¨	Diaresis
^ or or ˉ	Circumflex
˜	Tilde
ˉ	Macron
¸	Cedilla

Greek Alphabet

Alphabet and pronunciation

A	α	*A a*	alpha	*a* in *father*
B	β	*B b*	beta	*v*
Γ	γ	*Γ g*	gamma	*y* in *yes* before αι, ε, ει, η, ι, οι, ν, νι; ng in *singer* before γ, κ, ξ, χ; somewhat like *g* in *go* everywhere else
Δ	δ	*D d*	delta	*th* in *this*, except in νδρ, pronounced *ndr*
E	ε	*E e*	epsilon	*e* in *met*
Z	ζ	*Z z*	zeta	*z*
H	η	*H n*	eta	*ee* in *eel*; *y* in *yet*; when after a consonant and before a vowel
Θ	θ	*Θ θ*	theta	*th* in *thin*
I	ι	*I i*	iota	*ee* in *eel*; *y* in *yet* when initial or after a consonant, before a vowel
K	κ	*K k*	kappa	*k*
Λ	λ	*L l*	lambda	*l*
M	μ	*M m*	mu	*m*
N	ν	*N n*	nu	*n*
Ξ	ξ	*X x*	xi	*x* (= *ks*)
O	ο	*O o*	omicron	*o* in *for*
Π	π	*Π p*	pi	*p*
P	ρ	*P r*	rho	*r*, somewhat like the Scotch trilled *r*
Σ	σς*	*L s*	sigma	*z* before β, γ, δ, λ, μ, ν, ρ; *s* everywhere else
T	τ	*T (t)*	tau	*t*
Y	υ	*V v*	upsilon	*ee* in *eel*; *y* in *yet*, after a consonant and before a vowel
Φ	φ	*Φ p*	phi	*f*
X	χ	*X x*	chi	like a strong *h* (like German *ch*)
Ψ	ψ	*Y y*	psi	*ps*
Ω	ω	*W w*	omega	*o* in *or*

Source: United States Government Printing Office Style Manual (Washington, D.C.: U.S. Government Printing Office, March 1984).

*The character σ is used in initial and medial positions in a word. The character ς is used in the final position.

Standard Paper Weights and Sizes

Paper Classification	Standard Size (Inches)	Basis Weight (Pounds)
Book	25 × 38	30, 40, 45, 50, 60, 70, 80, 90, 100, 120
Bond	17 × 22	13, 16, 20, 24, 28, 32, 36, 40
Cover	20 × 26	50, 60, 65, 80, 90, 100
Bristol	22½ × 28½	57, 67, 80, 100, 120, 140, 160
Index	25½ × 30½	90, 110, 140, 170
Tag	24 × 36	100, 125, 150, 175, 200, 250

Source: International Paper Company, 891 New Brunswick Avenue, Rahway, NJ 07065.

Standard Sizes of Common Printed Material

BOOKS

5½ × 8½, 6⅛ × 9¼, 5 × 7⅜, 5⅜ × 8, 5½ × 8¼, 5⅝ × 8⅜

BROADSIDES

17 × 22, 19 × 25, 20 × 26, 23 × 35

FOLDERS

3½ × 6¼, 4 × 9, 5½ × 8½, 6 × 9, 8½ × 11, 9 × 12

FORMS

7 × 8½, 8½ × 11, 8½ × 14

CATALOG SHEETS

8½ × 11, 11 × 17

STATEMENTS

5½ × 8½, 7 × 8½

INVOICES

7 × 8½, 8½ × 11

LETTERHEADS

8½ × 11, 7¼ × 10½, 6 × 9, 5½ × 8½

BUSINESS CARDS

2 × 3½, 3½ × 4 (folder style)

ENVELOPES

Stationery: 4⅛ × 9½ (no. 10), 3⅞ × 8⅞ (no. 9), 3⅞ × 7½ (no. 8), 3⅝ × 6½ (no. 6¾), 3½ × 6 (no. 6¼), 4⅝ × 5⁵⁄₁₆ (no. 5)
Catalog and booklet: 6 × 9, 7 × 10, 8¾ × 11¼, 9 × 12, 9½ × 12½, 10 × 13

Metric Conversion Table

When You Know	Multiply by	To Find
Length		
inches (in.)	2.54	centimeters (cm)
feet (ft.)	30.00	centimeters (cm)
yards (yd.)	0.90	meters (m)
miles (mi.)	1.60	kilometers (km)
millimeters (mm)	0.04	inches (in.)
centimeters (cm)	0.40	inches (in.)
meters (m)	3.30	feet (ft.)
meters (m)	1.10	yards (yd.)
kilometers (km)	0.60	miles (mi.)
Area		
square inches (in.²)	6.50	square centimeters (cm²)
square feet (ft.²)	0.09	square meters (m²)
square yards (yd.²)	0.80	square meters (m²)
square miles (mi.²)	2.60	square kilometers (km²)
acres	0.40	hectares (ha)
square centimeters (cm²)	0.16	square inches (in.²)

When You Know	Multiply by	To Find
square meters (m²)	1.20	square yards (yd.²)
square kilometers (km²)	0.40	square miles (mi.²)
hectares (ha) (10,000 m²)	2.50	acres

Weight

ounces (oz.)	28.00	grams (g)
pounds (lb.)	0.45	kilograms (kg)
short tons (2,000 lbs.)	0.90	tonnes (t)
long tons (2,240 lbs.)	1.01	tonnes (t)
grams (g)	0.035	ounces (oz.)
kilograms (kg)	2.20	pounds (lb.)
tonnes (1,000 kg)	1.10	short tons
tonnes (1,000 k)	0.98	long tons

Volume

teaspoons (tsp.)	5.00	milliliters (ml)
tablespoons (tbsp.)	15.00	milliliters (ml)
fluid ounces (fl. oz.)	30.00	milliliters (ml)
cups (c)	0.24	liters (l)
pints (pt.)	0.47	liters (l)
quarts (qt.)	0.95	liters (l)
gallons, U.S. (gal.)	3.80	liters (l)
gallons, Imp. (gal.)	4.50	liters (l)
cubic feet (ft.³)	0.028	cubic meters (m³)
cubic yards (yd.³)	0.76	cubic meters (m³)
milliliters (ml)	0.03	fluid ounces (fl. oz.)
liters (l)	2.10	pints (pt.)
liters (l)	1.06	quarts (qt.)
liters (l)	0.26	gallons, U.S. (gal.)
liters (l)	0.22	gallons, Imp. (gal.)
cubic meters (m³)	35.00	cubic feet (ft.³)
cubic meters (m³)	1.30	cubic yards (yd.³)

Table of Weights, Measures, and Values

Long Measure

12 inches = 1 foot
3 feet = 1 yard
5½ yards or 16½ feet = 1 rod
320 rods or 5,280 feet = 1 mile
1,760 yards = 1 mile
40 rods = 1 furlong
8 furlongs = 1 statute mile
3 miles = 1 league

Common Metric Equivalents

1 inch = 2.540 centimeters
1 foot = 30.480 centimeters
1 yard = 0.914 meters
1 rod = 5.029 meters
1 mile = 1.609 kilometers

Square Measure

144 square inches = 1 square foot
9 square feet = 1 square yard
30¼ square yards = 1 square rod
272¼ square feet = 1 square rod
40 square rods = 1 British rood
4 roods = 1 acre
160 square rods = 1 acre
640 acres = 1 square mile
43,560 square feet = 1 acre
4,840 square yards = 1 acre

Common Metric Equivalents

1 square inch = 6.451 square centimeters
1 square foot = 0.093 square meters
1 square yard = 0.836 square meters
1 square rod = 25.293 square meters
1 square mile = 2.590 square kilometers

Solid or Cubic Measure (Volume)

1,728 cubic inches = 1 cubic foot
27 cubic feet = 1 cubic yard
128 cubic feet = 1 cord of wood
24.75 cubic feet = 1 perch of stone
2,150.42 cubic inches = 1 standard bushel
231 cubic inches = 1 standard gallon
40 cubic feet = 1 ton (shipping)

Common Metric Equivalents

1 cubic inch = 16.387 cubic centimeters
1 cubic foot = 0.028 cubic meters
1 cubic yard = 0.765 cubic meters

Surveyor's Long Measure

7.92 inches = 1 link
25 links = 1 rod
4 rods or 100 links = 1 chain
80 chains = 1 mile

Surveyors' Square Measure

625 square links = 1 square rod
16 square rods = 1 square chain
10 square chains = 1 acre
640 acres = 1 square mile
36 square miles = 1 township

Circular or Angular Measure

60 seconds (60″ = 1 minute (′)
60 minutes (60′) = 1 degree (1°)
30 degrees – 1 sign
90 degrees = 1 right angle or quadrant
360 degrees = 1 circumference

Note: 1 degree at the equator = about 60 nautical miles.

Dry Measure

2 pints = 1 quart
8 quarts = 1 peck
4 pecks = 1 bushel
2,150.42 cubic inches = 1 bushel
1.2445 cubic feet = 1 bushel

Common Metric Equivalents

1 pint = 0.550 liters
1 quart = 1.101 liters
1 peck = 8.809 liters
1 bushel = 35.238 liters

Liquid Measure (Capacity)

4 gills = 1 pint
2 pints = 1 quart
4 quarts = 1 gallon
31.5 gallons = 1 barrel
2 barrels = 1 hogshead
1 gallon = 231 cubic inches
7.4805 gallons = 1 cubic foot
16 fluid ounces = 1 pint
1 fluid ounce = 1.805 cubic inches

Common Metric Equivalents

1 fluid ounce = 29.573 milliliters
1 gill = 118.291 milliliters
1 pint = 0.473 liters
1 quart = 0.946 liters
1 gallon = 3.785 liters

Mariners' Measures

6 feet = 1 fathom
100 fathoms = 1 cable's length as applied to distances or
intervals between ships
120 fathoms = 1 cable's length as applied to marine wire
cable

7.50 cable lengths = 1 mile
5,280 feet = 1 statute mile
6,080 feet = 1 nautical mile
1.15266 statute miles = 1 nautical or geographical mile
3 geographical miles = 1 league
60 geographical miles or 69.16 statute miles = 1 degree of longitude on the equator or 1 degree of meridian
360 degrees = 1 circumference

Note: A *knot* is not a measure of distance but a measure of speed, about 1 nautical mile per hour.

U.S.-British Weights and Measures

1 British bushel = 1.0326 U.S. (Winchester) bushels
1 U.S. bushel = 0.96894 British Imperial bushel
1 British quart = 1.03206 U.S. dry quarts
1 U.S. dry quart = 0.96894 British quart
1 British quart (or gallon) = 1.20095 U.S. liquid quarts (or gallons)
1 U.S. liquid quart (or gallon) = 0.83267 British quart (or gallon)

Avoirdupois Measure (Weight)

27.343 grains = 1 dram
16 drams = 1 ounce
16 ounces = 1 pound
25 pounds = 1 quarter
4 quarts = 1 hundredweight
100 pounds = 1 hundredweight
20 hundredweight = 1 ton
2,000 pounds = 1 short ton
2,240 pounds = 1 long ton

Common Metric Equivalents

1 grain = 0.0648 grams
1 dram = 1.771 grams
1 ounce = 28.349 grams
1 pound = 0.453 kilograms
1 hundredweight (short) = 45.359 kilograms

1 hundredweight (long) = 50.802 kilograms
1 ton (short) = 0.907 metric ton
1 ton (long) = 1.016 metric tons

Note: The avoirdupois measure is used for weighing all ordinary substances except precious metals, jewels, and drugs.

Troy Measure (Weight)

24 grains = 1 pennyweight
20 pennyweights = 1 ounce
12 ounces = 1 pound

Common Metric Equivalents

1 grain = 0.0648 grams
1 pennyweight = 1.555 grams
1 ounce = 31.103 grams
1 pound = 0.373 kilograms

Avoirdupois-Troy Measure

1 pound troy = 5,760 grains
1 pound avoirdupois = 7,000 grains
1 ounce troy = 480 grains
1 ounce avoirdupois = 437.5 grains
1 carat or karat = 3.2 troy grains
24 carat gold = pure gold

Apothecaries' Fluid Measures (Capacity)

60 minims = 1 fluid dram
8 fluid drams = 1 fluid ounce
16 fluid ounces = 1 pint
8 pints = 1 gallon

Apothecaries' Measure (Weight)

20 grains = 1 scruple
3 scruples = 1 dram
8 drams = 1 ounce
12 ounces = 1 pound

Common Metric Equivalents

1 grain = 0.0648 gram
1 scruple = 1.295 grams
1 dram = 3.887 grams
1 ounce = 31.103 grams
1 pound = 0.373 kilogram

Paper Measure

24 sheets = 1 quire
20 quires = 1 ream
2 reams = 1 bundle
5 bundles = 1 bale

Counting

12 units or things = 1 dozen
12 dozen or 144 units = 1 gross
12 gross = 1 great gross
20 units = 1 score

Technical Abbreviations

---

a, amp.	ampere
Å	angstrom
ac	alternating current
af	audiofrequency
a-h	ampere-hour
a/m	ampere per meter
AM	amplitude modulation
at.	atmosphere
at. no.	atomic number
at. vol.	atomic volume
at. wt.	atomic weight
au	astronomical unit
Au	gold
av., avdp.	avoirdupois
a/w	actual weight

bbl	barrel
bbl/d, b/d	barrel per day
bdl	bundle
bhp	brake horsepower
bl	bale(s)
bm	board measure
bp	boiling point
Btu, BTU	British thermal unit
bu.	bushel
c	cycle (radio)
C	Celsius; Centigrade; centi (prefix: one-hundredth)
C/	case(s)
cal.	small calories
cd.	cord
cd. ft.	cord foot
cg	centigram
ch, c-h	candle-hour(s)
cl	centiliter
cm	centimeter
c/m	cycles per minute
cm^2	square centimeter
cm^3	cubic centimeter
cp	candlepower
d	deci (prefix: one-tenth)
da	deka (prefix: ten)
dag	dekagram
dal	dekaliter
dam	dekameter
dam^2	square dekameter
dam^3	cubic dekameter
dB	decibel
dBu	decibel unit
dc	direct current
dg	decigram
dl	deciliter
dm	decimeter
dm^2	square decimeter
dm^3	cubic decimeter
dr.	dram
dw	dead weight
dwc	dead weight capacity

dwt	deadweight ton(s); pennyweight(s)
dyn	dyne
EHF	extremely high frequency
EMF	electromotive force
esu	electrostatic unit
eV	electron volt
F	Fahrenheit; farad
fbm	board foot; board foot measure
FM	frequency modulation
ft.	foot
ft.^{2}	square foot
ft.^{3}	cubic foot
ft. H_2O	conventional foot of water
g	gram; gravity
G	gauss; giga (prefix: one million)
gal.	gallon
GeV	gigaelectronvolt
GHz	gigahertz
h	hecto (prefix: one hundred)
H	henry
ha	hectare
hf	high frequency
hg	hectogram
hl	hectoliter
hm	hectometer
hm^2	square hectometer
hm^3	cubic hectometer
hp	horsepower
Hz	hertz
ihp	indicated horsepower
in.	inch
in.^{2}	square inch
in.^{3}	cubic inch
J	joule
k	kilo (prefix: one thousand); knot; carat
kc	kilocycle
keV	kiloelectronvolt
kg	kilogram
kG	kilogauss
kgf	kilogram-force

kHz	kilohertz
kl	kiloliter
km	kilometer
km^2	square kilometer
km^3	cubic kilometer
kn	knot (speed)
kt	kiloton; carat
kV	kilovolt
kVa	kilovoltampere
kW	kilowatt
kWh	kilowatt-hour
l	liter
lf	low frequency
lin. ft.	linear foot
l/m	lines per minute
l/s	lines per second
m	meter; milli (prefix: one-thousandth)
m^2	square meter
m^3	cubic meter
M	mega (prefix: one million); thousand
ma	milliampere
mbar	millibar
mc	millicycle
Mc	megacycle
MeV	megaelectronvolts
mF	millifarad
mg	milligram
mG	milligauss
mH	millihenry
mHz	millihertz
MHz	megahertz
mi.	mile (statute)
$mi.^2$	square mile
mi./hr., mi/h	mile(s) per hour
min.	minute (time)
ml	milliliter
mm	millimeter
mm^2	square millimeter
mm^3	cubic millimeter
ms	millisecond
Mt	megaton
mV	millivolt

mW	milliwatt
MW	megawatt
μ	micro (prefix: one-millionth)
μF	microfarad
μg	microgram
μH	microhenry
μin.	microinch
μm	micrometer
μs	microsecond
μV	microvolt
μW	microwatt
n	nano (prefix: one-billionth)
na	nanoampere
nhp	nominal horsepower
nm	nanometer
nmi.	nautical mile
npt	nominal pressure and temperature
ns	nanosecond
oz.	ounce (avoirdupois)
p	pico (prefix: one-trillionth)
pc, pct., %	percent
pk.	peck
p/m	parts per million
ps	picosecond
pt.	pint
pW	picowatt
ql	quintal
qt.	quart
R	rankine; roentgen
rf	radio frequency
r/min.	revolutions per minute
rms	root mean square
r/s	revolutions per second
s	second (time)
sh. tn.	short ton
shp	shaft horsepower
sw	shipper's weights
T	tera (prefix: one trillion); tesla
tMW	thermal megawatt

u	atomic mass unit
uhf	ultrahigh frequency
V	volt
Va	volt ampere
vhf	very high frequency
V/m	volt per meter
W	watt
Wh	watt-hour
yd.	yard
yd.^{2}	square yard
yd.^{3}	cubic yard
z	zero hour

Computer Abbreviations and Acronyms

ABM	automated batch mixing
abort	abandon activity
ABP	actual block processor
abs	absolute
AC	automatic/analog computer
ACC	accumulator
ACF	advanced communication function
ACL	Audit Command Language
ACM	area composition machine
ADAPS	automatic displayed plotting system
ADC	analog-to-digital converter
ADIS	automatic data interchange system
ADP	automatic/advanced data processing
ADR	address; adder; analog-to-digital recorder
ADV	advance
AFR	automatic field/format recognition
ALCOM	algebraic computer/compiler
ALGOL	Algorithmic Language
ALP	automated language processing
ALU	arithmetic and logic unit
ANACOM	analog computer
AOC	automatic output control
AP	attached processor
APL	A Programming Language

APT	Automatic Programmed Tools (language)
AQL	acceptable quality level
ARQ	automatic repeat request; automatic request for correction
ARU	audio response unit
ASC	automatic sequence control
ASCII	American Standard Code for Information Interchange
ASDI	automated selective dissemination of information
ASM	auxiliary storage management
ASP	attached support processor
ASR	answer, send, and receive
ATLAS	Automatic Tabulating, Listing, and Sorting System
AUTODIN	automated digital network
B	bit; magnetic flux density
BA	binary add
BAM	basic access method
BASIC	Beginner's All-Purpose Symbolic Instruction
BC	binary code
BCD	binary-coded decimal
BDU	basic device/display unit
BIM	beginning of information marker
bit	binary digit
BIU	basic information unit
BN	binary number system
BOF	beginning of file
BOS	basic operating system
BOT	beginning of tape
bpi	bits per inch
bps	bits per second
BPS	basic programming support
BS	backspace character
BTU	basic transmission unit
C	computer; compute; control
CA	channel adapter
CAD	computer-aided design
CAD/CAM	computer-aided design/computer-aided manufacturing
CAI	computer-aided instruction

CAI/OP	computer analog input/output
CAL	computer-aided learning
CAM	computer-aided manufacturing
CAN	cancel character
CAR	computer-assisted retrieval
CAT	computer-assisted training/teaching
CDC	call directing code
CHAR	character
CIM	computer-input microfilm
CIOCS	communications input/output control system
CIU	computer interface unit
CLAT	communication line adapter
CLK	clock
CLT	communication line terminal
CMC	code for magnetic characters
CMND	command; instruction
CMS	conversation monitor system
CNC	computer numerical control
COBOL	Common Business-Oriented Language
COL	Computer-Oriented Language
COM	computer-output microfilm
CP	central processor
cph	characters per hour
cpm	characters per minute; cards per minute; critical path method
CP/M	controlled program monitor; control program/microcomputers
CPS	Conversational programming system; central processing system
CPU	central processing unit
cr	carriage return
CR	call request; control relay
CRAM	card random access method
CROM	control read-only memory
CRT	cathode ray tube
CSL	Computer-Sensitive Language
CST	channel status table
CTR	computer tape reader
CTU	central terminal unit
CU	control unit
CWP	communicating word processor

DAA	direct-access arrangement
DAC	data acquisition and control; digital/analog converter
DASD	direct-access storage device
DBAM	database access method
DBMS	database management system
DD	digital data
DDL	Data-Description Language
DDS	digital-display scope
DE	display element
DIP	dual in-line package
DLC	data-link control
DMA	direct memory access
DNC	direct numerical control
DOS	disk operating system
DOV	data over voice
DP	data processing
DRL	Data-Retrieval Language
DRO	destructive readout
DTR	data terminal ready
DUV	data under voice
EDP	electronic data processing
EOF	end of file
EOJ	end of job
EOP	end of paragraph
EOR	end of record/run
ESI	externally specified index
ETB	end of transmission block
F	feedback
FACT	Fully Automatic Compiling Technique
FDOS	floppy-disk operating system
FF	flip-flop
FIRST	fast interactive retrieval system
FORTRAN	Formula Translation (language)
GDT	graphic display terminal
GP	general program
GPC	general-purpose computer
GPR	general-purpose register
HSM	high-speed memory

HSP	high-speed printer
HSR	high-speed reader
IC	integrated circuit; input circuit
ID	identification
I/O	input/output
IOB	input-output buffer
IOC	input-output controller
ipm	impulses per minute
IR	infrared
ISR	information storage and retrieval
k	about a thousand (in storage capacity)
KB	keyboard
kb	kilobytes
KSR	keyboard send and receive
LCD	liquid crystal display
LIFO	last in, first out
LILO	last in, last out
LP	linear programming
lpm	lines per minute
lsc	least significant character
lsd	least significant digit
M	mega
mag	magnetic
Mb	megabyte
MC	master control
MCP	master control program
MIS	management information system
MPS	microprocessor system
msc	most significant character
msd	most significant digit
MSU	modem-sharing unit
MT	machine translation
MUX	multiplexer
n	nano-
NAM	network access machine
NAU	network addressable unit
NC	numerical control
NCP	network control program
NL	new-line character
NO-OP	no-operation instruction

ns	nanosecond
OCR	optical character recognition
ODB	output to display buffer
OEM	original equipment manufacturer
OLRT	on-line real time
OP	operations
opm	operations per minute
OR	operations research
OS	operating system
OSI	open-system interconnection
P	pico-
PA	paper advance
PC	program counter
PCI	process control interface
PCM	punch-card machine
PCS	punched card system
PDN	public data network
PERT	program evaluation and review technique
PIO chip	programmable input/output chip
PIU	path information unit
PRT	production-run tape
RAM	random-access memory
RAX	remote access
READ	real-time electronic access and display
REM	recognition memory
ROM	read-only memory
RT	real time
RTU	remote terminal unit
R/W	read/write
RWM	read-write memory
RZ	return to zero
SAM	sequential-access method; serial-access memory
S/F	store and forward
SLT	solid-logic technology
SOP	standard operating procedure
STX	start of text
TLU	table lookup
TOS	tape operating system
UCS	user control storage

USASCII	USA Standard Code for Information Interchange
VDI	video display input
VDT	video display terminal
WC	write and compute
WFL	work-flow language
WIP	work in progress
WO	write-out
wp, WP	word processor
WS	working storage/space
XMT	transmit

State Abbreviations

	Traditional	Postal
Alabama	Ala.	AL
Alaska	Alaska	AK
American Samoa*	Amer. Samoa	AS
Arizona	Ariz.	AZ
Arkansas	Ark.	AR
California	Calif.	CA
Canal Zone*	C.Z.	CZ
Colorado	Colo.	CO
Connecticut	Conn.	CT
Delaware	Del.	DE
District of Columbia	D.C.	DC
Florida	Fla.	FL
Georgia	Ga.	GA
Guam*	Guam	GU
Hawaii	Hawaii	HI
Idaho	Idaho	ID
Illinois	Ill.	IL
Indiana	Ind.	IN
Iowa	Iowa	IA
Kansas	Kans.	KS
Kentucky	Ky.	KY
Louisiana	La.	LA
Maine	Maine	ME
Maryland	Md.	MD

Massachusetts	Mass.	MA
Michigan	Mich.	MI
Minnesota	Minn.	MN
Mississippi	Miss.	MS
Missouri	Mo.	MO
Montana	Mont.	MT
Nebraska	Nebr.	NE
Nevada	Nev.	NV
New Hampshire	N.H.	NH
New Jersey	N.J.	NJ
New Mexico	N.Mex.	NM
New York	N.Y.	NY
North Carolina	N.C.	NC
North Dakota	N.Dak.	ND
Ohio	Ohio	OH
Oklahoma	Okla.	OK
Oregon	Oreg.	OR
Pennsylvania	Pa.	PA
Puerto Rico*	P.R.	PR
Rhode Island	R.I.	RI
South Carolina	S.C.	SC
South Dakota	S.Dak.	SD
Tennessee	Tenn.	TN
Texas	Tex.	TX
Utah	Utah	UT
Vermont	Vt.	VT
Virginia	Va.	VA
Virgin Islands*	V.I.	VI
Washington	Wash.	WA
West Virginia	W.Va.	WV
Wisconsin	Wis.	WI
Wyoming	Wyo.	WY

Note: Spell out names in general text discussion (Wyoming), but use the traditional abbreviation in footnotes and references (Riverton, Wyo.), and use the two-letter postal abbreviation in letter and envelope mailing addresses.

*U.S. territories and possessions (by treaty, the Panama Canal will revert to Panama by 1999). Guam and Puerto Rico are self-governing U.S. territories. American Samoa and three of the Virgin Islands (St. Croix, St. Thomas, St. John) are non-self-governing U.S. territories.

Abbreviations of
Foreign Countries and Regions

Africa	Afr.
Albania	Alb.
Argentina	Argen.
Australia	Austl.
Austria	Aus.
Belgium	Belg.
Bolivia	Bol.
Brazil	Braz.
Burma	Burma
Canada	Can.
Chile	Chile
China	China
Colombia	Colom.
Czechoslovakia	Czech.
Denmark	Den.
Dominican Republic	Dom. Rep.
East Germany	E. Ger.
Ecuador	Ecuador
Egypt	Egypt
El Salvador	El. Sal.
Europe	Eur.
England	Eng.
Finland	Fin.
France	Fr.
Ghana	Ghana
Great Britain	Gr. Brit.
Greece	Greece
Guatemala	Guat.
Haiti	Haiti
Honduras	Hond.
Hong Kong	H.K.
Hungary	Hung.
Iceland	Ice.
India	India
Ireland	Ir.
Israel	Isr.
Italy	Italy
Japan	Japan

Korea	Korea
Luxembourg	Lux.
Mexico	Mex.
Netherlands	Neth.
New Zealand	N.Z.
Nicaragua	Nicar.
Nigeria	Nig.
Norway	Nor.
Pakistan	Pak.
Panama	Pan.
Paraguay	Para.
Philippines	Phil.
Poland	Pol.
Portugal	Port.
Rhodesia	Rhodesia
Romania	Rom.
Scotland	Scot.
South Africa	S.Afr.
Spain	Spain
Sweden	Swed.
Switzerland	Switz.
Turkey	Turk.
Uganda	Uganda
U.S.S.R.	U.S.S.R.
United Kingdom	U.K.
Uruguay	Uru.
Venezuela	Venez.
Wales	Wales
West Germany	W. Ger.
Yugoslavia	Yugo.
Zambia	Zambia
Zimbabwe	Zimb.

Index

Ø

Self-Help Books from SIGNET